Simon Barnes was the chief s[...]
2014, having worked at the pap[...]
of numerous books, including [...]
Birdwatcher. He lives in Norfolk [...]

Praise for *Epic*

'Excellent . . . his insights are rarely less than wise and
informative, and often fascinating . . . It's very fine
sportswriting indeed. This may conceivably be
Barnes's best work yet.'
Daily Mail

'*Epic* weaves together many of the most iconic, controversial
and unforgettable moments that coloured the 30-odd years of
Simon Barnes' tenure as a sports writer at *The Times*. It is an
unlikely triumph . . . He has a sublime ability to bring
you ringside without ever involving himself . . .
A sports book like no other.'
Racing Post

'[Barnes] has re-examined many of the events he attended
and taken another look at the figures who tasted
glory, disappointment and downright failure . . .
this is sport's story . . . It truly is an epic tale.'
Sports Journalists' Association

'Brilliant . . . combining a journalistic eye for detail with
a poetic ability to convey the emotions of a unique moment.'
Choice magazine

'From Eric Bristow and Watford as the second best team
in England to Novak Djokovic resurgent and the Glasgow
Commonwealth Games, Barnes was there . . .
caustically brilliant.'
Glasgow Herald

Epic

IN SEARCH OF
THE SOUL OF SPORT
AND WHY IT MATTERS

Simon Barnes

**SIMON &
SCHUSTER**

London · New York · Sydney · Toronto · New Delhi

A CBS COMPANY

First published in Great Britain by Simon & Schuster UK Ltd, 2018
This paperback edition published by Simon & Schuster UK Ltd, 2019
A CBS COMPANY

1 3 5 7 9 10 8 6 4 2

Simon & Schuster UK Ltd
1st Floor
222 Gray's Inn Road
London WC1X 8HB

www.simonandschuster.co.uk
www.simonandschuster.com.au
www.simonandschuster.co.in

Simon & Schuster Australia, Sydney
Simon & Schuster India, New Delhi

A CIP catalogue record for this book
is available from the British Library

Paperback ISBN: 978-1-4711-6421-7
eBook ISBN: 978-1-4711-6420-0

Typeset in the UK by M Rules
Printed and bound by CPI Group (UK) Ltd, Croydon, CR0 4YY

For all good colleagues, who kept
me halfway sane on the road, and especially
for Jim, who always had my back.

Foreword

But what did it mean?

We seek understanding when it's over. While it's still going on we're too much caught up in what happens from day to day. That's true of a love affair and of a period in history, of a great life and of a small one.

And it really was all over: 32 years of watching sport across the world, following sportspeople wherever they led and trying to write about it all, ended in a brief and awkward phone call.

So what did it mean? How could sense be made of this vast chunk of experience?

Perhaps a memoir, rollicking about the globe in pursuit of other people's glory: a tale of deadlines missed (none), late-night drinking sessions on the Ramblas (more than none), rows with sports editors (one, maybe one and a half), dear colleagues who made life on the road possible (a select but splendid few), global scoops (a somewhat brief chapter), and a general celebration of the life of the sporting journalist and in particular of the author.

Who was a chief sportswriter, you know, for 12 years, can you imagine? And you've heard about the chief sportswriter with the inferiority complex? He thought he was just the same as everybody else.

Said that before, but no matter.

But who the hell cares about chief sportswriters? What matters is sport. What matters is not the people who write about sport but the people who do it. Because, in sport, truth is only and always in the action.

Said that before, too. And will say it again. Because that does matter.

So look at the sport, not the sportswriter – and sport had been telling its story to this sportswriter for every one of those 32 years.

At once it became clear. The task was to write sport's story, not mine. Or at least, to write the chapters that were told to me. Here, then, is sport's ghosted autobiography and I – and this is more or less the last time that pronoun will be used in this book – have the ineffable privilege of being the ghost.

Hear, then, what sport has to say.

The author or ghost was present at nearly all the events described. Where that wasn't the case, a reference to the television or photographic coverage will be found in the text. Most of the stuff between quotation marks comes from one-on-one interviews. The events of the book of necessity follow the author's career: which began with small stuff, rising to bigger stories, went through a period of relegation to a backwater and ended up with the big job.

At every stage, sport spoke. Here then is the story.

Prologue

Hail muse.

Hail athletes. Hail victors. Hail losers. Hail nearly-but-not-quiters, has-beens, never-wozzers, young hopefuls, wily old pros, contenders, 12th men, bench-warmers, reserves, mavericks, rocks, leaders, followers, lone wolves, last resorts, team players, rampant individualists, misfits, joiner-inners, fading stars, heroes, villains and victims.

Hail coaches, hail officials, hail the good administrators, hail all those who make it possible.

Hail those who write and talk and shoot and do all the other jobs that bring sport to the many.

Hail those who watch. Hail those who care, hail those who love, hail those who love too much. This is for us.

Done.

Begin!

Noon.

A gunpowder day. Everything you touched seemed liable to crack and burn. Events had been ratcheted up to the limit: one more turn and something would snap. The sky was perfect blue. Everything else was red.

The rich colour of the track underneath the merciless sun. The vest of the man we were all watching. The black skin beneath the vest seemed touched with red. And as we were to learn later, when we saw it on television, his eyes. Red tinged yellow.

1

Face like the face of a warrior from the Terracotta Army, though running away was his fierce pride. The impossible muscles of the red–black man in the red vest with the red eyes on the red track.

Eight men dropped to their knees. The man in red splayed his arms out wide, as he always did. Low to the ground, so that when he rose up and started to run it was as if he was bursting out of the earth, a chthonic creature hurtling into the light and travelling as if seeking the fastest possible return to the darkness.

It was a revelation of the marvellous. How many times does sport provide such a thing? Times without number if you watch a lot of it, if you spend your life travelling round the world to seek it, if you spend countless hours and years of your life thinking about it. Marvellous beyond measure.

Here were the seven fastest men on earth, and with them an eighth who made them look slow.

Marvellous, yes. Marvellous in a slightly frightening sort of way. He seemed to be running beyond the physical capacity of the human frame, so much so that you half-expected bits of his body to come flying off in the frenzy of his speed. Ben Johnson seemed to be running away from his own humanity.

Two final floating strides with his right index finger pointed at the sky – how much faster would he have gone had he raced to the line, without this premature celebration of dominance? His head lifted high, neck arched to the sun, an instant icon.

Victory.

But at what cost?

This was the final of the 100 metres at the Olympic Games in Seoul in 1988. Sport's primal scene.

~

BOOK 1

1983

They were seeking to be the best, or, at least, the best they ever could be. Of course they were, because this was sport. They were seeking excellence, both comparative and absolute. Above all, they were seeking victory. It was the Newquay Surf Classic and the restless sea was heaving beyond Fistral Beach.

For Chris Hines it was blasphemy. He looked out at the long line of Atlantic rollers but for once he had no wish to be out there. This wasn't a day to try conclusions with the ocean; God no, quite apart from all those competitors, these were no sort of waves. It'd be like surfing a washing machine. No one would go out into that. Unless he wanted nothing more from life than victory.

Hines's board was decorated with a view of sunset on Mars. It had a single fin, mark of a person who seeks to become one with the glory of the wave. Multiple fins are for those who prefer to tear a wave into shreds. For Chris, a surfing competition was like a love-making race.

'The wave has come to you across thousands of miles of ocean and no one will ride it except you. Surf it, and it's gone. You have a relationship with a wave, a complete involvement with it, and then it's broken. You know those insects that mate once and die? It's like that.'

~

He was the boy who won. He always would be. Knowing that nothing would ever be as good again. To fulfil your life to the very last degree is a fine thing – but if you're 21 when you do so, you have plenty of time to contemplate the meaning of triumph.

There were tears in his eyes. A café in Winchester, sitting in the June sunshine with the statue of Alfred the Great. He'd been working in Butlin's. Coaching kids. He liked it, liked it a lot, but that wasn't really the point, was it? Now he was talking about the great things he wanted to do, that he still had to do, that he needed to do. If only they'd let him.

Alan Ball. You've won it once, now go out and win it again. Instant mythology of our times: sport does things like that. For those were Alf Ramsey's words to his England team after they had conceded a late equaliser to West Germany in the World Cup final of 1966. They had the world and they lost it. Now it was extra time, 15 minutes each way and the whole world there to be won and lost all over again. Sport can be very cruel: after all, it's supposed to be.

Ball, the youngest player in the team, set out to win it again. And he did. He took on the task before him in a sporting frenzy, as if exhaustion had started to work backwards. As if running gave rather than devoured energy. As if giving everything meant only that you had more to give.

Like love.

Ball ran as if he was going to run forever. It was that state of infinitely vulnerable sporting perfection that has sometimes been called 'the rapture'. And through the rapture Ball won. He was the inspiration, he was the fightback, he was the cross from which Geoff Hurst scored. He won what is still remembered as the sweetest victory in English football, and sometimes as the sweetest victory in English sport.

'I can hardly remember a kick of the game. I went through the last half-hour with a combination of enthusiasm and the complete lack of fear you have when you're very young. I played in a kind of hypnotic trance of involvement. But I do remember waking up next morning and thinking: I've been the best in the world.'

Tears, Butlin's and imperishable glory.

~

'When Alexander of Macedonia was 33 he cried salt tears because there were no new worlds to conquer. Bristow is only 27.' Sid Waddell's commentary on televised darts, coming to the world through unguessable layers of irony. Eric Bristow had been world champion on five occasions. Champion of darts. The world laughed uneasily. How funny was this? If at all? How sporting was this? If at all?

They were getting ready to greet Bristow at the Freemasons Arms in London E14. An exhibition. It cost £500 to hire him for the night. Throw a few darts, sup a few pints. At last the great man arrived and changed into his Crafty Cockney darts shirt. 'I used to work round here. In a cash-and-carry, when I was about 15. Bloody awful.'

Perfection. Grace. Watch him side-on: that stillness, that balance. The head immobile. The body was like a statue, but the control lacked all tension. He looked like a figure on a Greek vase. Nothing moved but the right arm, and of that, little moved above the elbow. The strength of the wide shoulders made that possible, in combination with the finicky teacup-sipping delicacy of the fingers. He had refined a simple action until it could be repeated again and again and again, even under the stress of competition, when throwing a single dart to an accuracy of half a centimetre is the difference between defeat and victory. The indifferent muscles kept their control when the mind was raging.

Here it was nothing. Just throwing arrows with players from the Bow and District Friendly League. But this same easy action was his to command when the world was at stake.

'It was always darts with him,' said Pam Bristow, Eric's mother. An East End lady, so naturally she dropped in. 'It was dedication that got him where he is today. As a boy he spent hour after hour throwing darts. He never wanted to do anything else.'

Hour after hour after hour. A natural skill developed to an unnatural degree. A hyper-natural degree. A skill that could be taken into the most stressful times and places without breaking. Taking him to victory after victory after victory. And a kind of perfection. A kind of beauty.

~

A lovely bird alights, astonishingly close, and then, perhaps realising that you're looking, is already gone ... leaving you with a blurring image of perfection on your retina. It was like that with Tiffany Chin.

Chinese-American, as the name suggests. She was 15, and in the middle of a five-hour training session. Uncomfortable mixture of childish awkwardness and sexual awareness, the classic nymphet package. She could switch from one to another as you throw a switch. A practised if slightly uneasy word of farewell, a polite smile that revealed the brace on her teeth – the American chastity belt – and she was gone with a grace that made your head swim. For she had stepped onto the ice, gliding almost as a bird glides. It seemed that the blades on her feet had freed her not from friction but gravity. The real nature of her beauty was in movement.

It was wonderful to be so close to such beauty, not in the formal and rehearsed manner of performance, of competition, but here in practice. It was almost as if you had discovered the beauty for yourself, and that made it an oddly personal thing. As if she was dancing for you.

She was doing no such thing, of course. She was preparing for the Winter Olympic Games in Sarajevo the following year. She was preparing for glory. And for victory, yes, but more than that. Figure skating is sport, not performance art, and the performance is never entirely under the control of the performer. A certain number and quality of jumps are required in each routine, and a skater can fall on any one of these. A ballet dancer doesn't fall in the middle of an entrechat: for a skater, falling is part of the job. One definition of a champion is a skater who stays on the blades of her skates when gold medals are decided by fractions of a point.

But it's not just a jumping competition. 'People say she's got a triple this or a triple that, so she'll win,' Chin said. 'But I think that the artistic interpretation should be what makes the difference. Choreography is what matters, making everything beautiful. You just look at her skate past and say, wow! She's the champion.'

She stepped on the ice and turned in a single step from a pretty little girl to a creature half-woman, half-bird. And in that moment she was perfect.

~

Watford Football Club were guilty not of a tactical but a moral error. They were guilty of the lie in the soul that destroys the sport. They had finished second in the First Division that year: and this was appalling. Long-term observers of football found it hard to believe the evidence of their senses. Watford had ransacked the châteaux of the aristos with the weapons of artisans. It was against nature, against sense and against logic.

The villain at the heart of it was Wing Commander Charles Reep, who after World War Two put football to fierce analysis and found that most goals are scored after the completion of three passes or fewer. He concluded that it makes sense to kick the ball forward in the right general direction, for if you did that often enough you would surely win. He called the system POMO: Position of Maximum Opportunity.

Watford and their manager Graham Taylor put it into action wholeheartedly. The squad included John Barnes, one of the most skilful players of his generation, but that didn't let Watford off anything. The point was that Watford had to fail. It was essential. If they failed to fail, something close to a religious faith would be destroyed.

It was a faith in beauty. Football was a beautiful game and not to be profaned by louts from a no-account club hoofing the ball up the field and chasing after it like berserkers. Mere anarchy was loosed upon the world. It was a crime against beauty. It shouldn't be possible to win in this ugly fashion: *Swan Lake* in clogs.

Europe would find them out, that was the one great comfort. They would fall apart as soon as they tried their heresies on the sophisticated footballers on the far side of the Channel. POMO was a British aberration, one that shamed us all, but wrong would be made right when Europe came to the rescue. Watford, thanks to their position as Division One runners-up, were playing in the UEFA Cup, and already lost the first leg against Kaiserslautern 3-1. Thank God.

The return leg was at Watford, with the club hampered by a series of injuries. They promoted a few reserves, including Ian Richardson, and they all played like madmen. They whacked the ball upfield and chased it, headed it, hoofed it and headed it again. The ball occasionally touched the ground, only to be lofted again. No control. No beauty. No order. Watford won 3-0, Richardson scored twice.

There was beauty, perhaps even rapture in that sore night, but not everyone saw it that way.

- Alan Ball never found the success as a football manager that he longed for.
- Eric Bristow went on to suffer from a mental affliction called dartitis, in which he was unable to release the dart. 'I'd bring my dart back, get halfway through throwing it and could not let go. I don't know how I got it or how I got rid of it, but I had it for about ten years. I feel like I'm doomed.' He briefly regained the number one ranking but was never the same force.
- Tiffany Chin was ninth in the World Championships of 1983. She was fourth in the Olympic Games of 1984 in Sarajevo, third in the World Championships of 1985 and third again in the 1986 World Championships. Her jumping consistently betrayed her. She suffered from injury and was never quite the champion.
- Watford were beaten finalists in the FA Cup that season and finished 11th in the league. They were relegated in 1988, and returned to the top flight – by now the Premier League – in 2015. POMO did not become the new orthodoxy. Its shock value diminished, and it became clear that Watford's real edge was in fitness. Opponents got fitter and learned how to deal with them and with POMO.
- Chris the surfer continued his lonely colloquy with the sea.

~

BOOK 2

1984

A team of battlers. They put the opposition to the sword. He's a warrior, that one. The sort you'd want alongside you in the trenches. He left his opponent for dead. It was a war out there. The team kept soldiering on. Then they brought out the heavy artillery and blew their opponents away. They were doing well, but in the second half they just died.

But Bruce Grobbelaar didn't just die, and not dying defined his life in sport. He did, however, drop a cross going for a one-handed catch when playing in goal for Liverpool against Widzew Lodz in the quarter-finals of the European Cup the previous year. It cost them the match and the competition.

'You thought I was bad against Widzew Lodz? You should have seen me against Nottingham Forest last week. I didn't do one thing right. Every cross, I dropped it. Every shot, I fumbled. The ball was a bar of soap and my hands were covered in lather. They didn't score – I don't know how.'

A lot of laughter. Hard, dangerous laughter. Good company,

but with an edge. He wasn't playing by the normal rules of the sporting interview. You're not sure if you want to spend the evening in his company or get out while you're ahead. After all, he's left people for dead, this one. Killing them first.

Grobbelaar was born in Rhodesia. At 17 he was drafted into the army to fight the Bush War. He did his year, mostly on border patrols in Mozambique. Survived by a miracle or two. Then they demanded another six months. And after that, six more. Just like the book.

'I was certain I was going to die. A lot of my colleagues have been injured and maimed and killed ... I was helicoptered in on a village on the border. One of the enemy came at me and I shot him. I felt nothing but relief at the time. To say it changed me is an understatement ... I'm getting paid for a game I love and yet I reflect back to the army time and how many lives have been lost through a silly war. An absolutely stupid war ...'

Grobbelaar could take the responsibility for losing a football match in his stride. Even a game as important – yes, important – as a European Cup quarter-final. Football, after all, is an absolutely stupid game.

Just like all the others.

~

It was the worst nightmare in the world coming true.

Words of Peter Hobson, who destroyed a boat, the hopes of its crew and one of the world's major sporting events by means of his curious instinct for disaster.

A racing eight looks too tiny for its octave of giants; barely adequate for the shrimp of a cox at the back, shouting and operating the rudder. That last was Hobson.

It had happened before. That's what made it so odd, and perhaps so inevitable. He had even joked about it, listing his interests in the event programme as 'scuba diving and reshaping barges'.

This was the Boat Race, the annual aquatic competition between the universities of Oxford and Cambridge. Hobson was coxing for Cambridge. He was experienced, he knew that the minutes before the start are very difficult and very important: you must get your crew warm and loose, easy in their strength, united, balanced at that point just before eagerness becomes anxiety. Once they feel the boat moving on the water they'll be all right.

There's a moment just after the completion of a stroke and just before the crew eases forward again for the next: the moment between the drive and the recovery. At this point the boat is balanced on a knife blade, running sweet and true and impossibly fast: the power of the many in unison. Get the crew to feel that, and the minds don't just become quiet, they become one. Warm the body, cool the mind: bring them to the start ready to express the months of work that have brought them so far.

But Cambridge never made the start. They returned to the boathouse at Putney with the boat in ruins. The canary-coloured craft was broken: the bow three feet above the surface. It was bent at 45 degrees at a point just behind the seat of the bowman. Hobson had steered the boat into a barge. Reshaping the chances of this crew.

'It's the one day in the year in which the river is closed,' Hobson said. 'So I was steering my normal course. The last thing I expected was a barge in the way. It wasn't there the day before, and I just didn't expect it to be there. The crew were marvellous to me. Just marvellous. They pulled me right back. And I never thought of pulling out.'

Some disaster, that. And some courage.

~

Danny Blanchflower, former captain of Tottenham Hotspur, famously said: 'The great fallacy is that the game is first and last about winning. It is nothing of the kind. The game is about glory; it is about doing things in style and with a flourish, about going out and beating the other lot, not waiting for them to die of boredom.'

Perhaps there is something wrong in playing for the love of victory, rather than playing for the love of playing. Go for it, take a punt, have a dip. Go for glory, don't die wondering. Don't weigh up the percentages – open your shoulders and have a go.

Roundheads and Cavaliers. Engineers and poets. Those who play the percentages and those who play the ball. Those who pursue the joy of victory and those who pursue the purer joy of action. But the other kind win matches too. People for whom Blanchflower's fallacy is an eternal truth.

Steve Davis was playing Jimmy White in the final of the Snooker World Championship in Sheffield: best of 35 frames, or first to 18. It takes two days and when the first ended Davis was 12-4 up. He was always a percentage player: thoughtful, cautious, meticulous. He walked round the table in the manner of the instructor in Rembrandt's anatomy lesson. He never seemed to have a difficult shot to play. He had schooled himself to show no emotion. He had trained his mind to keep thinking. 'Anyone can miss a pot. But when you're thinking wrong you've lost.'

White wasn't thinking wrong. He wasn't thinking at all. And on the second day he played with the freedom of a man with nothing left to lose. It was thrilling, dashing and daring and it filled the intense little space of the Crucible Theatre with joy. He had plenty of difficult shots to play. He went for them all and he pulled most of them off. He was a man possessed by the rapture.

At last White was in Davis's slipstream and poised to overtake, the score was 17-16. White needed two more and looked unstoppable. Davis needed just the one and looked a beaten man.

Davis won the next frame, the match and the championship.

There was a real beauty in this defeat, a profound satisfaction in being the glorious loser. Perhaps it was here that White fell half in love with easeful defeat. Perhaps it was, in the end, more comfortable. Less lonely.

~

The doomed couple threw themselves into a volcano, plunged to their deaths, making a tryst with eternity and all in the name of sport. Anguish in their faces, desperation in their body language: the long climb up the slope before the last despairing dive into the molten lava as the horrors of love overwhelmed them. And in dying they left their opponents for dead.

It was perfection. Nothing less: nine sixes – the maximum – for artistic impression. And when they did a recap at Richmond Ice Rink a few weeks later there was still tension and terror in every sliding step. It still mattered. They had died once but another double death only made it truer. Richmond was an echo of that first rapture: this death was pure joy.

Here were Jayne Torvill and Christopher Dean. They had won the gold medal in the ice dance at the Winter Olympics in Sarajevo. In ice dance you dance. On ice. You don't jump, like Tiffany Chin, like figure skaters, so you can control your performance. They danced to a specially commissioned arrangement of Ravel's *Bolero*, cut from 18 minutes to 4 minutes 28 seconds: still 28 seconds too long. They solved the problem by kneeling on the ice at the start and swaying about, for the clock only starts once you're both on your skates. This slow start set the tone: something special was coming up. Something involving that weird stuff called art.

Most sports columnists hated it. For a start, women liked it, and surely that invalidated it as sport. It'd be better, ho ho, if opponents were allowed to tackle. Sport has to be governed by male values if it is to count as sport: that is to say, physical confrontation.

You mean like golf?

Arts commentators also hated it. It was sentimental, melodramatic and kitsch: Tretchikoff's *Chinese Girl* made flesh.

Torvill and Dean's aim was victory: but more than victory. They wanted to reach victory by the path of beauty, by doing it in style. And perhaps the subject of the dance – death – resonated with people who follow sport: for sport itself is a dance in which success and failure operate as metaphors of life and death.

It was bad art and bad sport, but it was great something. The spell of performance turned the commonplace Dean – a former policeman – into a tragic hero and turned the plain Torvill into a doomed beauty – the same aspect of will that turned Judi Dench – self-described as 'a menopausal dwarf' – into Cleopatra.

Bolero was never understood or accepted by the majority of art critics or sports commentators, but everybody else adored it. It wouldn't have been anything without the marks, without the victory, without the moment of tension before the marks were announced. That much was clear. But for the rest: well, if art has its eternal mysteries, then so does sport.

~

The Hong Kong Rugby Sevens tournament was first held in 1976. Some nations saw the event as the Olympic Games of rugby union, others as an opportunity to catch up on their drinking. New Zealand sent provincial sides out for a jolly, but as the standard of the competition got higher the policy became humiliating to both sides. One year the invitation for New Zealand was withheld. The New Zealand Rugby Union said all right, we'll send a national team, a proper All Blacks squad. Great, the organisers said. But not this year, thanks. Maybe next.

New Zealand were invited back and accepted. They also accepted that the event was now serious. Proper sport. Winning and losing and leaving the opposition for dead. They went to

Hong Kong to dominate the competition with brutal functionalism: three big ball-winning forwards and four backs who could run like the wind. It was all about straight lines and knocking people over. It was very well organised and very well executed and it took them to the final.

Fiji took another approach. They loved to be thrilling, dashing and daring. They did things in style. Beauty was their chief weapon, and it took them to the final as well.

The New Zealand teams were loved by New Zealanders. Everyone else loved Fiji: for Hong Kong was then the home of the free-booter and the maverick. Poets v engineers, etc.

Before the trial began a dozen drunken Kiwis tumbled shirtless from the stands to perform a rather poor haka. Perhaps that decided the outcome. The Fijians responded with their own war dance, sober, savage, serious. Deadly serious?

Straight lines against spirals. Sheet music against jazz. Science against art. Beauty against functionality. Or was it? Because this beauty was curiously functional, given that its function was victory. There is a mystery in all team sports, and it occurs when for no very obvious reason, every individual plays beyond his own limitations. It's as if excellence was a communicable disease.

Here a team found perfection. Rapture. Behind-the-back passes, through-the-legs passes, no-look passes: every audacity that had ever been tried on the training fields was tried for real and every one came off as if preordained. Fiji won 26-0. Glory, beauty and wonder.

And yet without New Zealand's brutal functionalism, there'd have been no need for such beauty.

~

The route was not beautiful. It led across the rubble through a hole roughly knocked in a wall. Beyond lay a brick-built shed. Once inside, the hogo of man sweat was like a playful slap. Bricks and metal: damp in the air: too cold. A clang and a crash and a welcome as the two men left off grunting for a moment. Let's call them Jim and Dave. There's such a thing as the Rehabilitation of Offenders Act, as well as common decency.

The room contained the basic training tools for sport. Well, any sport that requires strength. Weights. Heavy metal. Raised and lowered, raised and lowered: sometimes in pain, sometimes in self-approving vanity, sometimes in duty to the team and the cause of sport. Grunt and clank. Sweat and strain. Self-punishment, self-admiration: all for a distant goal of strength. And beauty too, of a kind.

But a weightlifter lifts weights in order to lift weights. In weightlifting the training is also the event. As if a Test match took place in the nets, as if football was a competitive passing drill, as if ice dance was a series of set exercises. It follows that a weightlifter has a very special understanding of sport.

'A lot of the time it is very boring indeed,' said Dave. 'There is only one way to alleviate the boredom, and that's by improving. Setting new personal bests is the only thing I don't find boring about weightlifting.'

The Olympic Games lay ahead, the goal of both men. Dave thought he had a slim chance of a medal, Jim was less sanguine. 'You learn all the technique when you're young, once it's there it should be there. Training is just lifting weights.'

Dave said he was better in training than he was in competition. That was something of a confession. Most sporting performers find their best in competition. They expand in the heated circumstances of confrontation and judgement. Training should be a base from which you arise: not an eminence from which you step down.

Arms like legs. Legs like half-grown trees. Muscles not for show but for use: for constant use, again and again and again. They looked hard as iron.

~

The Olympic Games of 1984 took place in Los Angeles. Avoid the false experience of being there. Better to share the real thing with the world – television.

Cheap witticism. But it was still participation in the common experience.

Whooo! Whooo! The televisions of the world echoed to the whooping of American spectators. This was not the brotherhood of nations: this was America against the world. America's triumph was made easier by the fact that much of the world failed to turn up: 17 nations boycotted the Games, including the Soviet Union, East Germany, Cuba, Iran and Libya. This was in response to the American-led boycott of the 1980 Games in Moscow, in which 65 nations refused to take part, though a good number of athletes competed as individuals under the Olympic flag.

Sport is a continuation of politics by other means. Who cares about the athletes who give their lives to sport? The competitors who live for one chance at the one event? For that is what the Olympic Games mean: all those athletes, lifting weights in sweat-stinking rooms for years, and all for an event they would never see.

~

Adrenalin – scientists use the more precise term epinephrine – is secreted by the medulla of the adrenal glands. Then, through a complex biochemical response, blood vessels are dilated, the rate and force of the contractions of the heart are increased and blood pressure is raised. The process that allows the mammal concerned to maximise certain physical responses. It is a time at which nothing on earth matters but the task in hand: and it's the reason for the stories about mothers lifting cars to rescue their trapped children. Adrenalin is associated with powerful and enduring memories, which explains the extraordinary vividness of everybody's sporting experiences – however humble – when recollected in tranquillity. (Alan Ball would have disagreed with this.) Adrenalin means that an athlete should perform better in competition than at any other time: and better in the ultimate competition of a lifetime than at any other time in the entire course of existence.

But sometimes it works the other way. Sometimes the stuff seems to work backwards, to disastrous negative effect: think of Eric Bristow and his dartitis. And then think of Sebastian Coe in the 800 metres at the Olympic Games in Moscow four years earlier. In the final he lost his head, failed to control the race with his vastly superior speed and was caught by the better sprinter, Steve Ovett. Coe's father Peter, also his coach, summed up the performance for all time: 'You ran like a cunt.'

Adrenalin is essentially connected to the fight-or-flight response. If you want to run away when you need to fight, or vice versa, you get the whole thing tangled up and disaster follows. Coe knew that as he entered the last lap of the 1500 metres a few days later. He was ignited by the terror of a second failure and ran as if the cheetahs of hell were after him. Terror and exaltation combined in that extraordinary grimace as he crossed the finishing line first, arms spread as if crucified.

It was different this time round in Los Angeles. His run to the line was fuelled not by fear but by anger. Not flight: fight. This time he ran as if blasting through walls. He didn't look as if he was running away from his enemies: he looked as if he was running towards them with a knife in his teeth. He marked the greatest victory of his career with a deranged rant at the press box, jabbing his finger to the air as if it were an enemy's eye. 'Who says I'm fucking finished?'

The lunatic and the athlete are of imagination all compact. Or to put that another way, don't expect exceptional people to be normal. Sport is a process of separating the exceptional from all the others. No champion is normal: that would be a contradiction. Everybody wants champions: we don't always like what we get.

In other walks of life, ultra-high achievers learn to hide their abnormality with urbanity and charm. An athlete in competition is naked before us: stripped bare by adrenalin.

~

Harley Street. Dr Peter Harvey. Consultant neurologist at the Royal Free Hospital. A stout, jolly man with a mind like a scalpel. He was talking of death. Living death, and the other kind. And sport, of course.

Doctors who specialise tend to have a special reverence for the bit of body they have devoted their lives to. Harvey talked about the brain as if it were the soul. As perhaps it is. He met an amateur boxer in the course of his professional life. Some years later, they met again. 'He had become a near-criminal, a tragic man. The brain-damaged boxer becomes a social responsibility and a menace. Often violent, often a drunkard.'

This meeting changed his view of sport forever.

He spoke of the delicacy of brain tissue, its vulnerability. All brain damage is permanent, he said. It's not like the films, when the hero is struck on the head, sleeps for a while and then recovers after a brief shake of the head. If that was the case, we would use rubber hammers – or boxing gloves – instead of anaesthetics in hospitals. Nor is concussion a comic episode that passes as if it had never been. All of which makes boxing unacceptable as a public entertainment, he said.

'People point out that rugby is dangerous, that National Hunt racing is dangerous. They are perfectly right. But the aim of these sports is not to cause injury. In boxing the ultimate achievement is to knock somebody out. And to knock somebody out is to injure their brain.'

There are two kinds of brain injuries. There is a traumatic kind that comes from a single fight, or even a single blow, which can sometimes be lethal. And there is subtle and cumulative damage that doesn't kill the person at once but bit by bit destroys his personality and his life. His soul, if you like.

'Boxing is a contest in which the winner seems often to be the one who produces more brain damage on his opponent than he himself sustains.'

The process of injuring an opponent's brain is much easier when you wear gloves: they protect the striker's hand, not the recipient's head. It's hard to cause real damage when you strike bone against bone. Protect the hand and you can strike with real force. Boxing helmets (worn in sparring and then in all amateur boxing) merely give the striker a bigger target to aim for and increase the torsional effect of a glancing blow.

Most sports are metaphors, often metaphors of life and death: battles, duels, sieges, last-ditch stands, assaults, hunts and great escapes. Boxing, alone among sports, is no metaphor. Boxing is the real thing. In boxing, you really can leave your opponent for dead.

On purpose.

- Bruce Grobbelaar won six league titles with Liverpool, also three FA Cups, three League Cups, and a European Cup. In 1994 he was accused by the *Sun* newspaper of fixing the results of football matches. The case went to court and he was cleared in 1997. He sued the *Sun* successfully and was awarded £85,000. This was reduced on appeal to £1, and he was ordered to pay the *Sun*'s costs, estimated at £500,000. He was unable to pay and was declared bankrupt. He has since moved to Canada.
- The Boat Race took place the following day. Cambridge were in a borrowed boat and lost by 3¾ lengths. Peter Hobson went on to cox internationally. He became a development banker.

- Steve Davis was beaten finalist at the World Championship of 1985, losing on the final black to Dennis Taylor in what's still remembered as snooker's greatest match. He won the championship three times in a row from 1987, making six in all. Jimmy White never won the World Championship; he was beaten finalist five times in a row from 1990.

- Torvill and Dean went professional and put on a series of shows. They made a comeback to competition when the rules about amateurism were changed, and won the Olympic bronze medal in 1994.

- Fiji have won the Hong Kong Sevens 15 times, the most wins by any nation. The Hong Kong Sevens inspired the development of the Rugby World Cup, which was first contested in 1987. Sevens became an Olympic sport at the Rio Games of 2016; Fiji won the gold medal.

- Jim and Dave, the weightlifters, were convicted of selling anabolic steroids illegally.

- Sebastian Coe went into politics. He was made a life peer. He ran the successful London campaign for the Olympic Games of 2012, and was subsequently in charge of the event itself. He then became president of the International Association of Athletics Federations.

- The British Medical Association continues to campaign, in a low-key but persistent way, for the abolition of boxing. The various organisations that run boxing continue to do a reasonable job of trying to abolish themselves.

~

BOOK 3

1985

Eamonn McCabe was a great sports photographer. His work is often graced with art and humour, but he was also a newspaper-man who knew what a story was. So when he saw a disturbance in the crowd at the football match he went into action without thinking about artistic values. He felt ever-so-slightly sick: he could foresee bad things. He walked to the other end of the pitch to check them out.

It was his habit to carry a snapshot camera in his pocket: a compact thing with a decent lens that used proper 35mm film. When congestion was too great for his big single-lens reflex cameras and heavyweight lenses, he would make a quick draw and use the little camera. It was ideal in the scrum around a trophy-waving lap of honour.

McCabe got to the end of the pitch where the ground staff were starting to be aware that something was amiss. He went for his camera with the speed and accuracy of Josey Wales and exposed a single frame before he was hustled away. It is one of the most terrible images in the history of sport.

Even one-handed in the midst of a melee McCabe was a good enough craftsman to hold the camera steady as a statue and to produce an image sharp as a stiletto. By doing so he created a masterpiece. A Goyaesque portrait of terror. It is a picture of people who know who they are about to die. Their faces stay with all those who have gazed on this photograph.

This was Heysel Stadium in Brussels, on the occasion of the European Cup final between Liverpool and Juventus. The trouble took place before the match when Liverpool fans invaded a neutral area, provoking a retreat. A wall collapsed. There were 39 people killed and 600 injured.

Juventus won 1–0, but it was never a penalty.

~

Linsey MacDonald was studying chemical engineering in Edinburgh. She was 21. When she was 16 she won an Olympic bronze medal running for Great Britain in the 400 metres relay. She also made the final of the 400 metres individual event. One of those who didn't boycott the Moscow Games, then. That same year, 1980, she set a British record of 51.16 seconds for the 400 metres.

Too much too soon. She went on to suffer serious injury, almost certainly from overtraining. After prolonged rehab, she went back to the track determined to run again. Well, jog. Attainable goals, you know how it's done, don't overface yourself. So she set herself a target of ten metres. And failed. The woman who aimed low and missed.

Next day, she managed it. All ten. But she failed to make the Olympic Games of 1984, when she might have been at her peak. She had, it seemed, been wasted. The victim of other people's ambitions. And her own, of course. 'When you're 16 and someone asks you to do something, you do it. That's where experience would have told. It was all so quick. I could, I suppose, have held myself up for the LA Olympics four years later – but then I could have got injured anyway. No, it was a chance to run in the Olympics. I paid for it, but it was definitely worth the price.'

With the Panglossian optimism of everyone involved in big-time sport, MacDonald was inclined to think it was all for the best, and that when she regained competitive fitness she would have a second athletics career. That was the way things seemed to be moving that day in Edinburgh. But part of her – the part she didn't show to the world, the part that she preferred to bury, the part that tends to crop up at 3.45 on a restless night – suspected that she had already reached her peak. That she was already in decline. That her life as an athlete ended at the age of 16.

Without cruelty there can be no sport.

~

Have you actually been to South Africa?

No.

Trying not to sound even remotely apologetic. Failing.

Ayyyoh.

Drawling contempt in that public-school diphthong. Enemy duly slain.

No point in saying you don't have to witness injustice to grasp the concept of injustice.

Have you read his stuff? And he hasn't even been there. He has no idea what it's like, to be out there on the front line beside the braai and the swimming pool. It's a great way of life they have out there behind the razor wire. Everybody has servants. Except the servants, of course. And they're happier that way. *Everybody* is happier that way. But if you haven't been there you can't possibly understand. If you haven't taken your glass of wine – and believe me their wines there are wonderful – from the black hand of a servant under a sky of cloudless blue, you simply can't understand South Africa. If you dismantle apartheid, the country will collapse in bloodshed. Margaret Thatcher had it right when she said: 'Anyone who thinks the ANC is going to govern South Africa is living in cloud-cuckoo-land.' And you see, she's been there, she goes there often, she takes holidays there, she knows the place, she loves it and she understands it.

And they've done a great job in the townships. White people have been helping black people in townships to play cricket. So that makes everything else all right. What can he possibly be complaining about? It's a view that comes from ignorance. And that, in my book, is prejudice.

The BBC's radio programme *Test Match Special* sounded at times a party political broadcast in favour of the National Party of South Africa. The sports pages of the national press were full of generosity and understanding towards the South African government. They're doing a great job in the townships. And that makes the whole concept of townships all right.

What? You disagree? Have you been there?

Ayyyoh.

~

The England rugby team ended their practice session. The head coach, Dick Greenwood, was happy with the way things were going, but then again, he wasn't. He knew his team weren't really much cop. A dull lot. No imagination. Wholly lacking in devil. They worked hard and enjoyed confrontation and were hot as hell on esprit de corps. But when they won, it was because they ground out a result. And when they were beaten they looked plain bewildered. They were a functional team, except that they didn't really function. France were the dominant force in northern hemisphere rugby, and played as if there were points on offer for style alone. But two weeks earlier, England had managed a 9-9 draw with France. Grinder-outers can sometimes get results. More than one approach to winning in sport.

Mind you, there was a period in a recent match against Romania when England had looked beautiful. That period of rapture had lasted for a full minute. 'No, it wasn't a minute,' Greenwood said. 'It was 47 seconds.'

England were facing a match against Wales in Cardiff the following weekend: 'The finest sound in the game of rugby is the silence of the Welsh crowd.' The Welsh team of the 1970s had played with style all right: and they were murderously effective, too. But perhaps England could grind something out. Or perhaps they might find 47 seconds of rapture.

'I'd be happy to win by an unjustified penalty,' Greenwood said. 'Except I wouldn't.'

~

'I'm not a natural athlete,' Sarah Springman said, an unexpected remark from the British triathlon champion. She was preparing to defend her title the following weekend: two-mile swim, 60-mile bike ride and a 15-mile run. She had been fitting training around her work as a civil engineer: a weekly regimen of 300 miles on the bike, 45 miles running and 10 miles swimming. She was in good shape, well prepared. It had been different the previous year, when work on her thesis for her MPhil at Cambridge rather got in the way.

'I handed in my thesis on Friday with two minutes to spare and then drove off to the race on Sunday. I was in no fit shape to do the race and I didn't want to do it either. I was 15 minutes ahead after the swim, but by the time I had finished the run I was only four minutes clear. Then I collapsed with dehydration and heat exhaustion.

'I really should not have got round the course. It was my mind that got me through.'

Mind and body.

How do you separate them? Can you train both? Questions that were now entering the mainstream of sport. Talent is never enough on its own: but Springman took that idea to an extreme. She said that she had almost no talent at all, not in the physical sense. Her talent was for achievement. For victory. It was a matter of will.

So an athlete can be whatever he and she decides to be? Like an existentialist? Perhaps not quite that, but you can't fulfil physical talent without mental ability. And both kinds of talent can be worked on: alone or with assistance.

The bodies of men and women are different. Are their minds different also? 'I don't feel a macho compulsion to go flat out all the way round. I often beat men who should beat me. They set off too fast and are dead for the run. I try to run my race in an intelligent fashion.' So that's mind as instrument of will and mind as thinking organ: two kinds of mind. The brain is better used in sport as a tool than a target, perhaps.

'Sometimes the mental battle is very hard – when you're swimming in the Cam in March, for example. People wonder what it is I am trying to prove. But I actually do enjoy doing it, you see. Sport defines your goals. You learn about your limits – and you discover that if you want to do something enough, there really are no limits.'

But perhaps an athlete has to think that way. Perhaps there is no other option. Perhaps a refusal to accept physical realities is a diagnostic trait of a successful athlete.

~

Somewhere off one of those ladder-steep streets of Merthyr Tydfil stood the home of the last British man to hold the world featherweight boxing championship. It was filled to the point of clutter with pictures and trophies and souvenirs: a shrine to his own past. He was a champion, but his career was defined by three protracted and bloody fights with Vicente Saldivar of Mexico. Howard Winstone lost them all. But he won ever-greater respect from each shattering defeat. In the first he lost on points after 15 rounds; in the second he lost by half a point; in the last he was knocked down in the seventh and again in the 12th round before his corner threw in the towel.

'I still think I could have gone on, like,' he said. Not accepting the physical realities. 'There's no doubt that I would have had more problems – but Saldivar said afterwards that he wouldn't have been able to come out for the next round.' Saldivar retired after the fight, though he made a couple of the inevitable – and inevitably disastrous – boxer's comebacks. Physical realities: the will is not enough.

Winstone carried on after the defeat and at last won his world title. Shortly after that he retired. He went to Mexico City for the 1968 Olympic Games as a spectator. 'First thing that happened when I got to my hotel was a phone call from Saldivar. He picked me up at the hotel every day and we went and saw everything and did everything. He had no-good English but we could communicate.

'I'm not surprised we became friends. He was a fellow I boxed, we were doing a job, and when it's all over, it's finished. I don't know anyone who doesn't feel the same about opponents, we're all good buddies. But Saldivar, he was the hardest, he was the strongest I fought against. He was a good champion.'

But it's not a job like painting houses or writing for newspapers. Something big is being shared. It's not just danger, as you get when riding horses over fences, or racing motorbikes. It's the business of deliberately inflicting pain and potentially lethal damage on each other that is so peculiarly intimate. Boxers often embrace and kiss after a bout: the closer and more brutal the fight is, the more effusive the boxers. In some ways sex is less intimate than a 15-round boxing match between two fighters of equal talent. These two men loved each other for the damage each had caused and that each had accepted.

You can make an unanswerable case for the abolition of

boxing. You can loathe the criminal traditions of the sport. You can feel disgust at the way that boxers have so often been the playthings of rich men, discarded when their usefulness is over. You can feel profound distaste for some of the people involved in professional boxing, and double that for the hangers-on. You can have serious misgivings about the people who pay to watch boxing.

But the boxers themselves, well, that's a different matter. Boxing is neither noble nor an art, but there is unmistakable nobility in the courage and the strange friendship of Winstone and Saldivar. Perhaps beauty as well.

~

How beautiful are the feet. An aria from *Messiah*, words from Isaiah: and if the feet are beautiful, how lovely must everything else be? Not that David Gower ever moved his feet much when he was batting. But never mind that: how beautiful are the runs. Not just the number of them or the fact that they allowed England to beat Australia: those runs were beautiful in themselves. In three successive matches Gower, England captain, scored 166 in a draw at Trent Bridge, then 215 and 157 in victories at Edgbaston and The Oval.

But why so lovely? Perhaps more than any other batsman, Gower brought off the illusion of complicity. When he hit a boundary with a flick-pull, the bat moving through an angle of no more than 45 degrees, the ball apparently acquiring a supernatural life of its own through this minimal contact, it seemed as if the bowler and the batsman were not in opposition but in collaboration, creating as lovely a thing as *Bolero*: a ritual dance with prearranged steps. The bowler was condemned to be part of this beauty.

No bowler ever cared for this – but there were times when the batsman resented it as well. Beauty was not Gower's weapon of choice. He was a man condemned: unable to free himself from the shackles of beauty. He could not make an effort of will and become somebody else: someone more reliable, less fickle, less in thrall to his own gifts. 'I tread a very fine line. My natural strength – and weakness – has always been my timing. If my timing is out, batting looks very hard indeed. At other times, timing is my best ally.'

There was a hint of despair in this self-analysis. A resentment of the lofty talent that made him so vulnerable. 'If you hit a four without moving your feet they say it's effortless. If you get out, it's a fault in your game. But the basis of my game has not changed in times of good form and bad.'

Gower was always being told to knuckle down, get his head down, concentrate, learn to be a grafter. No one ever told the grafters to snap out of it and be a genius. But perhaps grafters and geniuses are equally stuck in the trap of their own natures. Gower was doomed to beauty as others were to mediocrity. And the curse of it all was that Gower knew that such beauty – depending on such fragile nuances of timing – could only ever be intermittent. The rapture comes and the rapture goes.

Is beauty a higher cause than victory? No athlete would ever say as much: especially one playing a team game as captain. But in the heart of the action there are truths that never show up on the scoreboard or in the interviews or the match reports or the autobiographies. Did Gower move beyond his own hopes for victory and personal glory and feel a duty to beauty?

It always looked that way, but perhaps that was just another illusion. And perhaps not: the truth of sport as well as its beauty lies in the action, not in the assessment. It is all about what happens between the motion and the act. In cricket they call it 'timing'.

Cricket is a dance to the music of timing.

~

Graham Gooch told the story of his participation in what was called 'a rebel cricket tour' to South Africa in his book *Out of the Wilderness*. The tour comprised a series of unofficial matches played in a country banned from world cricket because of its policy of apartheid. The tour was set up by a laborious process of lies and deception, or as Gooch put it, 'almost deception'. 'But what else could we do?' he asked. What indeed?

He quoted a letter from the *Daily Telegraph*: 'Businessmen of all nationalities visit South Africa daily in furtherance of their commercial interests, so why not cricketers, as already do golfers and tennis players and so on?' Why not, indeed?

To summarise: Gooch was bribed to take part in Test matches that weren't Test matches, captaining a side that was mendaciously called 'England'. He was paid to pretend that South Africa was a normal place in which normal sport could take place. He was paid to show the world that apartheid was a damn good thing: and that England agreed with that assessment.

Some people agreed with the letter-writer. Many within cricket were quietly approving: after all, they're doing a great job in the townships, and what's so terrible about apartheid? You can't understand the system until you've been there.

But there were also objections to the rebel tour: and that's because sport is not the same thing as business. Sport has a meaning, even if we're never entirely sure what, and sport has a value, even if we're not entirely sure what – only that it's not a value that you can add up and stick in a bank.

That's why sport became the medium for expressing the world's disapproval of apartheid. Sport bore this burden with more resentment than pride. But sport had no option but to take it on.

Unlike business, sport has a soul.

～

Courage is a form of beauty, and courage is the business of the soul. Sport showcases courage in a million different ways, not all of them concerned with men attacking each other's brains. Courage – perhaps a higher form of it – can also be found in a lovely woman on a nice day in the country.

Fence four at Burghley was a brute. It was big and imposing, yes, but you expect that. It was also blind. Its upper half was a screen of birch twigs. You not only had to jump over the fence, you also had to jump through it. You and your horse, because this was the sport of eventing, perhaps the most dangerous sport in the calendar, certainly the most dangerous sanctified by the Olympic Games. It's also a rare thing because men and women compete on equal terms for the same prizes.

Fence four was what's technically known as a bullfinch. You have to batter your way through it, but the rider following you had no cause to feel happy about that. The fence attendants were equipped with bushels of replacement twigs to keep the fence big and opaque. It was – like so much of sport – a courage-opp.

Ride tentatively at the fence and your horse will get the message that there's something fearful ahead and stop instead of jump. Ride with the madcap boldness that is really fear in another coat, and you will overstride and take a tumble. Both approaches had their fans and the fence took a heavy toll. There was a second option: a long way round with an infinitely easier jump. That way the rider lost face and time and all chance of victory – but at least finished the course.

Ginny Holgate and Priceless cantered to the fence with a casual certainty that made you gasp. The drumbeat of hooves – the moment between the motion and the act – the silence in the leap – the crackle of twigs and then the drumbeat rhythm was picked up again along with the relieved roaring of the Ginny-loving crowd as Holgate, clad as ever for cross-country in purple, kicked on for fence five with Priceless calmly eager to leap again.

The rider must trust the horse to leap as she commits herself to the jump; the horse must trust the rider not to put him at anything beyond his scope. Trust is always a bilateral business: and in whatever form you find it, it is a form of courage. And a thing of beauty.

- After the Heysel Stadium disaster English clubs were banned indefinitely from European competition; the ban was lifted in 1990-91. Liverpool served an additional year; 14 Liverpool fans were found guilty of manslaughter and received three-year sentences. Heysel is now seen as 'the forgotten disaster'.
- Linsey MacDonald was never as fast again as she was at 16; her British record was beaten in 1997 by Allison Curbishley. MacDonald became a doctor and worked in Hong Kong.
- Wales beat England 24-15; England finished fourth of the Five Nations. This was Greenwood's last year as England head coach.
- Sarah Springman won 20 elite European medals. She became a professor of geotechnical engineering at ETH Zurich and was appointed CBE in 2012.
- Howard Winstone died in 2000, aged 61. There's a statue of him in St Tydfil's Square.
- Graham Gooch served his three-year ban, was welcomed back into international cricket and went on to become England captain.
- Ginny Holgate became Ginny Leng and is now Ginny Elliott. She won Burghley that year.

BOOK 4

1986

Weep for the beauty of it.

Even now, watching it again and knowing the result, you know he can't win. Not in a million years.

The race was almost run, a mile run and just half a mile to go, and he was 11th of 15 runners.

At the front a wall of green, three horses in near-identical colours, all owned by the Aga Khan: Shadari, Darara, Shahrastani. Behind them Triptych and Bering. And at this point Pat Eddery took a look – and tucked his horse back in again. You see courage in a thousand forms in sport: here was courage of a very rare kind: doing nothing in a time of the most strenuous action when nothing is the right thing to do.

One of the three horses with the green riders must win: but no, there was Bering swooping past them all as if he came from another order of being. It was all over in a second and it was wonderful enough in all conscience.

Then and only then did Dancing Brave make his move. It was

an instant of metamorphosis: he changed in a single stride from horse into archangel. From a damn good horse to a horse of all-time greatness. From a pretty sight to one of a beauteous wonder that hurt the eyes and made them moist. He had been the equal, or near-equal, of all the pretty horses in that race: now, a stride later, he was better than them all. Better than anything there had ever been before. This was the Prix de l'Arc de Triomphe in Paris and perhaps the finest horse race that had ever been run.

He was beautiful. But it was victory that made him so. Dancing Brave had run a similar race in the Derby a few months earlier when ridden by Greville Starkey and finished second. That wasn't beautiful at all. Something about victory, something about being the best of the best, was in itself beautiful. There was also beauty in the courage of Eddery, but the courage was only visible because he won. Perhaps in absolute terms Starkey was even braver than Eddery. But Eddery won, and that has made all the difference.

Dancing Brave was beautiful, but all horses are beautiful. The Brave was lovelier than the loveliest horse ever foaled because he won, and because he won in an especially lovely way. It was about that transition. That moment of revelation. Like the hero removing the girl's glasses and letting down her hair, but better than that. Here was a single step that took the occasion and the winner from commonplace to unique.

There was a sense of shared privilege in the stands, something common to every absolutely extraordinary sporting occasion. It is a sense of being blessed, the very pure joy of sharing something perfect. It wasn't about whether or not you had backed the horse. It was about being in the presence of perfect beauty – a revelation made possible by the perfection of victory.

~

There can be beauty in defeat but never in rout.

They were destroyed by their own inadequacies. They were

inadequate individuals, they were an inadequate team. The other factors – hatred, fear, greed, politics, star culture, personalities, journalism – were just so much more wolfsbane in the hell-broth of failure. In victory such things would hardly have been noticed.

The politics were about apartheid, of course. Two members of the England cricket team, Graham Gooch and John Emburey, had recently returned – been welcomed back – to the team after three-year suspensions for playing in South Africa. Caribbean politicians were not happy about their presence. There were threats to deny 'the rebels' entry into Trinidad and Tobago. There were promises of violent demonstrations.

In England football was still a game of fear and loathing. This created a star vacuum and the great – we owe him that at least – Ian Botham filled it. Botham scandals filled the media and he nursed bitter resentments. Newspapers sent scandal specialists to cover the tour of West Indies, ending the years of cosiness in which journalists shared the players' lives and kept their secrets. For more or less the last time, players and press shared a hotel, the Port of Spain Hilton. Botham operated under siege conditions, hiding in his room with a court of chosen companions.

But it was the cricket that caused the real pain. England had lost the first Test in Jamaica by ten wickets, scoring 152 and 159 against the uncompromising four-man fast bowling attack. Botham had a poor game, out twice to Malcolm Marshall.

Sport destroys people: and here in Trinidad people were being destroyed before the eyes of their public. Some of the players on that tour recovered, at least to an extent, but most were never quite the same.

It wasn't just defeat. It was the manner of defeat. They were humiliated by fast bowling, much of it aimed at the body. They were made to seem less than men. Every innings was a defiance of physical terror, a feat some managed more efficiently than others. David Gower was captain and his method was to see how many glorious shots he could play before the inevitable doom.

Quite a lot. Never enough.

Teams take their tone from the dominant individuals: and Botham's unhappiness was a frightening thing. In Trinidad he scored two in the first innings. When he bowled he tried a childish experiment, attempting to bounce out the West Indies openers. They acted as if he had insulted not their manhood but their intelligence. He made one in the second innings, and on the way back to the pavilion he made a pantomime to the press box: go on, then, you bastards – hang me! I know that's what you wanted all along.

But oh, the terrible beauty of Malcolm Marshall. Eight wickets in the match. Sending both England openers back to the pavilion with the match a few minutes old. Getting Botham twice. Again. He was cricket's master of terror. That was not his only weapon, far from it; just the most obvious. It began with terror: and continued with the skilful way he exploited terror. Terror was his edge. The bouncer the batsman could play, followed by the bouncer he only thought he could play. Terror opened the door for still more terrible possibilities of failure.

Here was beauty, though it was beauty of a cruel and terrible kind. But sport is cruel and terrible: it follows that its beauties must often be of the same sort.

～

What is it with you Brits and Dan Marino?

That's easy. He was around when there was a national hero shortage.

Hero-worship is a derogatory phrase. Most people stop worshipping heroes before they get into double figures: but if we remain human we have heroes still. We worship only gods, but we can esteem a hero without incurring lasting personal damage. It follows that human nature abhors a hero vacuum: and like Ian Botham, Marino was available.

Wait here. In a few minutes you'll be shown in. You'll have 15 minutes.

Marino was waiting.

Because it was hard to have a hero in football back then: the memory of Heysel was too sharp, the fact that English clubs were banned from European competition was too shaming. So people looked for something exotic: and it came in Channel 4's weekly highlights package of American football.

It was at once apparent that American football is designed to showcase a single player: the quarterback. The game is set up to create a single hero from the crowd around him. And then the throw: sometimes hurled like a dart, sometimes arcing into the sky towards a tiny distant figure running beneath it.

A sporting hero like so many others. Just wearing unfamiliar clothes.

Marino took the Miami Dolphins to the Super Bowl of 1985. He threw a then record 84 touchdown passes in the season. But the style of it mattered as well: apparently aloof, detached, indifferent, paring his fingernails: just waiting for the ball to come to him and then making it do his will, making all the other lesser figures do his will, while he waited, back in the place he had never left, arms now aloft to acknowledge his own distant triumph.

But how did he make such an impression on the British?

'Well, I guess it's partly because I'm a pretty good player.'

And so we were introduced to the way the heroes now speak. Whatever you say, say nothing.

Your 15 minutes are up.

Thank you.

Football's no good any more but we still have heroes. Not worshipping but esteeming.

~

Dan Marino was beautiful too. Or his passing was. Not just the long, high curve, the line of beauty that took the ball from his one hand to the two hands of his distant receiver. It was also the fact that he made every pass while bigger and stronger men were trying to hit him so hard that he never wanted to throw a football again.

What is sport without danger? Incomplete. What is a sport that doesn't require an element of physical courage even to take part? A lesser thing entirely.

Ron Fawcett, climber: 'It's a very personal thing, climbing: you against the rock. With ropes you fall, you get used to falling – but soloing without ropes is incredibly dangerous. You and your hands and your feet. You don't even fully control the risk: a hold could break, a bit of dirt on your boots could make you slip and you're gone ... but it's a charge. It really is. I used to think it was the best but I've broken too many bones.'

Gina Campbell, daughter of Donald: 'I remember looking at the sky as I came out of the boat and thinking ... Shit! Then I blacked out ... Five minutes before I had set a world record. Now I had written off the boat and was lucky not to write off my body at the same time. I would like to go the same way as my father. I have a feeling that I'll die a violent death. I don't want to get old, but I don't want to die ... there are so many nice clothes I want to wear before I go.'

John Francome, jump jockey, had a potentially fatal accident when he was suspended underneath a horse called The Reject. After he was disentangled, 'I walked far enough away from The Reject so he wouldn't walk on me and fell to my knees on the grass. I didn't know whether to laugh or cry and settled for swearing out loud that I'd had enough of riding.'

Jonathan Palmer, Formula One driver, and qualified doctor, had known people who have died in motor racing. 'It doesn't give me pause for thought, in that I might give up. It makes me angry. I feel sorry for the survivors, for the family, but more than anything else I feel angry at the unfairness of it all. Not angry at the car manufacturers or the competition organisers . . . angry at God, maybe.'

Charles Shea-Simonds, parachutist: 'Every time you step out of a plane it's a moment of truth. You know if you do nothing, you are dead. It's not frightening, not exactly. It involves – ah – an acute sense of apprehension. I always hated sport at school but the first time I saw someone drop from 5,000 feet, I thought, My God, I've got to do that. I don't parachute because I like the idea of dying. I parachute because I enjoy living so much.'

~

At the end the handshake, the embrace, the kiss. Enemies, yes, but all in the day's work. When the match is over, all friends again, or at least not enemies. Opponents are bound together in the conspiracy of sport: hardly foes at all because there are so many more things uniting than dividing them in their beautifully constructed artificial world.

As Howard Winstone knew, real enemies are oddly rare in sport. The faux enmities of competition seldom create real hatred. The best place to look for hatred is inside a single team.

Peter Roebuck once described his Somerset team-mate Ian Botham as a wonderful friend and a terrible enemy. Dangerous words. Roebuck, a fine writer, had that year published a celebration of Botham called *It Sort of Clicks,* which was also a celebration of the rapture. By the late summer they were enemies of the most terrible and enduring kind. Forgiveness was not a possible concept for either.

Roebuck, so charming, witty, spiky and brilliant in conversation, sought to bring off the win-double of intellectual and man of action. He combined this ambition with the desire to become a leader of men when he took the captaincy at Somerset.

Botham, then as now, was a man who had escaped the tyranny

of abstract thought. Botham was always so very cheery, so prepared to bring you into his inner ring of 'friends'. He believed that too much reflection was inappropriate: that was his great strength. It was also a weakness, though perhaps a minor one in pure sporting terms. But this was not just about pure sport.

Somerset contained three players you would pick for the world XI: Botham and the West Indians Viv Richards and Joel Garner. But they finished bottom of the County Championship and many felt it was time to change. The answer was to release – that is to say, sack – Richards and Garner. Scandal. Outrage. Botham's instant threat to depart.

Roebuck telling all; in private, in confidence. Sharing his never published diary of those troublous times. His appalled descriptions of what went on in the raffish Botham-centred Somerset, stories that are unpublishable even now. A leader in *The Times* (anti-Roebuck) was followed by the members' vote (anti-Botham). Not a clean break but a continuing sulphurous hatred.

Ancient feuds grow more pathetic with every year that passes since their inauguration. Was the annexation of a wife – even one as beautiful as Helen – worth ten years of slaughter? And was a disagreement about cricket strategy worth a lifetime of loathing?

For both men it was a matter of moral principle: Botham believed that Roebuck had betrayed men; Roebuck believed that Botham had betrayed moral principles. Roebuck believed he could bring about a solution by the force of his own nature and moral worth.

Two men, two very considerable men. One was a great cricketer, the other wrote a great cricket book, *It Never Rains*, a classic memoir of sporting anxiety.

Five years previously, Botham had turned around a Test series against Australia when all seemed lost – by, it seemed, pure will:

overflowing vitality and a jovially ferocious desire for victory. Roebuck tried to do the same sort of thing: to take a bad situation and make it into a good one, also by force of will. He proved that reality is less tractable than sport. Botham fulfilled his fantasies of how life should be because he stuck to sport and was a very considerable performer. Roebuck never fulfilled his.

~

If sport is anything at all it is fair. That is the point. An artificial world has been created in which everybody has an equal chance, the better team or the best athlete wins, virtue is rewarded and transgression punished. The playing field is level.

The concept can be a little fuzzy around the edges, but essentially sport is fair. Fairness is what sport is for: without fairness there is no sport. The assumption of sport is that cheats get found out.

He did it so well. When you see the footage it still looks fair. Certainly the BBC commentator, Barry Davies, thought it was fair. He had no idea why the England players were protesting: offside? Surely not.

Not offside. Handball. This was the World Cup quarter-final and England were playing Argentina. With the game still scoreless, Diego Maradona ran through onto a high, bouncing ball and nudged it over the advancing England goalkeeper, Peter Shilton. With his hand. That was quite clear in replay. But it was a goal: the referee said so.

It's been said that the first experience that victims of an earth-quake undergo – even before terror – is a sense of disbelief. The solid earth can't do this: the ground beneath my feet can't tremble and shatter and break. It can't betray me like this. The response to Maradona's goal had something of that: this can't be happening. It just can't.

The evidence of this sense of disbelief came in Maradona's second goal. It was a thing of beauty. Four minutes after palming the ball into the net Maradona dribbled through an England team that looked, in the words of an observer, like men who had just had their wallets stolen. He went past Peter Beardsley, Peter Reid, Terry Butcher, Terry Fenwick, Butcher again and then Shilton. These fine players all looked not like enemies but dancers whose job it was to set off the perfection of the principal. It was brilliant all right and England supporters turned to the brilliance almost with relief. It was easier to deal with than the bewilderment created by the unfairness of the first goal.

The response wasn't anger at Maradona's deviousness: it was disbelief that sport could let you down so badly. Maradona's second goal was the first symptom of disaster-shock: and it was accepted as some kind of atonement for his earlier sin. Sport without justice is a hard concept to comprehend: but beauty can go some way to healing such harms.

- Dancing Brave retired after the Arc. He was given what was then the highest rating ever bestowed on a horse, of 141. He had a comparatively modest career at stud in England and then in Japan.

- The England cricket team lost every one of the five-match series against West Indies; their second successive 'blackwash'. David Gower resigned as England captain the following year after England lost 2-0 at home against India.

- Dan Marino never won a Super Bowl, but is still regarded as an exceptional quarterback.

- Ron Fawcett had a modest success with a book called *Ron Fawcett, Rock Athlete*. In 2012 Gina Campbell published an autobiography, *Daughter of Bluebird*, which told of her strange relationship with her father, three failed marriages, and suicide attempts. Jonathan Palmer went into motor racing-related business. John Francome became a racing commentator and wrote an excellent autobiography, *Born Lucky*.

- Ian Botham became a television commentator. Peter Roebuck turned against England, perhaps because it let him down so badly. He became an Australian citizen. He was also a philanthropist, funding the education of young Zimbabweans. He committed suicide by jumping off a hotel balcony in Cape Town when police called to discuss allegations of sexual impropriety.
- Argentina won the World Cup, beating West Germany 3-2 in the final.

~

BOOK 5

1987

Las Vegas is a trick of the light. The sun strikes like a hammer, you scuttle for shelter. Once inside you are instantly robbed: robbed of light and dark and sun and moon and day and night: robbed of time itself. You are trapped in an unending present that can never progress or develop or change. It's always the same time of day, the same light, the same machines, the same gaming tables, the bars always open, the restaurants always ready: 'Yes, sir – we throw away 56 pounds of good meat every day!'

You seek redemption by turning to the ridiculous and the surreal. You look for self-mockery, self-awareness and humour, but you look in vain. Fear and loathing? Without psychedelic drugs only the latter remains: instantaneous and total: a visceral rejection that has nothing to do with moral revulsion. That comes later, though not much.

This, then, is the world's pleasure dome. Las Vegas is a bloated Mephistopheles, so accustomed to easy conquest that it has grown careless. Its ceaseless offering, ceaselessly accepted, of ultimate pleasure makes gambling, food, drink, entertainment and even sex unattractive.

Naturally, this is the world capital of boxing. There is no attempt to disguise the fact that it's all about money, starting with what's in your pocket. The lack of disguise is part of the attraction. The eternal lights beckon you to slot machines and gaming tables while the television screens, never out of your eyeline, showed an endlessly rerunning sequence of Mike Tyson knocking out opponents with ever-greater savagery. That was part of the pleasure.

Tyson was to face Tony Tucker and the winner would hold all three versions of the world heavyweight championship; boxing is as riven with schisms as the medieval papacy; there were for a while three simultaneous popes. Don King, the fight's promoter, was out there promoting himself: seeking power through buffoonery, a sinister figure with a long prison record and two killings on his CV. He called himself the only-in-America man.

Quite.

The Golden Gloves Gym had no facilities for gambling. Here at least was a kind of reality. Even in sparring the blows are frightening things to be close to, but those in attendance were blasé. Manhood was defined by your degree of comfort in these circumstances: wise cynicism; brain-damaged boxers and gangster influence were discussed in half-admiring tones.

The fight built its ritual tensions as the big night drew closer and more and more people flew in. The town and tables were busier by the day ... and it was all about Tyson's unequivocal reputation for ferocity. People were coming to see a man destroyed. To see a man suffer permanent brain damage deliberately inflicted.

It seemed, in the casinos and the bars and the restaurants, that the joy of violence had united the human race. Tyson's shocking, intemperate, unstoppable displays in the ring had the world joyfully anticipating a convulsive victory: one in which Tucker would suffer a defeat that changed him.

But Tucker turned out to be canny. He played a strategy of not losing; at least, not losing like that. He lasted all 12 rounds in an oddly pacific encounter that left the world dreadfully let down. Tyson won on points, bloodlessly. The wheels spun, the cards were reshuffled, the machines clicked and whirred, the bars served enormous glasses with enormous drinks hidden among the ice floes, the restaurant threw away 56 pounds of meat.

Here was neither truth nor beauty. Such things lay elsewhere, along with the daylight.

~

Some men talk of manhood as if men were complete on their own. Not better: complete. Complete in a world without the pernicious influence of women, free to exult in uncompromisingly masculine traits. These include carefully circumscribed violence and equally circumscribed camaraderie, at the same time homocentric and homophobic. All these things are made accessible by drink. Sport is about men's love for other men. It's a truly serious world because women are for once absent.

Those who restrict themselves to this view of sport find problems. They found themselves declaring that Glenn Hoddle was a bad football player, even though he was the best English player currently practising. He combined ball skills with an astonishing understanding of time and space; he was able to change a match with a single pass. But the ideologies of masculinity required the denial of his talent. It became important – essential to male pride – to state that Hoddle didn't get stuck in, he didn't tackle, he didn't hustle; he seemed to find the best of himself by being slightly apart from the rest. Like Dan Marino, aloof and paring his fingernails.

He talked while sitting on the bank of the practice pitch at the old training ground in Cheshunt. 'We start looking for faults as soon as we recognise a player's skills. I've had it pushed down my throat ever since I was a kid. Of course the runners and tacklers are part of the game, but people don't have a go at them if they can't play 40-yard balls or go past three men at a time. They don't expect them to do the things skilful players are good at ... that's the way we are in England.'

So instead of building the England team around the exceptional skills of Hoddle, a sequence of managers built it around Bryan Robson: a player of considerable but infinitely more humdrum virtues: a super-runner, a super-tackler. A bloke. A man's man. A player's player. Someone you'd like alongside you in the trenches.

Brian Clough said: 'You don't have to bare your false teeth to show you are a real he-man in football. Some people are morally brave and Hoddle is one of them.' But that was too outré a concept: sport in England has always had a default tendency to literal-mindedness.

England relegated Hoddle to a secondary role: too good to leave out, too challenging to trust. It came down to the quest for manliness. Robson looked like a manly man: Hoddle did not. Hoddle played with diffidence and the most extraordinary elegance. He wore his shirt outside his shorts, no doubt a tribute to George Best, though he always denied this. Shorts were short back then and Hoddle was long of leg: he looked as if he was wearing a miniskirt and his style and movement didn't entirely contradict this impression.

Hoddle was unacceptable because he was too beautiful.

~

Boris Becker won his 15th successive match at Wimbledon when he beat Karel Novacek, a player from what was then Czechoslovakia, in the first round. He completed the first set with a second serve ace. Stylish.

He won his first Wimbledon when he was 17: an outrageously gifted boy with pneumatic muscles and bones made of vulcanised rubber. He could dive and bounce and dive again, all in the same point. People liked to call him a man-child, precocious masculinity busting out of his shorts. The following year the wise wagged their heads and said that the second season was always the toughest: your novelty has worn off, you've been found out, you've no surprises left. And yet Becker won again.

In tennis, especially on grass courts, the serve is seen as an expression of masculinity. In those days the courts were fast as lightning and the big server dominated the lesser man in most matches. Your serve is your territory, which you must hold safe from marauders. To make inroads on your opponent's serve is to question his manhood as much as his skill. It is a violent invasion; it's the heart of men's tennis – and all that counts double on grass. Becker's serve was huge.

But in the second round, in a shock almost as great as his initial victory two years earlier, Becker was beaten in four sets by the Australian Peter Doohan. Becker's response afterwards is famous. 'I didn't lose a war, nobody died. I lost a tennis match,' he explained afterwards.

This was not so much philosophy as the removal of what theatre people call the fourth wall: the invisible structure that, by mutual consent, divides audience from participants. As Graham Chapman, dressed as the Colonel, marched into Monty Python sketches announcing, 'It's getting silly', so Becker told us that sport was not about actual death.

Only symbolic death.

Sport is action, which is why we do it. Sport is a trope, which is why we watch it.

~

Breakfast for 2,000: scrambled thoughts on toast. Donuts to follow: not-food as you pursue a not-story about not-sport. Media Day at the Super Bowl: 2,000 writers in search of an author.

What was the story? The consensus was this: the monster's

quest to destroy the hero; the hero's quest to avoid destruction and find the great prize. The part of the monster was played by Lawrence 'the Terminator' Taylor, linebacker for the New York Giants; the knight errant was John Elway, quarterback for Denver Broncos.

Turning Super Bowl XXI into the first battle of *Beowulf* was a pretty obvious way of interpreting the event; you didn't need to read Anglo-Saxon to see that. Overcoming the monster is one of the eternal myths of humankind: and that makes it one of the eternally recurring themes of sport, as David Gower showed when he batted against Malcolm Marshall in Trinidad.

The battle may not always be to the strong, but it's the right way to bet.

Sport recreates archetypal situations. Though not necessarily in the way you expect. In the event, the game wasn't decided by gallantry or monstrosity or genius or ferocity. It was decided by efficiency: a sporting quality that works and plays well but writes poorly. New York won the game thanks to the effectiveness of their offensive linemen, whose job it was to protect their own quarterback, Phil Simms. The good job they did freed him up, and he was able to show his considerable but rather humdrum qualities. So, as ever, the truth was in the action: but it gradually became clear that neither action nor truth really matters at the Super Bowl.

The monster was not Taylor but the event. The story was not the game but the story itself: the self-referencing tale of America's fascination for the Super Bowl and the extent to which players could cope with it. What mattered was not sport but the idea of sport. It was like modern Christmas: eternal anticipation of impossible glory that leads to an overwhelming let-down. The sport was almost incidental to the sports story, and perhaps the least interesting part of it. If you wanted to write about the sociology of sport and its relationship with the media and advertising and commerce, you were in the right place. The action was a mild distraction, but you could get over it.

It wasn't much of game, but at least it was true.

~

The trick with underdogs is never to give them a chance. That's what the Giants did to the Broncos; that's what Tyson did to a succession of opponents. That's what Boris Becker failed to do against Doohan. They already know they've got nothing to lose, so don't for God's sake let them think they can win.

St. Louis Cardinals were as efficient as the New York Giants. At the start of Game Six of the World Series they were leading the Minnesota Twins by three games to two and, by the fifth inning, by five runs to two. The underdogs had had their moment: now it was time for the big battalions. The battle to the strong. But the underdogs crept back into the game and even took a one-run lead. That's when the game and the series changed forever in a single instant. Baseball is good at such things.

Don't do it!

One of those fourth-wall moments when the audience freezes in horror at the errors of performers: as if longing to tell Gertrude not to drink from the poisoned cup and Hamlet to beware the envenomed rapier.

The Cardinals gave Don Baylor an intentional walk and so loaded the bases. Baylor has already hit a home run: by deliberately allowing him to get on base they were casting scorn on the batters who followed. You lot are not up to it. Not good enough. We've put your batter on base because you're a soft touch. You can't hurt us.

So it proved: Tom Brunansky popped out (gave up a routine catch) and Kent Hrbek came out to the plate: a big man in the middle of a huge batting slump. His team-mates called him 'Herbie', but those with a more elaborate sense of humour called him Kent 'Getta Vowel' Hrbek.

He took a swing at his first pitch – desperate? inspired? – and sent it into the crowd. Home run. Grand Slam. Four runs. Like hitting a six in cricket that's worth 300 runs.

Sport creates the same archetypal situations, no matter what game you happen to be playing. Here was one more: the man who saved the world: saved the world with a single blow.

~

It was getting dark, too dark to see. Or at least take pictures. Most of the photographers had packed up but Graham Morris carried on alone. After all, you never know.

So, from the boundary's edge in Faisalabad, Morris caught the confrontation that ignited like a petrol fire as the England captain Mike Gatting and the Pakistani umpire Shakoor Rana engaged in an eye-blazing, finger-jabbing row. It's an image that still haunts the sport.

Victorian educators loved sport because it taught the virtues needed to run an empire: sinking of self into common cause and unquestioning obedience to authority.

But here was the England captain disputing with authority. On the other hand, it was a Pakistani he was disputing with, and that made it all right. It was an accepted fact – at least in England – that Pakistani umpires cheat and English umpires, the best in the world, occasionally make mistakes.

The Pakistan cricketers saw it another way. They had requested third-country umpires in the previous series between the two countries in England, but England refused. They then asked for the removal of the umpire David Constant, who they mistrusted. This too was refused. English authorities were rather puzzled at the Pakistani failure to comprehend the superior nature of English cricketing culture. After all, the Empire had worked on the principle of keeping the underdog down, and if it had worked then, no reason why it shouldn't work now. This was a row generations in the making.

The squabble between Gatting and Shakoor Rana halted the Test match until Gatting finally gave a 'written apology'. His angry scrawl finally permitted continuation. The English governing body showed what they thought of it all by giving the players an additional £1,000 each for the tour. It was called a 'hardship bonus'. It was a calculated gesture of contempt for Pakistan.

Cricket is the game of Empire, and its abandonment. Sport is never pure and rarely simple. The truth that lies in the action was again obscured by everything that grows up around it.

- Mike Tyson's chaotic life needs no recapitulation here. He won 50 of his 58 professional fights, 44 by knock-out; he made around US$300 million in prize money and was declared bankrupt in 2003.
- Glenn Hoddle's career similarly requires little repetition. He played for England 53 times and was probably at his best in the 1986 World Cup, in which England were knocked out by Diego Maradona's handball goal.
- Boris Becker won six Grand Slam singles titles in total, including one more Wimbledon, in 1989.
- Minnesota Twins won the seventh, decisive game in the series with a superb pitching performance from Frankie 'Sweet Music' Viola. They won their third World Series in 1991 against the Atlanta Braves in what is remembered as a classic.
- Mike Gatting was sacked as England captain the following year after a tabloid newspaper reported a romp with a barmaid. Thus the cricketing establishment got rid of a man who was an embarrassment without seeming to give in to Pakistan. That's the way we do things over here, old boy.

BOOK 6

1988

Laugh at danger. Laugh at the near-death experience. Is this deep madness? Or a deeper sanity? Who cares, so long as you can do it again? Break machines, break limbs, risk worse: it's all one in the pursuit of victory. Victory and what else?

Steve Curtis was Class One powerboating world champion. 'Right from being a kid I liked to make things go fast. Everything I had, I made it go faster . . . and then broke it.' He took a gear from a moped and fitted it onto his push bike. No one could turn that gear on the flat but once you started going downhill . . . he broke the bike and bits of himself and then looked for the next adventure.

If you can't find a war for such people you have to find something else. Perhaps it's good that they're so rare. Not hard to find people who talk like that: not easy to find people who live like that. Life is too precious . . . too precious to enjoy, at least in the way that Curtis enjoys it. 'Crew abandon me. They think I'm going too fast. They're all very macho on the shore, but when they're out there they want to back off. I've had three drivers walk out on me, one after just one race ... Mind you, I wouldn't drive one of those things, not with me throttling. You've got no control over things, hardly at all. You'd have to be bloody mad.'

A Class Two powerboat. A joyride. A taste of what it's like. A Formula One motor car is fast all right, but at least the stuff underneath you is consistent. Unlike the sea. A rhythmic slamming, wave to wave, a series of short flights, each time a slam-dunk landing on concrete-hard water, an osteopath's adjustment every couple of seconds ... and every now and then, but at intervals elusive of prediction, a longer flight and a landing that shatters every vertebra. And Curtis laughing, always laughing.

'Some people go out to race really hard, but some don't want to. They just don't want to. Me, I pull out all the stops. If you have to scrap the boat after I've driven it in the World Championship I don't care ... In fact, they did scrap the boat after the World Championship in 1985.'

Sometimes it's best just to listen. Not interrupt, not join in, and certainly not judge. And the Boris Becker rule doesn't always apply here.

'A friend of mine was killed before the World Championship that year. But I didn't think about walking out. No. He wouldn't have walked out either. It's something you accept in this sport. I'm here to race and the dangers aren't something I think about. I just love the sport: five tons of boat leaping 20 feet in the air – there aren't too many sports like that. It's a neat feeling, running really sweet; it's a different feeling to anything else ...'

A pause, savouring it. Then laughter.

～

Ginny Leng had stopped laughing. She had also given up being charming. Walking the cross-country course at Badminton, two days before competition. The fences are much bigger on foot: you're looking up at them, not down. The easy ones look hard; the hard ones look irresponsibly dangerous.

Leng was champion here in 1985, one of the world's best. Slight, hard-looking athlete's body, sudden all-conquering smile, blue eyes that turn in an instant from ferocity to charm and back again. So be careful.

A dangerous sport. People get smashed and killed here. Horses too, sometimes, though the course designer, Colonel Frank Weldon, said: 'My aim is to frighten the wits out of the riders without harming the horses.' Often it's the moment of fear in the rider that persuades the horse to decline the jump. Horses respond to subtle, often unintended messages from their riders: good news to the brave, bad news to the fearful.

The bold take the faster and more dangerous options, the less bold go the longer and safer way, and it's an event judged by the clock. On your own, just you and your horse. Competing not against opponents but the course builder: the unseen enemy. 'It's your *duty* to go straight at the nastiest fence that Frank Weldon can devise.'

The walk continued, the eyes lost all sparkle. The mouth had gone hard and unkissable. Of all things, a fury: a mad sense of anger that she was to be put through so terrible an ordeal: an anger that tapped artesian wells of defiance. Then a fence called the Ski Jump. Leng looked at it, glared at it. Tried her hardest to believe what she was seeing. And then spoke.

'*Fuck!*'

A silence. Then a smile to slay giants and eyes that didn't quite soften. ''Scuse my French.' After that not a word, till the end of the course. A polite farewell, a handshake of not-unexpected power and a smile slightly off-target. Nothing existed save the task in hand.

~

A world untouched by the sordid things we meet every day in ordinary life: a world to keep forever pure.

No room for politics in sport, they say – and then they hoist the national flag above the field of play. Sport's separation from daily life – sport's purity, goodness and natural justice – has permitted the people who run it to perpetrate a history of injustice. Amateurism was a creed of purity designed to keep out the working classes.

In South Africa the policy of apartheid kept non-white people out of everything except work. But the British, the English and others were always ready to play sport with South Africa, because sport has nothing to do with politics. That changed after the D'Oliveira Affair of 1969, but English cricket retained a nostalgia for the old days. And perhaps an envy. In high places there was a feeling that South Africa's exclusion from Test cricket was Not Fair. Sport should be above such things as politics.

What possessed them to make Graham Gooch captain of England? Desperation, perhaps. This was the summer of the Five Captains. England lost four out of five Tests against West Indies, only saving the first because of rain. Mike Gatting was sacked after the first Test; John Emburey stepped into the gap for the second; Chris Cowdrey got the job for the third and fourth but then got injured and never played for England again. So in came Gooch. The fifth was Derek Pringle, who captained England in the field at one stage.

So Gooch had the job. Gooch, who had toured South Africa, captained the rebel team and been banned. So far as England were concerned, the completion of the ban made him a virgin again. He cancelled a contract to play in South Africa that winter, so that he could lead England on their tour of India. But India refused to grant visas to any cricketer with South African connections, especially Gooch, and so the tour was called off.

There was disappointment that India had brought politics into sport: like criticising the prime minister for bringing politics into a parliamentary debate. English cricket claimed a moral victory: doing so after making an appointment that demonstrated equivocal feelings if not clear approval of apartheid.

Gooch's appointment was bound to make trouble, so perhaps trouble was what they wanted. Certainly it showed a certain contempt for India, as well as for the wider world's feelings about apartheid. But England believed themselves pure. Everybody else was corrupt, bringing politics into sport. The objections to England's cheery thumbs-up to apartheid were – unsporting.

Sport is an emotional business. It's generally accepted that sport should not be corrupted by coherent argument. People respond to sport at a deep level: pre-thought, pre-verbal. Sport is an area in which the best of minds can be excused thought . . . as a malingerer in the army is excused boots.

~

There are times when not acting is the most devastating form of action. Not rescuing a drowning child, to take a melodramatic example. Not taking a phone call from someone you quarrelled with. Not going to fight in Vietnam.

Sport is about movement: but there are times when not moving is a devastating form of sport: like Pat Eddery on Dancing Brave. There are times when the task of not moving is as physically demanding as performing four and a half somersaults from the ten-metre diving board. Does sport contradict itself? Very well, it contradicts itself. Sport is large; it contains multitudes.

Most sporting performances are aided by the secretion of adrenalin. Most are performed with a high pulse rate and a high rate of respiration. Not here, though. Here the essence of the sport was to get as close as possible to the suspension of the processes of life. Victory goes to the person with the least obvious vital signs.

Rifle shooting. Three positions: prone, kneeling, standing. Each one increasingly difficult; with each one it is increasingly easy to move without wishing to. They sought perfect stillness: breathing with reluctance, heart slowed to the dawdle of deep sleep. Nothing moving, nothing save the few muscles that power a single finger: the shooter is hardly there at all, part of the living landscape, a gun emplacement, not a human being at all . . . save for the quiet mind hungering for glory and the finger taking up the first and then the second pressure on the trigger.

After the instruction to fire you have 30 seconds. A ragged volley broke out, taking about ten seconds in all. And most times, Malcolm Cooper, shooting for Britain, was not a part of it. In a leisurely way, as if stress was an alien concept, he would shift his body minutely. Standing directly behind him, you could see the far end of the gun with its sharp foresight shifting and wavering and then returning to the aim. Never satisfied that it was right, waiting, always waiting, for the optimum moment of perfect stillness in the perfect aim. And again and again, bang. Ten points.

Cooper looked like a gun emplacement: stocky, with immense breadth of shoulder. 'There's a fine edge between holding still and another wobble. That's why I take so long. If I'm not still, I aim again. That's much better than trying to hit on the move.'

The implication is that the others do try to hit on the move. Not what most people would call movement, but a fractional failure of balance and strength and concentration. And so, not knowing what it is to go beyond such limitations, you fire. You fire while Cooper re-aims.

Cooper won a gold medal for Great Britain at the Olympic Games in Seoul. He had won the same event four years earlier and made it clear for all time that the Olympic Games are a celebration of the biodiversity of excellence: at the many ways that humans seek physical mastery.

~

Something slightly dead behind the eyes. Something very still indeed. Something almost corpse-like. Perhaps it was because the owner of the eyes no longer inhabited the present. Perhaps it was because the people all around had no meaning. They had vacated your world.

Steve Redgrave talked well after the heats. He and his partner in the pair, Andy Holmes, had won convincingly. 'The Olympics. Big thing. A bit nervous at the start.'

A frail craft, you could put your fist through it. Two immense men; you wouldn't try to put your fist through them. There was the certainty of power in those hulking bodies, but there was also a sermon about the fragile nature of sporting ambition.

Was this something we shared? Or did Redgrave already know the result? Here was a man whose spirit was absent: gone racing, already living the final.

The same deadness behind the eyes of Florence Griffith Joyner. She had set a world record for the 100 metres in the United States Olympic trials, competing in one-legged tights. 'I spend a lot of time thinking. Maybe praying. Sometimes I'm just dreaming. Or maybe I don't want to share something.'

There was a stillness here, an inner quiet. Or deadness. As if she was under hypnosis. The press conference: packed, noisy, full of arguing journalists. And after every question, a pause of alarming length, followed by an answer in a voice of carefully cultivated softness, like the prime minister's and just as phoney. 'The main competition is myself. I'm just going to concentrate on myself.'

Not a thing hard to believe. She had improved vastly as a runner: and done so very suddenly. But it wasn't drugs. Of course it wasn't. It was all down to hard work, she explained. Every bit as plausible as the prime minister.

And the eyes said nothing to no one: a spiritual absence. An audience of two thousand, or of televised billions, were given nothing. Only words. The reality – the only reality – lay in a race a few days ahead. Nothing before mattered. Or after.

'It's a neat feeling, running really sweet, it's a different feeling to anything else ...' and everything, absolutely and entirely everything, your whole life for that one race. Sanity, madness – who knows? Or cares?

~

Disaster-shock. Yes, a bit like the England team after Maradona's handballed goal. Disbelief that so terrible a thing could have happened: a loss of confidence in your own powers to make things better.

Something like that happened after the night of the great telephoning. At two-thirty in the morning the phones started to ring across the press village in Seoul. Lights came on in ones and twos and then in dozens: a *son et lumière* of disaster. Hello, hello? The world has changed forever. Write the news at once. And in 45 minutes we'd like your considered piece.

The following day, unnaturally bright eyes at breakfast, thousands of them. Wondering about the follow-up story: and then, dizzyingly, wondering what to do about the sport that would be taking place all over the city that day.

Ben Johnson had failed a drugs test. The fastest human being on the planet was more than human. Or less. It was above all else a crisis of faith. Did the Olympic Games still mean anything? Did sport? Did our lives? What was the point of sport, of life, of anything? Like members of a cult whose sainted leader had been arrested heading for the airport with a suitcase of dollars and a couple of 15-year-old blondes, those who had devoted their lives to tales of victory and defeat in sport – in the world that should be forever untouched by the sordid matters of everyday life – had to wonder what their lives really meant.

Seek the normal. Seek the soothing routine of everyday life. Seek sport, which just keeps rollin' along, especially at the Olympic Games.

A few days earlier Greg Louganis, the American diver, had overdone the instruction to descend as close to the diving board as possible. He caught his head on the springboard and required three stitches. He refused painkillers lest they affected his balance; he refused to watch the replay lest it affected his confidence, and he won the gold. The day after the night of the revelations about Johnson, Louganis was in the final of the ten-metre platform diving event. Xiong Ni of China, aged 14, was three points ahead going into the final dive.

Xiong's last dive was a beauty. Louganis assumed the crucifixion position in preparation for his own final effort: a long moment of perfect stillness. Then he dived and he nailed it. He won the gold medal by 1.4 points.

Sport doesn't die so easily.

~

The captain, Richard Dodds, was a surgeon. The goalkeeper, Ian Taylor, was a teacher. Imran Sherwani, who scored twice in the final, was a newsagent. Sean Kerly was unemployed, ready to go to the Job Centre on his return to England.

There was a joyous feeling of innocence about the progress of the Great Britain hockey team. Was this what sport was supposed to be like? Was this the future of sport, or the past?

Australia were favoured to win the semi-final. Perhaps they should have done, but team spirit is one of the strangest phenomena in sport. Everyone knows what it is, but no one can define it, still less create it. It just happens, not in the victory but in the pursuit. We have often seen teams in which players play for their places, or to avoid mistakes and subsequent criticism.

Here at the hockey was the idea that Victorian educators strived for: 11 men for whom the common cause was all. Kerly completed his hat-trick with three minutes of normal time left: 3-2, Britain in the final.

The final was comparatively straightforward, a 3-1 victory over West Germany, and it was time to cherish the ordinariness of heroes. The innocence of the day contrasted with memories of Heysel and the recent trauma of Ben Johnson.

Is that how we want our sport? Essentially ordinary? Or do we come to sport in search of the extraordinary? Are we looking for ordinary people who can step up and do something special? Or are we looking for extraordinary people to make a mark in our lives that cannot be erased?

For there was also a kind of innocence in Johnson: willing victim of the world's hunger for heroes. Johnson was only trying to please us. We wanted a man who could perform miracles and he did all that was necessary to perform one.

Johnson was what you wanted. Johnson was what you got.

In sport we seek people prepared to push the boundaries, to do what's never been done and to win what's never been won. When they try too hard we complain, and say that what we wanted all along was the innocent boys of the hockey stadium.

Johnson is the name the world remembers from the Seoul Olympic Games: Ben Johnson, the alchemist who turned gold into base metal. His story, his victory, his defeat, his heroism, his villainy, is the story that we cherish. He gave us the greatest tale to be read from these Games, and so we despise him.

Hypocrites lecteurs as we are.

We are large, we contain multitudes.

- Steve Curtis was Formula One Powerboat world champion on eight occasions. He retired and went to work in the family firm, Cougar Marine.

- Ginny Leng – later Elliott – fell at the Ski Jump fence and damaged her ankle. She finished the competition the following day heavily strapped, jumped clear in the showjumping and finished third overall. Later that year she rode a heroic cross-country round as the British team won silver at the Olympic Games. She finished her career with three wins at Badminton, five at Burghley, three individual European Championships and one World Championship. She won four Olympic medals.
- More of Graham Gooch later.
- Malcolm Cooper founded Accuracy International, which produces rifles for military and law enforcement purposes. He died in 2001.
- More from Steve Redgrave and Florence Griffith Joyner later.
- Also more of Ben Johnson.
- Greg Louganis tested HIV positive six months before the Games. When he made this public in 1995, all his sponsors save Speedo dropped him. He was later inducted into the National Gay and Lesbian Sports Hall of Fame and appeared on the Wheaties cereal packet.

~

BOOK 7

1989

He stepped from the motorhome like a being from another planet leaving his spaceship. But he had no desire to explore or understand the planet on which he found himself: he wanted only to explain his mission. And then complete it. His eyes were focused on the distant galaxy he called home.

His name was Ayrton Senna, and he had won the Formula One World Championship for the first time the previous year. It was the day before the Canadian Grand Prix in Montreal and he chose the afternoon to stand in the sun and to tell the story of himself. He paused lengthily, spookily, after each question. When he spoke he looked far beyond his questioner, for that was where the answers lay.

He was mesmerising. Compelling. And quite used to mesmerising and compelling his auditors. He never sought to convert: he merely gave you the opportunity to believe. Knowing that you would. Because you had no option. You weren't humouring him: he knew you would listen to every word and find them all good.

It was like interviewing St John of the Cross.

'I don't know how far I can go. It is all a learning process, something I work very hard to keep clear in my mind. I aim to have a really realistic, clear understanding of what is going on, and what I'm doing – and what I can do. I can only try what I believe I can do, but by trying I often find I can do more. And then I have to readjust.

'On many occasions I have gained most satisfaction from beating my own achievements. Many times I find myself in a comfortable position – and I don't feel happy about it. I feel it is right to slow down, but something inside of me, something very strong pushes me on, makes me try to beat myself. It is . . . an enormous desire to go further and further, to travel beyond my own limits. Of course you are always compared to other people's limits – but when I establish limits that are higher than anyone else's, then I want to beat them, I want to beat *myself* . . .

'Every time I have an idea about where my limits are, I go to check it. And most of the time I am wrong. So I have to adjust myself to going even further. It is very exciting and a non-stop process.

'Power comes from my education, which you'd say was privileged. I was privileged to grow up in a happy and healthy environment. I had my family always behind me, helping me when I have some doubt, some question . . . And on top of that I have been able to experience God's power on earth.'

Then he walked away as graciously, as kindly, as he had come.

∼

No place for death in sport. In sport, deaths are metaphorical: a defeat, a batsman's dismissal, even a boxer's brief period of unconsciousness. Then you get up and start all over again. A death in pursuit of sport is wrong on some cosmic level: it seems to trivialise life and make death itself a frivolity. It follows that when deaths in sport occur they inspire bewilderment and anger.

In a godless society we still grieve, and we must find a way of expressing our grief without help from God. Anfield that day opened its doors without thought of charging for admission and mourners came by the thousand. Who started it? Who first wove a scarf into the netting of the goal? Who brought the first flowers to a football ground? Who was first to lay team favours in the goalmouth?

By the end of the day the football ground was a Hindu temple. The dominant glowing red was picked out with white: colours of conquest and joy that were now the colours of solidarity in the face of death. This was the English football club that had been involved at Heysel four years earlier, but no one mentioned that.

You'll Never Walk Alone, it says on the gates, in reference to the great godless hymn of Liverpool Football Club: well, the 96 people killed at Hillsborough football ground the previous day didn't die alone. They died in crowds of fearful proximity, and they were mourned by crowds who needed their mourning to be a shared and public thing.

Behind the sadness was a great anger, and it was an anger that never faded. It won't finally die until the last person who knew and loved one of the victims is also dead. Even in the silence – the eyes cast down on the ground, the wringing hand-shakes, the embraces shared with people who'd never embraced before – the reason for these deaths was clear to every person who walked through the temple, who walked away having left scarf, flowers, favours, who walked away not alone.

And it was contempt.

No escaping it. Not that day, nor in the days and the years that followed. These 96 people died because the people who went to football matches were considered contemptible. They were accommodated in horrible places, confined behind bars and policed as if a taste for football deprived you of human rights. The government wanted all football's followers to carry identity cards: football was being criminalised. Football supporters were redundant people – so they were driven into a dangerous place where they died.

The occasion was not war or earthquake or famine. It was the FA Cup semi-final between Liverpool and Nottingham Forest, played at Hillsborough, a neutral ground in Sheffield. Here 96 people died of contempt.

~

Miami paid £1.1 million for the right to hold Super Bowl XXIII. Good for the image of the city. On the Tuesday before the game the accredited media, a gathering of 2,200 people, were given dinner in a genuine imported Italian Renaissance palazzo.

That same night in the same city eight people were shot: in Overtown, which was having its third riot in six years, and in another area of Miami called Liberty City. And they say Americans don't do irony.

The previous night police officer William Lozano took a pot-shot at a speeding motorcyclist called Clement Lloyd. Lloyd was 23. It was suggested that he gave the policeman the finger. The single bullet hit Lloyd in the head and killed him instantly. It was the shot of a lifetime. The pillion passenger was catapulted into an oncoming car, received head injuries and died the following day.

Three days of rioting followed, with 310 arrests. Cars in flame, liquor stores liberated. It was a continuation of the tensions between the people of Hispanic extraction who dominate Miami, and the much poorer blacks.

Sport tries to separate itself from the real world, but the real world has never respected that wish. Part of sport's enduring beauty is this separation: it's all play, it's always fair, it's about joy, its deaths are metaphorical along with its victories and conquests and its promises of immortality.

Sport must be separate from the real world if it's to have a meaning: and yet it can never complete that separation. So sport has settled on the illusion of separation, even though this illusion must be shattered again and again. In any American football game, the athletes fall over and then get up and then fall over and then get up. Temporarily slain, they rise again. This sits awkwardly in a world where real deaths can occur so casually, so easily, so close and for a gesture.

Sport and the real world have never really got on.

~

There were three minutes and ten seconds left on the clock. The San Francisco 49ers had 92 yards to go if they were to win the Super Bowl in Miami. They were dead and buried.

Then Joe Montana walked into the huddle. Even from the top of the stands there was something compelling about the way that Montana, the 49ers quarterback, carried himself.

There are times when calmness seems irrational: when rationality itself seems irrational. To think and to act clearly in times of maximum stress seems impossible, unimaginable. It's the If Test: If you can keep your head when all about you are losing theirs ... Rudyard Kipling wrote the perfect to-do list for sports psychologists.

Those who have the gift of clear thought and right action under extreme testing often seem a little otherworldly: not quite part of the same universe as you and me. And often ever-so-slightly dead behind the eyes. You wouldn't think, from the press conference clichés, offered with complete absence of irony, that Montana was capable of such thought, such action. 'Oh, I got enough problems without worrying about the opposing quarterback,' he said.

The opposing quarterback was Boomer Esiason. 'I can remember somebody saying that all quarterbacks deserve skirts. Well, I think it's easier to give somebody a hit, than to sit there and take it.' People often get sporting courage wrong, and confuse it with some dream of masculinity. Ask Ginny Leng about courage sometime; people really die in the sport of eventing.

But Montana filled his unforgiving three minutes and ten seconds with 92 yards of distance run. He turned them into beauty and glory and victory. And he started to throw. Not hit-and-hope passes: short, fierce, stinging passes that ate up the yards and marched his team up the long, striped field. Pass by pass the 49ers advanced. They might have tried for a tying field goal but instead they went for the lot. A final pass: hurled like a javelin straight down the middle, double-bluffing the opposing defence to find John Taylor and victory.

It's been called Joe Montana's immortal drive.

All one for Clement Lloyd.

~

A young man entered the building that stands at 1235 Bay Street, Toronto. He wore a dark suit, white shirt, unmemorable tie. He spoke slowly, with care, a touch jerkily, in an attempt to keep his stutter under control. The Jamaican tonalities in his voice were muted but clear enough.

Anabolic steroids?

'Yes.'

And human growth hormone?

'Could be.'

You don't know?

'If Charlie gave them to me, I took them.'

Once a confession begins, it moves from trickle to flood in a matter of moments. 'Charlie said that the whole world was using drugs. The only way I was going to be better was to take them.'

And being better is what it's all about.

This was the Dubin Inquiry: a public investigation into the use of performance-enhancing drugs by athletes representing Canada. The witness was Ben Johnson. Charlie was Charlie

Francis, his coach. It was not a legal process. There were no adversary tactics. It was slow, relaxed, friendly: Charles Dubin, the good cop, was in control. It was a leisurely business: like a shoal of fish contentedly picking the bones of a drowned man.

Johnson had already done all he could to satisfy the world's hunger for heroes, perhaps unaware that the world has a still greater hunger for villains. Perhaps it's easier to be a villain if you're black and a poor speaker in public.

If you have been disappointed in love, you blame your former partner, rather than your own unrealistic hope. Sport had disappointed the world and the world needed Johnson to suffer.

Johnson trusted. Johnson believed. Who hasn't done so? If his trust and his belief were self-serving, they sprang also from a deep desire to please, just as he tried to please Dubin and the watching world by confessing. He tried to please Francis, he tried to please Canada, he tried to please the world by becoming the greatest hero sport had ever seen.

He surrendered autonomy over his own body, but we all do that when it comes to medication and surgery. And yet to the world it seemed that Johnson had gone far beyond anything normal humans considered acceptable, just as he had previously gone beyond anything that humans considered possible.

How majestic he had looked in that red arena in Seoul: that impossible speed in which it seemed that the bang came from the power of his start rather than the starting pistol, the hopeless slowness of the seven other fastest men on the planet, the red track that lay between Johnson and the rest, and then again that final floating stride, the index finger raised as if to poke out the eye of the sun. And then in that square room in Toronto, how diminished. Not defiant, not regretful: seeking only to please.

He had been a symbol of aspiration and achievement; he was now seen by many as a symbol of pure evil. Sport certainly does a fine job in satisfying the world's hunger for symbols. He seemed a man bewildered. Whatever the world gave him, he took it.

~

A club defines itself by those it excludes.

Rochester is an ordinary town in the United States. In other words, it's not safe to walk around downtown after dark. But the place was jumping that week, because the US Open golf tournament was being held at Oak Hill Country Club, out in the suburbs. It was perfectly safe to walk around Oak Hill Country Club, once you had paid your entrance money.

All the good hotels were full, but the bad ones had the odd vacancy. The Hotel Cadillac, $20 a night, was full of people who had come to town for the golf. All of them caddies. All of them black, a tight bunch walking in and out of the lobby talking shop.

The bar was cheerful, welcoming, noisy, much used. Those who went to bed before midnight were woken by a bang. Not a car backfiring. Not a starting pistol. A man was shot dead just along the street.

But everything was lovely under the trees and along the sterilised lawns of the country club. Jack Nicklaus was to turn 50 next year and had as big a comet tail as any of the golfers who might actually win. His followers were looking not for great sport, or even the memory of great sport, but some sort of infection from his glowing nature. They walked after him, scarcely believing their own privilege, and at intervals shouted, 'Great galf shat!'

They wanted to be like him. They wanted to dress like him. Jeff Andress, marketing director of Golden Bear International Inc, said: 'He isn't going to wear anything he's not comfortable wearing. His shirts have a full-cut body and are made of a poly-cotton blend. His slacks are a poly-wool blend.'

Tom Place, the director of information for the Professional Golfers' Association, said: 'We're doing a lot of things right now.

Apparel is one of them. We're clean-cut guys – well-groomed, well-dressed. It all ties in. This is a classy sport and it goes with the image.'

No room for politics in sport, no room for real life in sport, no room for real death in sport. But always room for money.

~

She was unable to press the lift button with her fingertip so she knuckled it. Her nails, twisted, lacquered, a good two inches long, prevented her from using the lift as everybody else did. How did she cope in more private moments?

We all know you're taking something, Florence. You can tell me. Is it rocket fuel? Is it essence of panther?

Florence Griffith Joyner kept eye contact for a moment and then lowered her gaze shyly. Yes, shyly. Like Lady in *Lady and the Tramp*. A soft giggle. She had plenty of brothers, she knew what teasing was. 'Ohhh nooo.' The voice husky but controlled, consciously mellow. 'I just gave it my ahhhlll.'

Like Michael Jackson she seemed neither black nor white, neither male nor female. She had recently retired from athletics. She did so at precisely the same time that it was announced that athletes would be tested for drugs out of competition. 'People need to be educated about drugs. There must be more research – people just speculate and guess. And that's very sad.'

She had made her bid for eternal glory and set world records and won gold medals, but she had reckoned without Ben Johnson. In the post-Johnson era, running fast was prima facie evidence of wrongdoing. It was as if winning had become the most shaming thing in sport.

She'd been giving motivational speeches for IBM. 'I tell them if you're looking for a way to better yourself, first you have to set yourself a definite goal. Then put in the time to work at it. It took me 20 years. People think I came into track and field in 1988 but that's not true; I've been running since I was seven.

So I tell them about having a goal and keeping focused on it. Putting in the hours, four hours, six hours, maybe more on the track. Two hours in the weight-room. Going home on the run for the second time. It's all part of the Attitude.'

An embodiment of romantic success, then. Rags to riches. Stay cool and follow your dream, as she said in her pre-Olympic press conference. Hers was a perfect story. She ran after jack rabbits when she was a little girl, and eventually she caught one. So why didn't they love her more?

It's been said that acting is a shy person's opportunity to show off. Something of that is true of sport, certainly in this case. She was able to present herself as a shining icon of self-help. She embodied the notion that glory is at everybody's fingertips. And always that hint of shyness, that vulnerability. She was a glorious figure of achievement. She had done everything she wanted and everything the world could possibly expect of her. She was strong, triumphant, glorious, perfect. There was no flaw in her. She preached her gospel of giving 100 per cent and so inevitably reaching your goal. Here was a figure of ultimate achievement.

And yet you wanted to give her a hug and tell her that it was all right, really it was, even though you thought it quite possibly wasn't.

- Ayrton Senna finished second in the World Championship to Alain Prost that year after the two crashed at Suzuka. Senna finished first in that race but was disqualified for a push-start and other infringements.
- A new inquest into the 96 deaths at Hillsborough ran from 2014 to 2016. It rejected the previous verdict of accidental death and concluded that the people were unlawfully killed as a result of the negligence of police and ambulance services. There was profound and widespread criticism of the attempts to cover up facts of the disaster.

The Heysel disaster, which was caused by the violence of some Liverpool supporters, is seldom mentioned.

- Ben Johnson made a comeback to athletics in 1991. He failed to make the final of the 100 metres at the Olympic Games of 1992. He failed another drugs test in 1993, this time for excess testosterone. He was banned for life but contested this. In 1999 he failed another drugs test for a banned diuretic.

~

BOOK 8

1990

Down the Spanish Steps. Across the Piazza del Popolo, along with, it seemed, half of the population of Rome. Cut across to the Tiber, and over the bridge into the Foro Italico. *Forza Azzurri!* And then enter the Stadio Olimpico.

The World Cup. Surely Italy must win. Somewhere across the country a team called England were playing football, but what did that matter?

Italy had beaten Austria by a single goal in their first match, also in Rome. And then the United States by the same margin. Italy were favourites and they were overwhelmed by hope. They had won the World Cup eight years ago in Spain, but this was different. This was home. This was frightening.

Czechoslovakia: and an early goal. Italy, the Azzurri, were leading after nine minutes. But what followed was hard and bitter agony, missed chances, rejected penalties, a disallowed goal, a disallowed goal for the other team. Why watch it if it's such agony? Sport's never-to-be-answered question.

Roberto Baggio. *Il codino divino*: the divine ponytail. Loved and hated in a land that has never concerned itself overmuch with moderation, especially in sport. Italy has never come to terms with the question of why a very good player can't be even better, and why a player can be great at one moment and quite ordinary the next. Perhaps that's the great problem for all watchers of sport: to become reconciled with the fallibility – the humanity – of the participants.

Why is it that in one moment, it can seem that an athlete in competition is touched by the finger of God?

There were 11 minutes left to play when Baggio took the ball about 35 yards out on the left. He cut in, left a Czech player on his back, and then ran on into the middle with the ball at his right foot. Took on the centre-half and turned inside him, as if this was a ballet the two had been rehearsing all month. His low shot made the score 2-0.

Victory. Victory today, victory in the group, and with this second goal a typhoon of optimism shook the stadium and the land: for with a goal of such beauty, how could the ultimate prize escape? This was the greatest footballer on the planet playing for the greatest team on the planet in the greatest city on the planet.

Have you ever drunk a glass of champagne on an empty stomach at ten in the morning in bed with your beloved? Held your first child in your arms? Had your first novel accepted? Seen a blue whale close enough to touch? Had a flight of cranes overfly your garden?

Sport brings joy of a kind that makes a sober person dance in the street, makes a shy person kiss strangers, makes a person full of legitimate sorrows rejoice, at least for a while.

Walking back. Crossing the Tiber, the Piazza, the Steps: a Hallelujah Chorus of ten thousand motor horns: a joy-filled traffic jam, and who could fail to rejoice? Weeping, singing, slaloming round the stranded cars in the manner of Roberto Baggio, the city gorged on joy.

Sport can do such things.

~

It shouldn't have mattered. Things like this aren't supposed to matter. Certainly they were never designed to matter. But if you walked around Kensington Oval in Bridgetown, Barbados, that evening as the sun was coming down, there was no escaping the truth that it mattered a very great deal. Life and death? Sure, why not?

The most dangerous time is the period when the glory has gone but you haven't accepted that fact. Hell, you haven't even noticed. You think you're still great but you're not; the rapture comes and the rapture goes. Beauty and glory and triumph and wonder are slipping through your fingers and you still think you've got them fast. How long can you hold a draught of champagne in your hands? How long before it has all trickled away between your locked fingers?

Calypso cricket. That's what people said West Indies used to play. Cheerful, happy-go-lucky, win if you can and don't worry if you lose. Way out of date. The previous decade had celebrated another kind of music: get up, stand up – stand up for your rights. Get up, stand up – don't give up the fight.

At its crudest, this was the slaves rising up against the slave masters. At a more subtle level, it was a celebration of a changing world. When the great West Indian bowlers bowled, wrong was made right, winter met its death, spring was come again and all harms were healed. Sport is living mythology – but it's never quite under anybody's control.

How could England have won that first Test? How dare they think they might save the fourth? There was something amiss in the fabric of the cosmos: something that needed to be put right. How was that? Not out. How – was – that? Oh, all right, out.

Lloyd Barker, home umpire, surrendered to the second appeal from Viv Richards, West Indies captain.

Awful decision, terrible, shameful. Came off the thigh pad, Rob Bailey never hit it. Fellow doesn't know what he's doing. Criticism from polite white voices. Especially from the BBC cricket correspondent, Christopher Martin-Jenkins, a man with often-stated sympathies for South Africa (they're doing a great job in the townships). He thought he was the ultimately reasonable man: others saw him as an overt supporter of apartheid. So, by extension, this was South Africa waging war on West Indies: this was the white world turning on the black world once again: trying to put time into reverse.

The rest day that followed was not restful for anybody and the story hotted up and the politicians weighed in. England began the last day 15 for three. Their job was to bat all day and save the Test. That way they would go into the final Test with a 1-0 lead: defeat in the series no longer a possibility. But this wasn't a test of cricketing skills: it was a trial of righteousness. It was a battle between the knight and the dragon for possession of the virgin of truth.

It was also a day of heroic defiance from Jack Russell and Robin Smith – but most of the audience at the Kensington Oval in Barbados saw them as the enemies of freedom and the champions of the oppressor. It didn't help that Smith was born in South Africa.

If you play backgammon you can change the stakes by means of the doubling cube – and it's shocking how fast you can escalate things. Six faces on the die, the first reading two. Produce the cube and it already matters twice as much as it did before. The sixth face reads 64. Make just five turns of the cube and a simple game of chance and skill has become a struggle for all you possess.

By the evening of the last day of the fourth Test the die was showing its final and most terrible face. That was when Curtly Ambrose found his greatest abilities. He took five wickets in five overs of frenzy, power, speed and brilliance. How could a game with a bat and ball matter so much? This wasn't fun. This wasn't even joy: instead there was a fierce and terrible relief each time a wicket fell.

It was a battle against time and history: a desperate attempt to prove that the sporting world had not changed, that West Indies were still masters of the cricketing world. It was majestic and terrible: and truly frightening. The frail, tottering Heath Robinson structure of sport was not designed to carry this load of significance. Sport was invented to pass the idle hours: but now it was a theatre of cruelty in which ancient and terrible wrongs were symbolically avenged.

The glory was going, but it hadn't gone yet. Not quite.

~

It was a game of rugby, and it was about a battle that took place in 1314. It was also about the prime minister, a new form of taxation, a rekindled sense of political identity and the cancellation of a football fixture. And a folk song.

Partisanship is not quite the lowest level of pleasure that comes from watching sport. That's schadenfreude, of course. But partisanship brings more spectators to the stadiums and the screens than anything else.

Scotland v England: Bannockburn, Margaret Thatcher, poll tax, Scottish nationalism, and the loss of a traditional opportunity for expressing local differences in sporting form when the annual football fixture between the two nations was cancelled the previous year.

'Flower of Scotland'. This skirling nationalist ditty was used, for the second time, as Scotland's anthem before a rugby match. A crowd lashed itself into a state of passion: a closed feedback loop in which love of Scotland and hatred of the English fed on each other ravenously. In sport bigotry is acceptable. Sport is a bigotry-opp. After all, it's cut off from the real world. After all, it's only play . . .

The crowd was not on the pitch making tackles and scoring tries. But they changed everything.

If you're Scottish the match turned on a brilliant try: Gavin Hastings and his kick to Tony Stanger. If you're English it turned on the moment the England captain, Will Carling, failed the If Test. He called Simon Hodgkinson to kick a penalty and then sent him back to think again, overruled by his gung-ho forwards who wanted to go for the try. They came up empty.

Anyone is allowed to miss a pot. After all, mistakes happen. It's when you're thinking wrong that you're in trouble. Carling's thinking, England's thinking, was forced into error by the depth and power of the emotions in the crowd. And Scotland's defining moment of brilliance: did that too come from the crowd, from the love and the hate that came flooding down from the stands?

~

It began with incredulous frenzy; it was brought to an end by scrupulous calm. The penalty-taker seldom seeks inspiration. All he needs to score is the performance of certain well-rehearsed motor skills. All he needs is the talent to withdraw from the hurly-burly of the action and to perform this simple closed skill. With a penalty, only failure is worthy of comment.

Cameroon came into the World Cup as cannon-fodder: a team from the developing world that was offered the privilege of being beaten by the world champions Argentina in the opening match. It was a gift they declined, preferring instead to win 1–0 on a night of rare frenzy.

Football invites the Lord of Misrule into its proceedings more often than any other sport. Few sports are so responsive to sudden inexplicable surges of corporate inspiration: those curious passages of play in which, for no very clear reason, each player on the pitch becomes one-eleventh of a genius.

The best player in the world could do nothing against such forces. Diego Maradona may have been eleven-elevenths of a footballing genius, but he could do nothing in the face of this frenzy. Cameroon qualified for the round of 16 and then beat Colombia 2-1. It seemed that they could beat anybody. Every time, every expert predicted that they would fall at the next challenge, but they kept on not falling. They seemed to be operating in defiance of football's law of gravity.

Against England they were leading 2-1 with eight minutes to go. The semi-finals beckoned: and beyond that . . .

Hot v cool. Calmness v passion. Preparedness v inspiration. A penalty conceded. Gary Lineker both earned and scored the penalty.

The word clinical means 'of or pertaining to the sick-bed'. Inexplicably, in football it means the calm, apparently emotion-less scoring of a goal: the opposite of frenzy. Perhaps the idea is that the goal is scored with the calm precision of a scalpel, in which case 'surgical' would be the correct word. But football annexes words and changes them for its own purposes.

And so to extra time, and a pass of perfect inspiration from Paul Gascoigne. Taken up adroitly by Lineker – who was again fouled in the penalty area. He got up and scored the penalty. Clinically.

It was all so wonderful while it lasted.

~

One player can't be a team, but one player can be its heart, its meaning, its soul, the sun around which ten planets revolve.

Some athletes have a strange ability to turn their fantasies into actuality. Ian Botham in 1981: it's as if these unusual people give the entire world a duty to humour them.

I'm glad I'm a gamma . . . that was the motto of the England football team, comfortable in their role of second-raters: a duty they had been committed to since their defeat to West Germany in 1970.

But Paul Gascoigne had a fantasy about winning the World Cup. As a result England were in the World Cup semi-final, playing – West Germany. He was capable of having big thoughts, and believing them. He seemed capable of anything.

Gascoigne played as if England were the natural champions of the world. He played as if he believed England were Brazil and he was Pele. There was a touch of madness in it: reality was becoming a purely subjective concept. Gascoigne didn't play to the consensus: he attempted to make his own reality. And nearly succeeded.

England fell behind; England drew level, a goal stirringly completed by Gary Lineker. Extra time: and here the story that was revealed to millions was denied to those in the Stadio delle Alpi. The booking, yes, that was clear: but Gascoigne's subsequent breakdown, no. That was a television thing: clear demonstration that what matters in sport is the pictures, not the reality. Or perhaps television is the reality.

The story of Gazza's tears enraptured all England. That, and Puccini, for the World Cup broadcasts on BBC were preceded by the aria, 'Nessun Dorma', and that ear-busting music changed perceptions. Gascoigne and Puccini made football acceptable again. Not just acceptable: glorious, soul-lifting, beautiful, terrible and, above all, shared.

Then penalties. Stuart Pearce, his shot saved. Chris Waddle, the ball soaring over the bar into the Italian night.

~

All the confrontational sports require a relish in, or at least an indifference to, the suffering of your opponent. That's a trait shared by boxers, tennis players and chess grandmasters. It's war on a board, said Bobby Fischer, world champion from 1972 to

1975. 'The object is to crush the other man's mind. I like to see 'em squirm.'

When there is almost no physical action at all, very small acts – acts that would pass unnoticed at the next table in a restaurant – become almost suffocatingly dramatic.

The Hudson Theatre on 44th Street in New York was packed. They were all watching two men sitting at a table. In the intervals they were talking about running scared, all over him, can't land the knock-out blow. He's afraid to.

Watch the eyes. Always watch the eyes. Garry Kasparov kept his eyes on the board, wouldn't look anywhere else. But the eyes of Anatoly Karpov kept flickering from the board to his opponent and back. Kasparov was squirming. He didn't want to miss that.

Chess is an adrenalin sport. That was very clear. Karpov, so close to victory, could sit no longer. He got to his feet and paced the stage. He wanted to smash something – someone – physically as well as symbolically and mentally. His excitement was so great he could hardly control himself.

Then Kasparov moved. He raised his hand, stretched out towards a piece – and then snatched it back, as if suddenly aware that the knight or bishop was wired to the mains and would deliver a lethal shock. This shocking, apparently quite involuntary moment of indecision was the climactic moment of the game. Piano openings, gambits, the rich, subtle patterns of movements, the mathematical intricacies, the tricks within tricks within tricks, all this came down to a single moment of self-doubt, the sort of thing that you see at Wimbledon or Las Vegas or on any other sporting field of action.

These two knew each other in terms of a very special intimacy: more intimate, in some ways, than any two other individuals in history have ever known each other. The score in games between them at that point stood at 70½ games to 67½ in favour of Kasparov. Cain and Abel knew such intimacy only once: here these men, the letters of whose names uncannily intertwined, had attempted to murder each other 138 times already, and were looking forward to more. They knew each other's mind, each other's strengths. Both had seen the other man squirm. Neither was tired of the sight.

Unsated. That's one of the ways you tell a great champion. They never get bored with victory; they never get tired of the sight of a defeated opponent.

- Italy were knocked out of the World Cup in the semi-finals. They drew 1-1 with Argentina in a rather fearful display, and then lost 4-3 on penalties. The final was a memorably dreadful match, in which West Germany beat Argentina 1-0, the only goal a penalty.
- After drawing level in Barbados in the fourth Test of the five-match series, West Indies won the final match in Antigua by an innings.
- Scotland completed the Grand Slam by beating England and so won the Five Nations Championship. England were second.
- Garry Kasparov and Anatoly Karpov left New York with the score between them 6-6. The match continued for another 12 matches. Kasparov won 12½ to 11½.

BOOK 9

1991

A single well-struck tennis shot sounds like a small explosion. When 74 courts are in use at the same time it sounds like a Gatling gun with a hopper that never empties of ammunition. This was the Bollettieri Tennis Academy at Bradenton in Florida, with 225 students aged between eight and 18. A dream factory. At least for parents.

There was an English girl there. Talk to her, then. A wish that brought, like the demon king from a trapdoor, a tennis parent: in this case with Midlands vowels and Clint Eastwood haircut. She's contracted with IMG and we like to con-*trowel* the press. Well, not exactly con-trowel, but we're keeping her *oonder wraps*.

They'd sold up: the house, everything, to give their daughter her chance. Staked it all on their daughter's ability, their daughter's temperament, their daughter's hunger for the fight. Those things, and Bollettieri's reputation. Buy your dreams a dollar down.

It's like McDonald's. Words of Nick Bollettieri himself,

stalking round his territory stripped to the waist and with Oakley shades surgically implanted. 'I can't make you a champion but I can make you the best tennis player you could ever be.' Star names are part of the Bollettieri stock-in-trade: back then Agassi, Courier, Seles. 'Look around. Talk to anyone. Write what the hell you want. If you think it sucks, write it, OK?'

Little girls with big rackets, grunting, always grunting. This little lad looks good, what's his name? That's Tommy. Tommy what? Haas, I think his name is. Good kid.

A whistle sounded. A Bollettieri clone walked across. Stripped to the waist. Oakleys in place. Shouting. 'OK! Let's go!' The English girl had to go for her footwork class. Schoolwork gets fitted in round the tennis. Bollettieri came back: 'Hey! C'mon over here! Getta a look at this!'

A clay court, secluded, its wire fencing shrouded in canvas. Two little girls with four large, solemn eyes. Beads in their hair. One was ten, the other eight. Bollettieri's voice was as hoarse as a professional wrestler's from constant professional shouting, but it dropped to a soft, eager growl for these two. 'No, that's your old grip you're going back to. That's it! That's it! I love it!' And the eight-year-old hit 30 successive volleys straight back at Bollettieri: rat-tat-tat, a Gatling gun made for two. 'Get outta here! That's terrific! Terrific!'

And that's the heart of the business, of course, that and the dreams. The fact that Bollettieri was forever thrilled by coaching, forever in thrall to the heady concept of taking something good and making it better. And in sport you can actually measure the degree of improvement, for the only truth is results.

Most fail. At least, most fail at the highest level. That doesn't make the academy cruel, or the hot-housing system cruel. What's cruel is tennis, what's cruel is sport, what's cruel are dreams . . .

What were the names of those two little girls? The ones you

were coaching on the clay court? Oh them two. The big one's Venus, she's going to be real good. The little one, she's Serena. She's going to be a whole lot better.

~

'Moreland was fond of quoting Nietzsche's opinion that there is no action without illusion.' A line from Anthony Powell's *A Dance to the Music of Time*, one that skewers sport for all time. Sport is not only illusory: illusion is its founding principle – and yet people take up sport in their millions and they perform actions that are sometimes beautiful, sometimes heroic, sometimes many other things.

To step from Seventh Avenue to Eighth takes five minutes, but it is a dramatic transition from comparative wealth to comparative poverty. In this poor quarter, at Eighth and 40th, stood the Kingsway Gym. It was on the first floor, above street level, floor-to-ceiling windows giving the passer-by a foreshortened view of the mysteries within. There was a handsome, intelligent, thoughtful man explaining why he was going to risk permanent brain damage.

It's a classic boxing gym. They're always almost wilfully sordid, no matter how great the champion. It would be wrong to train in comfort. You must maintain the links with poverty, with deprivation, with desperation. You need the smell of men's sweat, the hogo of embrocation, the bare changing room, the inadequate shower, the shuffle of the skippers, the rattle of the speed-ball, the crump of the heavy bag, the self-absorption of the shadow boxers before the mirror, the grunts and sharp exhalations. It's all part of it and good. Every successful boxer has to feel poor again before going into the ring.

Boxing admires a clever fighter, one who 'outsmarts the game', gets out with his mind and his fortune undamaged. Yet here was the smartest of them all preparing to go through it all again. Sugar Ray Leonard was getting ready to fight Terry

Norris. He was 35. 'It's my job. I can't understand what's so bad about me doing this. You ask me why I still do it – I ask, why even ask me?'

Fair point. But we must ask. 'It's the American Dream – I guess it's the universal dream – that you get a million dollars in the bank and after that you sit around on some island drinking pina coladas. That's not my perception of life. I'm still working. I ain't been laid off yet.'

But there are other ways of working. 'Nothing will ever give me the same satisfaction as what I do here. I don't care if I do the greatest movie and win an Oscar. It wouldn't be the same satisfaction. It would be foolish to say that it could be.'

What was he addicted to? Not to money. Surely not adulation. To glory? Risk? Fear? Pain? Perhaps to the process itself: the long anticipation, the sudden explosive release. 'Nothing compares to this. All this.' His gesture with his well-wrapped paw took in the gym and the street beyond.

Out there a blizzard was getting into motion, yet 20 or 30 people were standing on the corner, muffled and hooded, watching the training a floor above street level, giving a cheer or two, clearly audible within, as Leonard went through his workout.

'And if your son wanted to become a professional boxer?'

'I'd lock him up.'

~

The people who run sport don't really like sport. Which seems odd, at first sight. Most people watch sport in search of some kind of pleasure. Most people who work in and around sport do so because sport is pleasurable, even though it's many other things as well. But those who become presidents of international sporting federations often seem to have no liking for and very little interest in sport. Whatever interest they had has long been subsumed by more pressing concerns.

The fact is that presidents become president because they like being presidents. What they happen to be presidents of scarcely matters. Primo Nebiolo, president of the International Amateur Athletics Federation (subsequently International Association of Athletics Federations), was unapologetically sleazy. Philippe Chatrier, president of the International Tennis Federation, was devastatingly charming, somewhat reckless, and giving out the vibes of a man you could rely on as far as you could throw the Philippe Chatrier Court at Roland Garros. Jean-Marie Balestre, president of the Federation International de l'Automobile, was declamatory and dictatorial and, of the three, the most clearly mad – power drives you mad, absolute power sends you completely barking.

Joao Havelange, president of Fifa, said that what gave him most pleasure in sport was discipline. Imagine that – you look at football, the most emotional of all sports, and the most inspiring thing you see is discipline. His favourite team at the 1990 World Cup was England, because they were the most disciplined. (He didn't try to explain Paul Gascoigne.) He sat in Fifa's palace in Lausanne, a big man, consciously erect with a huge head like a troll, and with a troll's mannerisms: unhurried and deeply conscious of his own mastery. He made a series of statements in stately French, frequently falling back on the same word: *indisputablement*. In conversation with Havelange, you have a choice. You can agree with him, or you can drop the subject. *On ne dispute pas*.

He didn't talk football. But then he was never a footballer. He played water polo, but he was soon aware that the route to power doesn't pass through the water-polo pool. Instead, he talked money. But not money for what it can buy, money for what it can do. He liked money only because money is power. That was the reason for his long-running crusade to make football matter in the United States, where the World

Cup would be held in three years' time. It wasn't enough to bring football to football-lovers. Football also had to reach the football-indifferent and the football-hostile as well. So long as they were rich, of course.

Havelange was equally keen on developing nations. These may have no money, but they have votes and votes are also power. His loud support for such nations won their uncritical support: forging links of self-interest and gold. He brought Coca-Cola, Philips and JVC into football as major sponsors, and he expanded the World Cup to 24 nations. More room for developing nations.

All of which might be good or bad, whether done for bad motives or good motives. A question about morality, then: and an unexpected response. 'You must lead a healthy life. I am 75 and I have never smoked. When I did swimming and water polo I had a lung capacity of seven litres. Today I still have a lung capacity of five litres. I walk every day for an hour and cover five kilometres. I do 20 minutes of gymnastics every day. Every day I swim a minimum of 1,000 metres.'

A question about jingoism: another odd response. He talked about the doctor who examines his arteries every six months. 'So I hope you will feel as my doctor does – and not that you fail to report something negative. You must be pleased to report what is positive.' Was there a threat buried in there? So let's talk about football, and his idea of bigger goals to make for more scoring, or dividing the game into four quarters of 25 minutes each, to make television advertisers happy, especially American ones. Football people could discuss either subject for hours, but Havelange was not a football person. He just explained that the committee was looking into them. 'I do not see any problems for the future because I work from day to day.'

Well, what about corruption, then? Accusations of personal and corporate corruption were already part of Fifa routine.

'When the day arrives that someone is not criticised, he is about to die.' So no criticism of any kind has any meaning whatsoever. Therefore criticism doesn't exist. Therefore there is no corruption. Therefore Havelange is right.

Indisputablement.

But what about football? What about sport?

Thank you, Mr President.

The great head nodded.

~

Frank Bruno was dressed as a chef and surrounded by bottles of HP Sauce. There was a good deal of local unease because he wanted to do the clearing up and they wouldn't let him. His attempts to do so were not of the kind you are meant to refuse, and that got everyone confused.

Brunoburgers. That's what was on the menu. Principal ingredients: minced beef and two tablespoons of *cette sauce de premier choix*.

Bruno was acting. He was acting Frank Bruno – 'Yeah, right, keep duckin' an' divin', know what I mean?' But he wasn't acting when he tried to clear up. That was a sense of his obligations.

Lovely man, sweet man. Even nicer than I *thought*. 'One of God's people,' said his one-time cornerman, George Francis.

Here was a British heavyweight boxer who was genuinely loveable, going to considerable pains to present himself as loveable. 'He's everything we are and what we wish to be known for,' said Chris Bruce, marketing director of HP Sauce. 'Homely. Unpretentious. Well-loved. And, of course, very British.'

Perhaps the best-loved British black man in history. 'That's nice. That's really nice. If people really think that, that's really nice. The way I see it, though, it's about keeping my feet on the ground. One day you might be the best this and that, next day you might be the best nothing. I don't want to get big-headed, and out of order, but if what you say is true – it's very, very nice.'

And yet there was a certain uneasiness about the whole thing. It's so hard to look back and retain a clear memory of what that meeting felt like; at such moments, knowing the terrible things that happened later.

He wanted to box again, and it seemed clear to most of us that he'd boxed enough already. We do everything to make a man into a professional fighter, and then we are shocked when he doesn't want to stop. Boxing wasn't just what Bruno (or Leonard) did. It's what he *was*. 'Boxing's my job. It's in my blood. I'm 29, I still train every day, and I miss boxing.'

He'd done panto and television adverts. He'd made money by becoming a professional character, with all the know-what-I-mean-'Arry stuff. He had a genuine sweetness and innocence, but the awkwardness around him wasn't imaginary, nor was the sense of danger. There was a moment of misunderstanding, a nanosecond in which his pupils seemed to go crescent-shaped – and then no, surely you imagined it, it's Frank! Good old Frank, with his bottles of HP Sauce, know what I mean?

'I worked on a building site and now I go to hotels like this. What matters is keeping your feet on the ground. Being level-headed, being grateful for what you've got.'

~

The world will end if you don't kick the ball against the patch of white paint on the wall. The nuclear holocaust will overwhelm us all: the bomb is wired to this wall, and the only thing that can defuse it is the striking of my football against the white bit. It's televised, the world is watching. You place the ball precisely, walk back, eye the ball formally. The world holds its breath but you, alone in the world, are calm. You know how good you are. You know the world is safe.

Almost . . .

There comes a time in the lives of most children when such games lose their charm. You lose the ability to believe in it; kick it anywhere, let the world go hang, I've carried it on my back for long enough . . .

That happens in professional sport too. You realise in defeat that nobody died. You understand – as you never did before – that there's no earthly reason to flog your body and put your heart and soul and mind through the routine tortures of sport. It simply doesn't matter.

For some, it's the realisation that frees and opens the way to the loftiest achievements of a late flowering. For others, it's the beginning of the end.

Night match at the US Open at Flushing Meadows. Jimmy Connors, beloved in these parts, against Patrick McEnroe. And when McEnroe was two sets up, two-thirds of the audience left. There was a pause during the change of ends, and then a sudden invasion: those in the cheap seats at the top came surging down to the posh seats close to court. And somebody called out: 'We're staying, Jimmy.'

That should have been his moment, but it wasn't. Connors lost the next three games and was love–40 down in the fourth. Defeat was no longer probable: it was certain.

Now.

That was his moment.

Why was it that when Connors was trying his best before, his best shots were flying long and hitting the net? Why did they now seem to be laser-guided onto the target? Why was it that, before, his best efforts seemed to get in the way of achievement? Why, now he was trying even harder, did achievement become inevitable? Before he had been seeking the old thunder in vain: now he was threading that same old thunder through the eye of a needle – and just turned 39.

The night matches here, with the black sky and the lights, have a gorgeous theatricality, and Connors had always loved to strut and fret here above all places. Here he was again, landing combination punches on the unoffending air, and performing pelvic thrusts at a partner none of us could see.

Last set. Saved a break point in the sixth game. Another in the eighth. Now at last serving for the match – and finding himself love-40 down again. Only then, only then was he able to win.

And there was praise for him as the old street-fighter, the brawler, the man who loves the rumble above all else ... but his life and health were never in danger, not like Sugar Ray Leonard and Frank Bruno. His brain was safe, and with it his mind. He was not going to be destroyed. Everything he valued was safe. This was a metaphor.

The world did not end that night, and nor was it saved.

~

History came to a crossroads in Indianapolis, in a sporting event that shadowed or parodied those of the greater world beyond. This was the first time that South Africa had taken part in a legitimate global sporting event since before 1964, when the country was banned from the Olympic Games in Tokyo. It was also the last time the Soviet Union participated in such an event.

The Hoosier Dome was the stage for the World Artistic Gymnastics Championships. Here, great political statements were made by little girls in make-up performing routines of devastating courage and beauty.

Worlds were colliding while the somersaults – tucked, piked, straight, forward, back and sideways – were thrown beneath the lofty ceiling of the vast dome. The South African Gymnastics Federation brought six gymnasts, all white, but they would soon change all that, they said. Black coaches were being trained in a programme that dated back to 1983; legislation explicitly forbidding racial demarcation was introduced in the 1960s.

Svetlana Boginskaya was the top performer for the Soviets. She was a Belarusian; not one of the six members of the Soviet women's team was from Russia, though they all trained at the centre near Moscow. Boginskaya had unreasonably lofty cheekbones and captivating elegance of style; at 5ft 2in getting on for a foot taller than some of her competitors, and nearly three stone heavier than a few of them. In other words, gymnastics is harder for her; the same movements are a great deal more difficult to pull off – but, when performed well, incomparably more pleasing to watch. She won gold in the team event and on the balance beam.

The championships marked a world in flux. But then, when Boginskaya performed three successive walkovers on the beam, making that slim finger of wood look as wide and solid as a dance floor, the world seemed simple enough: all its woes forgotten in momentary perfection of movement. And of course victory.

And history is about the victors, is it not?

- Nick Bollettieri's tennis academy is now the IMG Academy, where people are trained in all sports. Bollettieri was still coaching in 2017, aged 82. The British prospect, best not named, never came out from *oonder wraps*. The two little girls, Venus and Serena, got to be quite good.
- Sugar Ray Leonard got down to 154 pounds to fight Terry Norris at light middleweight, and, though favourite, he took a savage beating. He made another comeback and in 1997 and fought Hector Camacho; he lost after the fight was stopped. In retirement, he runs a boxing promotion company and is a respected motivational speaker.
- Joao Havelange served as Fifa president until 1998. In 2012 it was revealed that he and his son-in-law Ricardo Teixeira received US$41 million in bribes. He died in 2016, having achieved his century.
- Frank Bruno won the WBC heavyweight championship

after beating Oliver McCall in 1995, and lost it in his next and final fight. In 2003 he was restrained under the Mental Health Act. He was found to have bipolar disorder, exacerbated by use of cocaine.

- Jimmy Connors got to the semi-finals of the US Open that year, where he was beaten in straight sets by Jim Courier. It was the last glory: he retired, rather reluctantly, the following year.

BOOK 10

1992

He never looked like a footballer. He didn't look like a football manager now. He looked like the author of a great European novel: serious-minded, rather uncomfortable company, not given to compromise, brilliant without apology. He would have got the Nobel Prize for football, for sport, if such a thing existed, for he reinvented it, making it wiser, more meaningful and more beautiful as well as more effective.

Total football.

The finest system ever devised: rapture as basic tactic. Every outfield player was capable of playing in any and every position. It was as lovely – visually and conceptually – as it was devastating. There was only one snag. It didn't really work without Johan Cruyff.

Even when Cruyff was playing football there was an element of detachment. It was the same now that he was manager of Barcelona. His heart condition 'was a technical problem, not a problem of stress. I don't get stressed from watching a game.

I have had all kinds of tests during matches. For example, my pulse is 74 at rest, and no more than 85 at a match. No stress. I do not look at a game in an excited way. I am always analysing. If you can't do anything, there is no point in getting nervous.'

There was a spooky echo of Joao Havelange here, though the health stuff was a response to a question rather than a gratuitous offering. But that detachment was a trifle unexpected; Cruyff, whatever else, can never be accused of being a water-polo man. Football was his life. Perhaps it was also his passion, but, if so, he was not passionate in the way that most of us understand the term. Cruyff was always the most singular footballing man. He was in Britain because he was manager of Barcelona and Barcelona were due to play Sampdoria in the European Cup final at Wembley.

Was Cruyff the best footballer of all time? Very close, certainly – and, of course, it's all about the grounds on which you make your judgement. When it came to ball skills, George Best was better, though not vastly. Diego Maradona, too, though almost entirely one-footed. Pele remains more or less untouchable. In recent years Lionel Messi and Cristiano Ronaldo both scored more goals, but both are compromised, one by his diffidence, the other by his self-regard.

Self-regard is all very well, so long as it is linked to accurate understanding of your capabilities. Cruyff ran the show, not because he had a driving need to be the main man, but because he knew the show was better with him in charge. In footballing terms – though only in such terms – he was the egoless leader. And if you judge greatness in football by the extent to which a player creates, shapes and drives the team all around him, then Cruyff and the total football teams of Ajax and Holland make Cruyff the best of all.

He never won the World Cup, though Holland should have done so under Cruyff in 1974, when they were beaten finalists.

Ah, but then greatness is most readily appreciated when it comes with a flaw: like Sir Donald Bradman's sub-perfect batting average of 99.94. Now Cruyff was bringing his extraordinary footballing nature into management.

The greatest novelists invariably leave us with at least one flawed masterpiece. And the more you read, the more you understand that this is not an oxymoron but a tautology.

~

And the frightening thing is that he's only going to get better.

Tribute to the young Graeme Hick. Hick scored 405 runs in a single innings for Worcestershire while he was preparing to make his debut for the England team. He was Zimbabwean and so condemned to wait seven years – like one of the plagues of ancient Egypt – before he was eligible.

Waiting for Hick. All the troubles of England cricket would be at an end once Hick had qualified. It was like waiting for the judgement in Jarndyce versus Jarndyce: cricket found itself living in a future world of comfortable imaginings, which was so much easier and pleasanter than the vexatious present.

Hick was at last able to play for England in 1991. As malign luck would have it, England's opponents that year were the still fearsome West Indies. Hick, like Bruce Grobbelaar, was a white boy brought up in what was then called Southern Rhodesia, under the white supremacy rule of Ian Smith. Was that why the West Indian bowlers let themselves go a little? Or was it just the pleasure of dealing with England's ultimate (and ultimately unEnglish) weapon? Hick scored 75 runs in his first four Tests. In New Zealand – not a place renowned for pace like fire – he made 134 in three more. In the World Cup final of 1992, England lost to Pakistan as Hick was bowled by a googly from Mushtaq Ahmed for 17.

Pakistan were back in England and Hick was once again batting for the country that had waited for him so avidly for so long. The occasion was the first match in a one-day series. He made three runs in 14 minutes and nine balls before being undone by Wasim Akram, apparently while trying to get out of the way of the ball. It was clear that here was a man who was broke.

As Hick first made his way in international cricket, it became obvious that he had technical limitations – big, immobile, front-foot heavy – but plenty of great batsmen, plenty of great athletes in all disciplines, have been limited players. The trouble was that Hick's mind was also limited. He was not given to soaring across the vast open spaces of top-level sport. Or perhaps it was just self-consciousness: a sense of embarrassment at being the centre of so much attention. He was essentially, by upbringing, by nature, by choice of English domicile, a small-town man, Hick by name.

Hick represents the eternal mystery of talent. His career was one long asking of the great sporting question: why do some people have the talent for possessing talent while others do not? He remains a sporting archetype, was skewered for-ever in a single phrase by John Bracewell, writing in the New Zealand press.

Flat-track bully.

An athlete who is superb – and merciless – when the odds are stacked in his favour, but lacks whatever it takes to deal with more demanding occasions. A terror to the weak who suffered the contempt of the mighty.

But then it is a hard thing to be promising. Whom the gods wish to destroy they first call promising, wrote Cyril Connolly, and poor Hick had seven long years of promise. Perhaps it was that – and not the West Indian bowlers – that destroyed him.

~

The problem for those with a financial interest in sport is sport's uncertainty. You don't know the result. You don't know what happens next. Even in the most promising circumstances you are at the mercy of a thousand unknowns.

But at the Barcelona Olympic Games they found a way of doing away with sport's vexatious uncertainties. They brought in the Dream Team. They turned the Games into the perfect American fantasy of money, glamour and global dominance: all the more vivid for the fact that this was the first Olympic Games since the Berlin Wall came down. Magic Johnson, Air Jordan, the Bird, Clyde the Glide, 'Sir' Charles Barkley and Karl 'the Mailman' Malone (he *always* delivers) were all in the same team. This, American writers solemnly declared, was bigger than the Olympic Games.

America tends to focus on its own domestic products. In sport that's American football, which they call football, Major League Baseball (which generously includes Canada), and to a lesser extent ice hockey, which is called hockey. And basketball. Basketball as played by the teams of the National Basketball Association. It's interesting that in all these games the players tend to be larger than average men, and in two of these games they wear gear that makes them look still larger. All these games tend to set off the skills of a single dominant individual. It follows, then, that gathering all the dominant individuals in basketball into a single team representing the United States was a big deal.

So long as you're not interested in sport. Or at least, sport in the sense of competition. 'I don't know anything about Angola,' said Barkley before their first match. 'But I know Angola is in trouble.'

He was right. Angola went through 16 years of civil war after independence from Portugal in 1975; half a million people died, two-thirds of them women and children. They had their first multiparty election in 1991. Disease and shortages of food and medical supplies completed an evil cycle. In Angola basketball represented a small freedom, a tiny piece of sanity and a smidgen of hope: an antidote to despair and killing cynicism. The Angola team coach was Victorina Cunha, a white Angolan of Portuguese descent. 'In this country, basketball is the only thing that makes something great,' he said. 'People have so many difficulties. But when I win, they win.'

Dunks, jams, lay-ups, rainbows from three-point land: the Dream Team won 116-48, at one stage putting up 33 unanswered points, which is just not supposed to happen in basketball. It was a dream all right. A marketing man's dream.

~

The bus plied a circular route around the summit of Montjuic. It didn't matter whether you got off at the Estadi Olimpic, the Institut Nacional d'Educacio Fisica, the Palau de la Metal-lurgia, the Palau dels Esports, the Palau Sant Jordi, the Pavello de l'Espanya Industrial, the Piscina Municipal or the Piscines Bernat Picornell – whichever you chose, you would walk in on the most important day of someone's life, the day for which all other days had been but preparation. It was on this bus, rather than in the vast press conference given by the Dream Team, that you could learn why the Olympic Games, why sport, has its strange meaning.

The Greco-Roman wrestling was at the second of the venues listed above. It has claims to be the oldest sport at the Games – and perhaps it's the most important. It's wrestling standing up, using upper-body strength, as opposed to freestyle, which is all rolling about on the floor. Greco-Roman wrestlers don't use their legs for anything other than standing on; their opponent's legs are out of bounds. It's stylised combat, not a death duel. It's not boxing.

Aleksandr Aleksandrovich Karelin was a Russian fighting for the Unified Team, the hastily improvised entity put together for the Games after the collapse of the Soviet Empire. He was in the 130kg section: the ultra-heavyweights. He listed his hobbies as reading, classical music and writing poems; he favoured the romantic Russians and the writing of Mikhail Bulgakov. He was also keen on throwing 20-stone men on their backs – the reverse body-lift is usually only seen in the lighter categories of this sport, but Karelin made it something of a signature move.

Most dangerous opponent? His fridge. It was delivered to his flat on one of those Soviet days when the lift was out of order. 'It was a huge fridge,' he said. 'I carried it myself up eight flights of stairs.'

The audience in the Institut Nacional d'Educacio Fisica was small, the place only half-full. The competitors went through the day of vast significance without too many people noticing. Not much money was made. And yet the significance of it all was overwhelming: almost oppressive, the weight of centuries, the weight of sport's meaning. The obscurity of the event, the modest size of the audience added to the day's significance. No doubt you could put together a collection of all the sports that gather vast audiences and offer the world a Showbiz Games with immense names, and measure it all by commercial success, and no doubt they soon will. But it would lack meaning.

The Dream Team made its mark because the Greco-Roman wrestlers were also there. Because Karelin was there. Such dignity as the Dream Team possessed came from the wrestlers.

~

In Linford Christie's pre-race ritual he turned every other living thing in the world into dross. Nothingness. He willed them out of existence, or at least into perfect insignificance. At the start of the race he would stand and stare back down the track. The world would be reduced to a tunnel 100 metres long and one Linford-wide. He stood tall and imposing, a near-miraculous physique, while his eyes destroyed everything that was not Linford.

It was the mark of a man of very great certainty; of many great uncertainties.

He won, that night in Barcelona at the top of Montjuic. Gold medal. No one really expected that, but Ben Johnson was banned and Carl Lewis had failed in the extraordinary system by which the United States pick their athletics team. He would have been favourite had he qualified, but he didn't. He was there, competing in the long jump, but not in his best event, although he was fully fit.

So Christie was lucky but one of the great skills of life is to seize your luck and your moment on the rare occasions they are there to be seized. Fight or flight? This contradictory demand had brought many difficult, awkward and rather unpopular champions to the sprint: Lewis, Johnson and now Christie. Christie was surly, awkward, difficult, chippy and, often enough, plain bloody rude. His contempt for the white press was deeply self-protective, but so well done it had become genuine. His victory brought him straight out before people he despised.

Which gave an added pleasure to proceedings, but an added pain, too. In this great moment it would have been nice to have unadulterated goodwill.

Christie had done something exceptional, proving himself to be an exceptional man. Exceptional men are people out of the common run, obviously enough. People in sport who seek popularity as well as success tend to find some way of covering up their exceptional nature, or at least of presenting it in a socially acceptable form – just ask the Dream Team, for as Michael Jordan pointed out, Republicans also buy sneakers.

But Christie, it seemed, wanted only one thing, and that was a gold medal. It was what he was for. He seemed content in that post-match moment of mutual hate. There is gold; the rest was dross.

Especially you.

~

It was the women who had the best of the running in Barcelona; perhaps it was the first Olympic Games in which women dominated events in and around the athletics stadium. In Barcelona this was set at the top of Montjuic. It was a tough climb for spectators and a brutal ascent for the runners in the marathons as they approached the finishing line inside the stadium.

Valentina Yegorova, a Russian athlete representing the Unified Team, duelled every inch of the last two miles with Yuko Arimori of Japan. Yegorova made what looked like the decisive break, was caught, fell back, came again. The pair swapped the lead again and again all along the refined cruelties of the slope, until at the last Yegorova made a second break and with it broke – cruel word, cruel business – Arimori. At the end the pair embraced, sobbing.

Hassiba Boulmerka of Algeria was unable to train at home for the usual reasons in an Islamic society, but she won the 1500 metres in a performance that radiated strength of mind, of purpose and of body. Some runners seem scarcely to touch the earth: Boulmerka ran as if she was bulldozing her way through the stuff.

How sport loves a symbolic moment. Britain's Liz McColgan had been strongly fancied to win the gold medal in the 10,000 metres and she set the pace more or less from the gun, but she was broken – heart and spirit and all – when Elana Meyer went past her with nine laps to go: a stunning and courageous move. Meyer was a white South African – for South Africa were back at the Olympic Games, now that apartheid had ended and the first free election was being planned.

The only runner to go with her was Derartu Tulu, aged 20 from Ethiopia. She was wearing a tee-shirt under her singlet, obviously feeling the chill of the Barcelona summer. She hadn't built up much of a reputation, very few people in the stadium knew even if she had a finish. She seemed to have trouble keeping up – but then, with a lap to go, she was transformed. It was as if the bell took the previous 9,600 metres from her legs, as if the nearness of the finish had taken all the weight from her body and mind. Meyer looked as if she had run every inch of the way, Tulu looked as if she was just about ready to start, and she fairly cruised away from Meyer and won by an ever-growing distance. She was the first black African woman to win an Olympic gold medal.

For a moment or two the pair celebrated together, Tulu with the Ethiopian flag, Meyer not with the banned tricolour of South Africa – still the official flag – but the Olympic flag, and they linked hands and for a second or two it seemed as if all the troubles of the world had been ended.

～

John McEnroe galloped towards the ball to execute a classic running pass. Missed it. This was practice, the day before the start of the Davis Cup final, in Forth Worth, Texas, with Switzerland the opposition. So there was some intimacy in the circumstances: the near-empty arena, no members of the public, very few people at all, just a few who could stroll up to the courtside, within touching distance, whenever they liked. So close it was possible to see the rage that crossed McEnroe's face like forked lightning: and to hear and be genuinely alarmed by his roar of self-loathing.

This was practice. It didn't matter; but of course, it did.

Very few people bring their game close to the level of perfection. Those who do usually play with an essentially limited method, achieving near-perfection in a small arc of the game's possibilities; a strategy that can bring considerable rewards. But occasionally you find people who seek perfection in every single aspect of the game they have embraced, and McEnroe was one of these.

Total tennis.

Rapture or nothing.

There is craziness in the ambition because it is doomed to failure. Few people have taken the game to such heights: few tennis players have hated themselves for their failures as McEnroe did. He knew he could hit perfection sometimes: why couldn't he do it every time? The thought was destroying him. To chase perfection is a noble thing, but it involves the need to embrace perpetual failure.

Victory is no vindication: merely a break in the routine of self-loathing.

There were other reasons for McEnroe's incandescent unhappiness. The news of the failure of his marriage to the former child film star Tatum O'Neal had just broken: tennis was a retreat into a different kind of unhappiness. Meanwhile, two jolly little lads, Sean and Kevin, were playing with a tennis ball at the back of the court; McEnroe's two sons, there with his daughter, Emily.

Marriage, like sport, requires a colossal – almost unrealistic – level of optimism. Although a great deal of realism is also helpful in keeping things going. But when optimism is dead, so is sport and so is marriage.

McEnroe looked in that practice session like a man who had had optimism surgically removed from his life. Maturity had been hard won in this unquiet man: and once achieved, it wasn't all it was cracked up to be.

But perhaps a brutally tough game of tennis would for a while block out the failure of real life to reach perfection.

- Johan Cruyff's Barcelona team won the final of the European Cup against Sampdoria 1-0. In Cruyff's time with Barcelona they won La Liga four times in a row. He created the modern Barcelona team, gave them an identity, a style and a swagger that eventually made them perhaps the finest football team ever put together.

- Graeme Hick played 65 Tests and 120 one-day internationals and scored more than 40,000 first-class runs. His first-class average was 52.23; his Test average was 31.32.
- The Dream Team won the gold medal in Barcelona, and a team with a broadly similar line-up won the gold medal at the Atlanta Olympic Games in 1996. In 2000 most of the big names did not participate; the Dream Team was no longer cool, or for that matter, profitable.
- Aleksandr Karelin won the gold medal in Barcelona, and again in Atlanta, making three in all. In 1999 he entered politics at the request of Vladimir Putin and was elected to the state Duma.
- Linford Christie tested positive for drugs in 1999, by which time he was no longer competing seriously.
- Derartu Tulu was fourth in the Atlanta Olympic Games, running with an injury, but she won gold again in Sydney in 2000. She won the Tokyo and London marathons in 2001.
- John McEnroe only played the doubles at the Davis Cup final. His match took place on the second day with the score tied at 1-1. He and Pete Sampras lost the first two sets but came back to win, and the United States went on to win the tie and the cup. McEnroe then retired. He had seven Grand Slam singles titles, and went on to a career in broadcasting that, a trifle unexpectedly, made him both respected and loved. After the divorce he had custody of the children and later married the singer Patty Smyth.

BOOK 11

1993

The more serious the occasion, the closer you are to farce. Funerals, weddings, speech days, church services, formal dinners: farce is always waiting in the wings. And of course, the portentous nature of great sporting occasions means that grotesque humour is perpetually ready to pounce. What happened in Mumbai would have been comic in any match, but given the almost endless subtext, it was more like one of those brisk switches between tragedy and comedy that you find in Shakespeare.

This was the third Test in a series of three and England were already two down. It seemed clear that Graham Gooch's time as England cricket captain was coming to an end and his entire sporting philosophy was open to question. Gooch demanded hard-working, hyper-fit players with – above all else – the right attitude. Attitude being far more important than talent. David Gower had been dropped for the tour, a move that caused much dismay: no room for one of the finest players in the world in a team that modelled itself on Boxer in *Animal Farm*. They worked harder all right, but they lost twice. So now what? And who should take over the captaincy from Gooch when the time came?

Two choices: the current vice-captain, Alec Stewart, a Gooch man by choice, or the previous vice-captain, Michael Atherton. Stewart was Gooch's sergeant-major; Atherton represented a less circumscribed, less football-centred approach. There was, as always in English cricket, as always in England, a class thing going on. Atherton was a Cambridge graduate; Stewart was not.

It was the final match of a bad tour. Defeat seemed the only option, the world was black and any change was a change for the better. No one was quite rational. Following the English tradition, the team resented above all the country they were travelling in: making an enemy of their own present. This was India, so resentment settled on bowel movements. Farce had already been touched on in the previous match, when Gooch took a dish of prawns – do you think that's wise, sir? – at his pre-match dinner. He fell ill, Stewart captained in his absence and the team lost heavily while the England management served a special lunch in the pavilion: corned beef, baked beans and naan bread dished out by the tour manager, Bob Bennett, the physio, David Roberts, and the chaplain, Andrew Wingfield Digby. It was *Carry On Up the Khyber*.

The final Test began in sulky mood. The plane home beckoned as an illusory sanctuary. Gooch, recovered from his battle with the prawns, won the toss. He chose to bat, opened the innings and was out for four – leaving Atherton and Stewart batting together. Stewart called Atherton for a quick single; Atherton responded, changed his mind and turned back. Stewart just carried on. Both players ended up at the same end: the other end batsman-less and bail-less.

It was one of those eternal sporting tableaux: a double Rodin statue, title *Innocence*. Both players leant on their bats, ankles crossed, determinedly not looking at each other. It was as if the fate of the cricketing nation was hanging in the balance – after a piece of rather especially inept cricket. A moment for the judgement of Paris: who was the most beautiful goddess of them all? Playing the part, we had the umpire Srinivas Venkataraghavan. He decided that Stewart was out. By most reckonings, including *Wisden*, he got it wrong both technically and morally. Stewart certainly thought so, prodding his own chest in a classic 'who, me?' dumb-show. He was out for 13, Atherton made 37 before departing himself.

It was the dawn of a new era. As Macbeth's reign began with the drunken porter, so England's new start began with the glorious sight of both alternative futures marooned at the same end.

~

The English have always envied the Irish, at least when not trying to kill them. So there was a strange feeling of acquiescence in Ireland's defeat of England in the rugby union Five Nations Championship. The large English contingent at Lansdowne Road stadium in Dublin mysteriously changed sides; defeat of their own seemed a thing of joy and Dublin was every English spectator's home city. Allegiance and nationality in sport are strange things, in which antagonisms can be an aspect of distorted love as well as an expression of millennia-deep antipathy. Here the traditional English envy of the Irish was given perfect sporting expression.

Ireland hadn't won a match in either of the past two seasons and were favourites for last place this time around. But sport has its own logic. You play well because you're playing well, and so you play better: how can anyone explain that? Further mysteries, like team spirit, are equally elusive of explanation: the magic just descends and everyone is doing everything right, mixing selflessness and responsibility in precisely the right proportions.

The better team is often beaten in football, but this is much rarer in rugby, and all the more to be cherished, even by the defeated overdog. In Dublin the underdog bayed and England offered their throats.

Such occasions need a hero: and here was Eric Elwood, the fly half. To kick Ireland to victory was a hard task – certainly harder than his day job, which was selling Jameson whiskey to the Irish. He succeeded triumphantly in both: two drop goals and two penalties as Ireland won 17–3 to create a day of sporting euphoria. There was, as always in Irish sport, as always in Ireland, especially when the English are involved, a politico-historical thing going on, usually a North–South thing. The Irish rugby team represents a united Ireland, one of the few things that does. Rugby union was once considered a game for West Brits and proddy dogs, but television has democratised the sport and made it a spectacle enjoyed all over the island. And beating England: well, who can't relate to that?

But it wasn't a vindictive, spiteful, defiant sort of rejoicing: just a revelling in the countless and boundlessly unpredictable joys of sport, which were inextricably mixed with the complications of national identity. The English felt honoured to be a part of it: celebrated alongside their victors in Guinness and Jameson.

~

There's a story about a footballer who went to the theatre to see the play *Thark*. He was asked: 'Was it a farce?' 'No – it was quite good, actually.'

The Grand National was the perfect farce. It was Brian Rix with his trousers round his ankles, it was Feydeau with every character in the wrong bedroom, it was the classic pastiche, *Chase Me Up Farndale Avenue, S'il Vous Plaît*, it was Ben Travers's haunted mansion. It was a man in a bowler hat and a riding mac like a small tent – appropriate dress for farce – waving a flag that failed to unfurl. As a result he failed to halt a madcap cavalry as

Britain's most famous horse race set off without his permission.

There had already been one false start. The starting gate, a single strand of rain-soaked elastic, had got tangled round a few jockeys. Further delays had been caused by animal rights protesters. All this added to the hell-broth of tensions created by the uniquely demanding and dangerous circumstances of the race. The horses were lit up like torches; the jockeys wanted to steal the best position right from the off. Then, as they approached the fateful gate – immortally described by the trainer Jenny Pitman as 'sixty yards of faulty knicker-elastic' – the jockey Richard Dunwoody got the elastic round his neck – that'll teach you to be so eager.

The starter was Captain Keith Brown. He waved his recall flag. But it didn't unfurl, so 30 of the 39 jockeys set off to win the Grand National quite unaware that the race hadn't actually started. Further down the course was Ken Evans, a casual worker earning £28 for his shift as recall man. He was supposed to back up the starter's recall signal by waving a flag of his own. Certainly he failed to stop the race. Most of the riders completed the first lap but realised after the final jump, the water, that the race had been called off at the start and so they pulled up. But 14 of them went on to take part in a second circuit. Esha Ness finished first – the word 'won' is inappropriate – in the second fastest time ever. The race was declared void. Brown then suggested that the race should be restarted, with only the nine runners who didn't set off taking part. It was later suggested that the crowd would have burnt Aintree to the ground if that had happened, but the grand author of the farce decided that enough was enough. No sense in overegging the pudding.

Racing went into a series of classic ruling-class evasion tactics, absolving everyone of blame except the 28-quid man, Evans. A report said he failed to wave his flag; Evans always denied this vehemently, but who cares about him? It was made very clear that the good captain — so unfairly called Captain Cock-up in the popular press — was more to be pitied than blamed. But somehow he never started the Grand National again. It's the way we do things, old boy. We act with self-serving cynicism and call it duty. And what's so funny about that?

~

We live in a dream of flight. The holiest beings after God we called angels and gave them wings. Our stories and our mythologies are full of flying creatures. Every time humans have tried to express a thought that was magical and full of meaning, the idea grew wings. Every culture on earth brings us creatures that waged war on gravity and won. The West has fairies, dragons, harpies, hippogriffs, witches, the phoenix, the sphinx and Pegasus, latterly Harry Potter and Superman.

Inevitably, we have tried to fly in play, and then we turned this play into games: who flies best? The National Exhibition Centre in Birmingham staged the world flying championships, otherwise known as the World Gymnastics Championships. The greatest prize on offer was for the all-around champion: the male gymnast who mastered all six pieces of apparatus and the woman who mastered all four. The apparatus in question are all flying-opps: different ways in which the human being can take on gravity in a straight fight.

Vitaly Scherbo of Belarus won the men's competition despite a poor opening performance on the rings, in which he finished 12th. His performance brought one of sport's Decisive Moments. It was suddenly obvious that the result had already been decided: from that point on the competition was a ritual procession. It came when Scherbo finished his floor routine with an enormous double-layout — two somersaults performed with straight legs, more or less in the position of attention. Nailed the landing. Pause. Thunder of applause. All over.

Top-level — top-*flight*, that's the mot juste — gymnastics first makes you doubt the evidence of your senses. But you make a strange adjustment: impossible things become normal and the minute error you noticed deservedly costs the flier marks, victory and hope. Then the champion steps in – and the fantastic nature of each and every contestant becomes once again overwhelming: and more so than before.

Shannon Miller of the United States won the women's competition. 'My parents took me to the gym when I was five, because I was wrecking the furniture,' Miller said. Most children wreck the furniture, very few become champions. Miller was 16, and with a slightly spooky quality about her ... though that's something you find with very many top athletes. Linford Christie has no monopoly on such a thing.

Not quite there. Not breathing quite the same air as you and me. And you're never sure whether such people are to be envied or pitied. Then you watch Miller's tumbling on the floor exercise – the floor which she seemed scarcely to touch – and you remember those dreams in which you swooshed across the floor and soared without effort – dreams Freud said were always about sex, not a fact that ever diminishes their charms – and you realised that where you dreamt, she did.

~

Hang time.

It's an illusion, of course, and it's the illusion of flight. Mostly it's an illusion that comes from television, which does curious flattening things to perspective: a man running and jumping towards the camera doesn't seem to be moving in the manner of the long jumper: he just goes up and apparently stays up. It's an error, but a highly vivid one, and it has helped to make basketball a hugely successful television sport.

The master of hang time was Jordan. Michael Jordan. Michael 'Air' Jordan, a nickname full of flight that was bestowed on him not by the will of the people but by the company that paid him to wear their plimsolls. His team, Chicago Bulls, had reached the NBA finals against Phoenix Suns and, for once, Jordan was getting criticised. He had taken part in ultra-high-stakes golf games, and that was considered unacceptable. After all, he was a role model, whatever that means. And when his team lost Game Three of seven, and this one at home in Chicago, it was somehow Jordan's fault. He was trying too hard, they said. He was feeling the weight of responsibility, for in basketball a single individual tends to dominate the team. Jordan was the game's highest scorer with 44 points from his team's 121, but he also missed a lot: from 43 shots he landed only 19, and that was the margin between victory and defeat with some room to spare.

Pressure.

Always in sport they talk about pressure. How shall we define it? It's the notion that certain circumstances make it harder to perform sport's basic skills. It's harder to convert the fifth penalty in a penalty shoot-out because of the pressure, it's harder to bowl 'at the death' because of the pressure, it's harder to rip the fifth and final dive at the Olympic Games because of the pressure, it's harder to fire an ace on the last point in the Wimbledon final than it is on the first.

So here is one of sport's eternal mysteries: the 'pressure' that inhibits some athletes inspires others. The ones we call champions. The circumstances that make others perform worse makes them perform better.

In Game Four Jordan scored 55 points, Chicago won 111-105 and went 3-1 ahead in the series. As an individual's dominance of a team game it was complete. That doesn't mean it wasn't close. With 33 seconds on the clock, the Suns were only two points behind and had possession. But then a steal from B.J. Armstrong, a pass to Jordan, and Jordan was once again going in the hard way, straight through the middle, fake the pass, fake again and soar, taking it on himself. As he took off, he received an almighty shove from Charles Barkley, and that skewed him off balance. He twisted in the air – and then dropped the ball into the basket over his head while facing the wrong way. He landed and took the free throw for Barkley's foul and it hit nothing but net.

Paul Westphal, the Phoenix coach, was asked if he was surprised at what Jordan did to his team. 'No. I'm amazed – but I'm not surprised.'

~

The afternoon shopping streets of the city were their usual humdrum selves: people walking in and out of Boots and WHSmith, people in the supermarkets, soldiers fully armed. To an outsider they looked like people horribly early for a fancy-dress party, but for the people of Belfast it was just a day in the life.

It had been that way for years, but right then, there was a faint and deeply unfamiliar scent in the air. The name of that smell was hope. Politicians and others had been speaking as if peace was not an entirely impossible concept. It wasn't that some people dared to hope: it was more that some people, some rare people, seemed – at least for the moment – to be immune to the weariness and despair of troubles without end.

So the gods of sport decided that this would be a good time for a football match: a World Cup qualifier, and not one involving a team representing a united Ireland. The Republic of Ireland played Northern Ireland in Windsor Park, Belfast, and the hardcore supporters of the home team dressed for the occasion in red, white and blue. It was a ceremony of division: a celebration of the causes of troubles.

It was rather like setting out a keg of dynamite in a room full of chain-smokers and hoping no one would drop a fag-end. As ever in this stressed-out place, the crowd in the ground and the people of the city were torn between the many who just hoped there would be no trouble and the few who hoped there would. Trouble is an addiction like any other.

No surrender!

The cry itself surrendering any hope of union. Loud singing of 'The Sash My Father Wore': one of the many hymns of division. The football ground was deep in a loyalist enclave. And when Northern Ireland took the lead, a group of 300 supporters clad in their Union Jack colours turned on the press box and hammered on the glass walls, faces alive with the joy of battle and desperate for a visible enemy to fight, or at least taunt. Good glass in that press box: it rang and it banged and it rattled, but it never gave. Eventually the banging lost its point and, besides, there was a football match going on.

No one died. Sport lived, not least because Alan McLoughlin bagged an equaliser and the score stayed at 1-1 and in the end it was all – just – sport. The seeds of violence never germinated, not there, not then.

Some of the crowd sang 'One team in Ireland'. It was utterly appropriate to the occasion, and perfectly ambiguous. There is one national rugby team, but there are two national football teams . . . and after this result, only one of them was going to the World Cup finals in the United States the following year, and that was the team representing the Republic. The other lot. The lot whose supporters wear green and don't sing 'The Sash'. And for that matter, there was only one team, from the group of islands and nations that's sometimes called the British Isles, that was sending a national football team to America. Not Wales, not Scotland, not Northern Ireland and most certainly not England, whose team, under the management of Graham Taylor, the former manager of Watford, had failed to get through the qualifying tournament. Republic of Ireland were not the only football team in Ireland, but they were the only one going to the World Cup.

The football match ended. The din died down. By then we could all do with a bit of peace.

~

The doomed comeback is one of sport's ever-repeating fables. Whatever the reason for leaving sport – injury, burn-out, disillusionment, surfeit of defeat, surfeit of victory, too easy, too difficult, too destructive, too time-consuming, too soul-consuming – there's always a terrible discovery when the comeback gets into full swing. Like the woman giving birth to a second child, they had forgotten it was this hard. And, unlike that woman in childbirth, they can always stop. Or at least not try so much that it hurts. Has the physical commitment gone? Or mental commitment? Or spiritual commitment? Something has changed. Is it sport? Is it you? Is it your opponents? Is it the nature of the game you play? Is it the nature of sport itself? Or is it just the nature of time?

No one ever knows. All that remains is the truth that a real comeback is the hardest thing in sport.

It was rules, not ennui, that drove Katarina Witt out of competitive ice skating; she needed to earn money by skating and the sacred codes of amateurism forbade such a thing. But the Olympic movement did away with amateurism as a concept – abandoning its previous policy of blind-eyeing professionalism – in time for the 1992 Olympic Games, and that made the Dream Team possible. Now the Winter Olympic Games were scheduled for 1994 in Lillehammer, and skaters who had worked as professionals found themselves eligible once again.

So Witt was once again a virgin, joyful concept. What called her? Was it the bugle call of competition? The heroin-hunger for adulation? The chances of more money? Or all three? Witt won one gold medal when she skated Maria from *West Side Story* at Lake Placid in 1980 and another four years later as she skated Carmen in Sarajevo. Now she was taking part in the German

Championships. Her aim was to qualify for the Olympics the following year.

She was noted for grace of movement – that is to say, she skated so perfectly she didn't stick her arms out as balancing poles. You just looked at her skate past and said, wow! She's the champion. She was also noted for a knowing sexuality and a smile like opening the door of a blast furnace.

But she chose to come back as something rather different. For her short programme she dressed up as Robin Hood and skated like the principal boy, and for the second piece, she wore a long, high-collared dress and danced not sex but world peace, to 'Where Have All the Flowers Gone?' The dances were lovely, the costumes were lovely, the skater was lovelier than anything you could ever dream of – but the jump was gone. The event was won by Tanja Szewczenko, aged 16, who stuck her arms out and landed six triple-jumps in the final dance. Witt attempted four, and two of them were flawed.

It's all very well being sad, sexy, graceful and beautiful, but if you can't jump, you can't win, and you can't win because this is sport. Sport is at heart a brutal business – and that's as true the day you make your debut as the day you make your exit wondering why almost all sporting careers end in failure. And why almost all comebacks do.

Where have all the flowers gone? A most pertinent question.

- Graham Gooch resigned as England cricket captain after four Tests against Australia the following summer; Michael Atherton was appointed his successor.
- Eric Elwood won 35 caps for Ireland and went on to be head coach of Connacht.
- Keith Brown retired as a starter that year. It was generally accepted that the procedure rather than the individual was at fault. The width of the Grand National start was

reduced from 60 to 40 yards, with a triple-stranded starting gate. There were two false starts in 2009, both successfully recalled.

- Vitaly Scherbo stopped his career a couple of years later after his wife was involved in a bad motor-car accident. As she recovered, she told him to get back in training. He did so, winning four bronze medals at the 1996 Olympic Games. Shannon Miller won two gold medals at the same Games.

- Michael Jordan retired from basketball that year to play baseball in the minor leagues. Perhaps he needed something to fail at. He later made a fully successful comeback, leading the Chicago Bulls to three more NBA Championships. He then retired – and, later still, he made a third comeback, this time for Washington Wizards, donating his salary to charities for victims and survivors of 9/11.

- The Republic of Ireland reached the round of 16 at the 1994 World Cup. Northern Ireland have not qualified for the World Cup finals since 1986.

- Katarina Witt qualified for the 1994 Winter Olympic Games and finished seventh. Her free dance, to 'Where Have All The Flowers Gone?', was widely praised for its beauty, but was short on technical content.

BOOK 12

1994

People talk about despair in sport but they don't really mean it. A despairing dive, despair at match point, despair on the podium because it's not gold. But that's not despair. That's just defeat. That's just disappointment. For the spectator it's symbolic despair, metaphorical despair, despair that can touch you, and perhaps make you shed a tear or two – but it can never persuade you, even for an instant, to take it seriously.

And yet in Pasadena on a football pitch the real thing was there for all to see: not despair in losing a match, but despair at the total futility of life, the pointlessness of continuing to exist, the utter uselessness of keeping the show on the road for a single second longer. Here was a football team that had lost the will to carry on. Why kick a ball? Why run? Why breathe? Nothing was left but the grey horrors of desolation.

It was like looking at a friend suffering from concussion: the shell is there but the spirit is absent. Here was one of the finest football teams on the planet and they weren't playing football.

They weren't trying to play football. Even though this was a crucial match in the World Cup.

Colombia were playing the United States in a group match in California. Before the tournament began, Colombia had beaten Argentina 5-0 in a tumultuous display from Carlos Valderrama, Faustino Asprilla and Adolfo 'El Tren' Valencia, and Pele said they would win the World Cup. They lost their first match against Romania, to a combination of stage fright and the brilliance of Gheorghe Hagi. But against the USA they were infinitely worse.

There was no fist-pumping, no arm-waving, no shouting, no reckless (despairing) tackles, no (desperate) attempt to turn the tide. The coach, Francisco Maturana, also a professor of dentistry, said afterwards, when asked why he had taken the radical step of making two substitutions at half-time: 'Because you are permitted to make only two substitutions. I would have liked to have made 11.'

Gabriel Gomez had dropped out of the match two hours before kick-off. He had received a threat that his family would be blown up by terrorists if he played. 'My football career is as good as over,' he said.

The USA won 2-1. They went ahead though an own goal from Andres Escobar; Earnie Stewart scored the second. Valencia put away a rebound to score in the last minute, a goal that could not obscure the true nature of the match. It had not been contested.

The Colombian team's despair affected everyone in the stadium. There seemed little point in discussing the game or discussing football or discussing life. What had happened? The obvious explanation – that they had been bribed to throw the match – didn't feel right. It was more that they had no option. In a place as lawless as Colombia was then, you didn't have to spend good money to make people do what you wanted. Here was a football match in which the best lacked all conviction. Worse was to follow.

~

'Here are the high-wire artists of the soul, people who can do the impossible, who are on another plane. They are flawless only in their expression of their sporting excellence.' This is how Eric Cantona chose to be seen. He quoted these words, from a French writer Jacques Thibert, in his autobiography.

For Cantona, every game of football was about him. That's supposed to be blasphemy, contrary to everything team sport is about. But Cantona's vision of himself as a solo performer on a crowded stage was what possibilised the great revival of Manchester United. He created a team because he was not a team man: his only interest in his team was that it gave him something to stand out from.

Cantona didn't think he was the best. He knew it. It was a conviction that went soul-deep, and that's why he was able to extort from the world a duty to humour him. Anything less would have been – well, rather unmannerly. Everything Cantona did reinforced his own personal myth: the upturned shirt collar, the way he stood with his shoulder blades almost touching, the way he walked as if smearing insects with every step.

In another team or on another day or another stage in history, this would have been insufferable. But Manchester United were rising from a long barren period – and Cantona was the difference between the dreary past and the glorious present. Because of Cantona, Manchester United began to see themselves as champions as of right. His swagger became the team's swagger, his self-loving mystique became everybody's mystique; his sense of being special to the point of being untouchable was Cantona's gift to his team-mates.

This was the second season of the Premier League. Cantona

was not the best player in the league, but he thought he was, and that was enough. He scored 25 goals in all competitions that season, but above all he set the tone: for his team, for the emergent self-regarding league. The paradox of the disguised back-heel was his signature. Every trick was an epigram designed to reveal the ultimate truth: and that truth was the greatness of Cantona.

Manchester United won the Premier League. It had existed for two seasons and Manchester United had won both of them. They also reached the FA Cup final against Chelsea. Penalty! Up strode Eric. A right-footed player with a taste for trickery will tend to put his penalties to the goalkeeper's left, the non-obvious way, the paradoxical or epigrammatic way. Cantona did just that and beat Dmitri Kharine, who bought the look to the opposite corner and dived the wrong way.

Penalty! Again! Up strode Eric to take the second.

How's this for arrogance, for swagger, for self-conceit, for self-belief, for a high-wire artist of the soul?

He delivered exactly the same penalty. Kharine gambled that Cantona would play a bluff within a bluff; but no, there was a bluff within a bluff within a bluff. Kharine went the same wrong way; Cantona scored on the same opposite side.

After a sending-off in France a few years earlier, someone passed judgement on Cantona: 'You can't be judged like any other player. Behind you there is a trail of the smell of sulphur. You can expect anything from an individual like you.'

It was intended as devastating condemnation. Cantona took it as a compliment.

~

What Eric Cantona wanted to be, Ayrton Senna was. His mystique was global, not local. He was adored at a level at which the idea of worship loses facetious or metaphorical possibilities. He had enemies enough to give a double-savour to every triumph – and even these acknowledged him as one of the best, if not the very best, ever to have attempted his sport. Cantona was a senator who thought he was an emperor; Senna was an emperor who thought he was a god.

The sight of Senna using his car like a razor to slice through backmarkers – and double that when the race took place in the wet – made it clear that he was a technician at the very highest level of his craft: at a point when craft is close to art. But not art of the decorative kind: everything that Senna did was functional, frill-less, pared to the bone.

Senna believed in his own uniqueness: in his special status among drivers, among men. He too extorted the duty to humour him: after all, he was specially blessed. It was impossible to deny that: especially in that still, certain presence.

That's why his death seemed an affront to reason. It was so important to humour Senna that everybody assumed he was – well, perhaps not immortal, but certainly let off the rules that govern the rest of us. When Roland Ratzenberger was killed in an accident during qualification on the Saturday before the race at Imola, it was a terrible thing, but back then it was not unknown for a racing driver to die in action. It was a terrible business, but part of the natural order of things.

Senna's accident during the race itself the following day was a different matter, even for the millions who saw it happen on television. His subsequent death was not an easy fact to assimilate: he seemed a thing that could not feel the touch of earthly years.

Those words, spoken on the Saturday before the Canadian Grand Prix a few years back . . . 'Every time I have an idea about where my limits are, I go to check it. And most of the time I am wrong. So I have to adjust myself to going even further. It is very exciting and a non-stop process.'

Here was a high-wire artist of the soul, one fully realised. There was in Senna something of the quality that made saints a few centuries back: that certainty, that sense of destiny. Did Cantona envy the still greater power of Senna's personal myth? Did Cantona in the end envy his martyrdom? But no matter. Senna's life tells us what separates high-wire artists of the soul from the rest. Senna's death tells us what we all have in common.

~

Sometimes the high-wire artist of the soul comes in a plain wrapper: without drama, without grandiose statements, without impossible behaviour. Sometimes you get only the excellence, and when it comes in this form it's easy to miss.

Eventing tests the bonds between two species, specifically between human and horse. It's about trust. And trust as a two-way street, for there is great peril to both parties in the neck-breaking discipline of cross-country. Horse and rider also need a deep mutual understanding to perform the balletic and gymnastic requirements of dressage, and at the last, they must both shake off physical and mental exhaustion to give everything that's left to the stride-counting fastidiousness of showjumping.

The bonds between individual horse and individual rider are established over time: years that involve daily schooling over jumps and on the flat, competing the horse up through the lower grades until both parties are capable of riding in the most demanding events of all, the four-star challenges of Badminton or Burghley.

Mark Todd did not claim a special relationship with God, or that his brilliance gave him the right to behave as he chose. He was a lanky New Zealander who looked too tall for every horse he ever sat on, laconic in manner. He was not given to extravagant imagery; big words don't make horses jump higher. When he won gold medals at successive Olympic Games, he said it was all down to his horse, the incomparable Charisma.

Badminton starts on a Thursday. On the Wednesday before,

Todd sat on Horton Point for the first time. He was offered the ride after Lynne Bevan broke her collarbone in a fall. Todd and Horton Point were accepted by the organisers, but because they were a new entry they had to ride the cross-country first: to be the path-finder. This is a considerable disadvantage, denying you all kinds of useful knowledge.

Horton Point was a decent horse. He had finished Badminton ninth, 16th, 13th and 16th again, generally jumping clear with plenty of time faults. Todd set the tone by riding an impressive dressage test. This was merely unlikely. On Saturday he did something considered impossible: he rode a very fast clear round over the cross-country course, going all the short routes on offer – more difficult, more dangerous – and setting a driving, ground-eating gallop in between.

He completed all this in his usual matter-of-fact, what's-all-the-fuss way. That's sometimes the way with supremely gifted individuals: they take their own gifts for granted, and have no idea what existence would be like without them. Nor are these gifts obvious to those watching: Todd just sat there and didn't seem to do much. It was just that the horse did everything he asked.

It's an illusion, of course. Riding a horse involves an endless series of corrections. After a while, the beginner starts to make corrections earlier; by the time he reaches competence many corrections are pre-emptive. The correction is made before the fault is committed – so it looks as if the horse was always going to stay on the straight line, make the transition to canter, put in the required number of strides, leap the precise distance from the obstacle and land without touching it. Todd's level of skill was allied to a near-miraculous balance, and that allowed him to make corrections whenever they were necessary. After all, he never had to adjust his position. As a result he looked as if he was doing nothing. The horse did it by himself. Todd, the athlete, the champion, the hero, was more or less refined out of existence by his own excellence.

~

'I predict that within ten years we will be among the ten wealthiest clubs in the country. We will be competing in Europe and will have one of the finest stadiums.' Burning sincerity. Total conviction. Not a scintilla of doubt. You have to admire that in any sporting context. He stopped talking, but only for a moment, and gazed out at the pitch and the stands of Carlisle United Football Club. 'We've just finished the new restaurant and corporate facilities and my priority now is to create one of the greatest football clubs in the country.'

Only one of the greatest? Not the stand-alone unquestioned supreme of the supreme? What's wrong with the man? Has he no ambition? All the same, here was the man who in 1989 came within an ace of buying Manchester United for £20 million. Michael Knighton announced the takeover and celebrated at a home match by running onto the pitch in Manchester United's first-team kit, sprinting the length of the field, doing a bit of keepy-uppy and then kicking the ball into the net. He ran off blowing kisses.

He left Manchester United after achieving all he wanted to achieve, he said. Now he was relishing the chance to perform the same trick with another club still more in need of his gifts. 'I am not a wealthy man, I am a modest millionaire. I had invited a few of my close friends to participate in this project . . .' In the end his takeover at Manchester United was prevented by a high court injunction. 'I got slaughtered for talking about peripheral income streams – now everyone is doing it. With all respect they didn't have the foresight to understand what I was all about . . .'

Knighton is another man with the gift for making reality conform to his own fantasies, at least to an extent, at least for a while. He too imposes a duty on people to humour him: that at least is the only explanation for his brief period as chairman of Manchester United. Sport is a fantasy world in which many people long to live; business is another world that attracts fantasists. When the two worlds collide – well, you brace yourself for a legion of Knightons, though few get as far as he did. He sat back at his desk and gave everything he had to the task of leading Carlisle United to eternal glory: a world of money and goals and power and love, and all because of him. How could the world deny him so simple a dream?

~

A tiny cottage in a Knightsbridge mews – you more or less had to walk sideways to get inside. Still, nice to have a *pied* in London, you can get very fed up with hotel living. It belonged to a quiet-mannered American, polite, welcoming and making absolutely no effort to impress or even to be liked. It was his sincere belief that there was too much money in sport.

This was Mark McCormack, founder of International Management Group or IMG, the man who invented the principle and the methods of turning sport into money: 'monetising' sport, to use some of the jargon of the trade – jargon McCormack avoided. He spoke plain commonsense in plain commonsense terms, but absolutely without aggression. He seemed an egoless tycoon: a Lao-Tzu of sports business.

'I am concerned about the kind of money paid for indifferent performances. It means that players can earn vast sums of money without doing very well. That's not right. The pendulum of supply and demand has a way of swinging back. That will happen. I don't think it will continue rising any further. I think we are about there.'

The classic example of McCormack's skill as a sporting entrepreneur is the World Match Play golf tournament. It was once called the Piccadilly World Match Play, sponsored by the eponymous brand of cigarettes. McCormack invented the tournament, put up the prize money, paid Wentworth golf course, put up the stands, collected the gate money and the television money and just happened to own most of the golfers who took part ... that is to say, he had them under contract, representing them in the commercial world and taking his percentage.

'I am a great traditionalist in sport. One of the reasons that we have had a certain amount of success is that we do not try to upset the traditions of sport. I try to bring the traditions into the 20th and the 21st centuries.' That skill has allowed Wimbledon tennis tournament and what Americans call 'the British Open' golf tournament to become huge financial successes. 'The most dramatic change I ever made was to move the men's singles final from Friday to Sunday.'

McCormack was like a financial version of nature: abhorring a financial vacuum. He had to fill sport's money vacuum because it was against his own nature to leave it alone. He could see the love the world had for sport and its stars; he could see that there were opportunities to use this love to make money. So he did it, in the instinctive way that you lift a fallen child to his feet or help an old lady across the road.

Now McCormack was growing concerned that he had succeeded not wisely but too well: and that pretty soon, sport would cease to make money incidentally, but become a business whose sole purpose was money. McCormack knew that sport had a soul. It wasn't his fault that people who play and (especially) people who run sport believe that the soul – like everything else – is a commodity with a price.

- The Colombia coach, Francisco Maturana, later said he had thought about resigning the day before the match. There had been other death threats connected to another player. The threat to bomb the house of Gabriel Gomez was received by fax at the hotel on the morning of the match. Nearly 20 years later, the Colombian tourist board campaigned under the slogan: 'The only danger is wanting to stay.' Shortly after the World Cup, Andres Escobar, one of the players, was shot dead in Medellin. The murderer shouted 'Gol!' at each shot.

- Eric Cantona was later made club captain. He won two more championships with Manchester United and then retired from all football at the age of 30.

- Ayrton Senna's status as one of sport's great mythological figures was secured by the feature-documentary *Senna*.

- Mark Todd finished his career with four Badminton victories, five Burghleys and five Olympic medals. He competed for New Zealand in Rio in 2016, his seventh Olympic Games.

- Carlisle United were promoted to Division Two in 1995, were relegated again and then promoted again. Michael Knighton took over as manager and coach in the 1997-98 season, in which Carlisle were once again relegated. He sold his interest in the club in 2002 after the club went into voluntary administration, giving himself over to the creation of art and poetry.

- Mark McCormack's business interests expanded beyond sport; he handled special projects for Margaret Thatcher, Mikhail Gorbachev, Pope John Paul II and Tiger Woods. He died in 2003 aged 72.

~

BOOK 13

1995

Sport cherishes its mythologies. It holds onto them indefinitely, in defiance of objective truth. What actually happens is largely irrelevant. What matters is what you believe happens.

Nobody can explain why a ball swings. Well, that's the notion that cricket has always cherished. Swing is a form of magic: an object travelling in uniform motion in a straight line will, for no reason that can ever be understood, veer laterally from that straight line, forcing the batsman into error. And while swing bowling is difficult to play, what really troubles the batsman is *late* swing: when the ball travels in a straight line for most of its flight and then, at the last moment, deviates, leaving the poor batsman undone.

The Institute of Physics held its annual conference at Telford and devoted the occasion to the physics of sport. Dr Rabindra Mehta explained the elementary fact that a ball swings because of the surrounding flow of air. What matters is whether that flow is laminar – smooth – or turbulent. If you can create a differential between those two types of flow – 'If you can trip the boundary layer,' Mehta explained – the ball will swing.

If you roughen one side of the ball, you will create that differential. If you polish one side of the ball and not the other, you will create the same thing. The difference is that the first of these actions is illegal.

The previous year the England captain Michael Atherton had been caught applying dirt, stored in his pocket, to a cricket ball. 'The naughty thought occurred to me that positive roughness is just as effective as negative roughness,' Mehta said. In other words, sticking stuff onto a ball is as good as scraping stuff off if you want to create a differential. The problem is that both are illegal. But as soon as you bowl a ball with positive roughness – dirt on the surface – the evidence vanishes.

As for late swing, that is a matter of perception. The more a bowler is able to bowl from wicket to wicket, the later the batsman will *perceive* the deviation. The ball will appear to swing late, even though it's swinging at a uniform rate throughout its flight. It's where the ball starts relative to the batsman that makes the difference in perception.

All these things are known and accepted in physics, but cricket people still talk of late swing – perhaps because it's easier to understand some truths by means of an error. And sport will always print the legend rather than the truth, the truth being less attractive – and probably less true.

~

A sports administrator's first duty is to the administration. He must see himself (it is usually he) as a guardian of the higher hypocrisy. The abiding moral principle is 'thou shalt not rock the boat'. So if you had been a member of the Rugby Football Union committee during the appropriate years, you would have been required to connive at apartheid, to turn a blind eye to covert payments made to players while stressing the pure-souled virtues of amateurism, to praise at all times the higher morality of your game – I thank God we are not as other games are, especially football and rugby league – to soft-pedal the issue of player violence and, above all, to despise the players. They are young, you are old: are you not then wiser? The game is about administrators, personal power and glory and privilege. Players are a distraction. Player excellence belongs in the past and maybe the future – certainly not the present.

So naturally they sacked the England captain Will Carling when he called the RFU committee '57 old farts'. He did so after a dull, even by the standards of the genre, television interview. He had taken off his lapel mike and was chatting afterwards with his interviewer, Greg Dyke. But the mike was still live and picking up the conversation. Channel 4 made their own decision about what was and what was not on the record and broadcast this indiscretion.

This was three weeks before the World Cup in South Africa. Carling had been made captain of England at 22, and under him England had won three Grand Slams – winning all four matches in the Five Nations Championship – the most recent that same year. But players are nothing, results are nothing, the public are nothing: what matters is the dignity of the administrators. Sport teaches unquestioning obedience to authority: that's the whole point of sport, isn't it? The matter was over, finished, dealt with: now we can move on. They went to bed on their decision, much in the way that Louis XVI wrote the word '*rien*' in his diary for 14 July 1789.

They woke up the next day to discover that not only were they living in the 20th century, but that the century was almost over. The condemnation was universal. Their problems were made worse by the fact that no player was prepared to accept the captaincy in Carling's place. Carling offered an apology of sorts, and was reinstated two days after being sacked.

Sport is about players.

~

Sport is a performance. We can take part in it, we can watch it. It is artificial by nature. Its goals are unreal and its achievements are without significance or meaning outside sport's own points of reference.

Sport gives to spectators the illusion of participation. Spectators empathise with the goalscorer's joy or the goalkeeper's anguish; they wince when the tackle lands late, though they feel no pain themselves. Many utter involuntary cries at great moments in sport. Shoot! Run, you're on your own! Knock him over! Man on! Cheat! Dirty cheating bastard!

The fourth wall is more porous in sport than in the theatre. People who go to football matches call themselves supporters, in the belief, perhaps, that the sporting edifice will collapse without them – as perhaps it might. Advice, encouragement and accusation are bandied about freely in many sports: supporters are participants yet not participants.

Eric Cantona's crime was to break that fourth wall. He leapt into the audience at Crystal Palace and kicked an abusive supporter named Matthew Simmons. He was sentenced to two weeks in prison, an absurd sentence for common assault. It was the violence he did to our conception of sport that caused so much outrage. A spectator no more expects to be kicked by a footballer than to have Hamlet charging off the stage with rapier and dagger in his hands, ready to sacrifice a member of the audience for covert support of Claudius.

L'affaire Cantona made it plain that people who play professional sport are fair game; those who watch them are protected, licensed by the phenomenon of sport to abuse their betters – for the people who play professional sport are certainly better than the audience at the sport the audience loves so well. Part of the job of every person in big-time sport is to be abused. Sport as a profession would not exist otherwise.

No politician can resist sport. In every great sporting victory there's a politician sneaking into shot like Benny Hill's Fred Scuttle. They want to be associated with the victorious athlete's aura of success and virtue.

Rugby union has always been good at self-righteousness. Rugby people traditionally believe that anything that suits rugby is by definition a force for moral good. Which brings us back uncomfortably to apartheid: abolished but impossible to forget. Rugby was ever the heartland sport of the Afrikaners. It was the emblem of the way they faced life: a band of brothers fighting the world together in faceless, self-sacrificing unanimity. The scrum was a living, moving symbol of the way life should be lived: and the more the world turned against South Africa, the more the Afrikaners believed they were right. *Skrum, skrum, skrum!* The cry of a people at bay: defiant to the last.

If an ordinary politician had been imprisoned for 24 years before becoming president of South Africa, the first item on his agenda would have been the criminalisation of rugby union. Partly from spite, partly from a political need to disempower the Afrikaners and partly as a statement to the world that all those who supported apartheid by means of sport – and their name was legion – must suffer.

The picture went round the world: Nelson Mandela at the Rugby World Cup final wearing a Springbok shirt, the hated symbol of his – everybody's – former oppressors. On its back was the word 'Pienaar', a reference to Francois Pienaar, captain of the South African rugby team. They were playing in the final against New Zealand. Pienaar was an Afrikaner, of course.

The symbolic power of sport is breathtaking, especially when it's bound up with the identity of a nation: W.G. Grace for Britain's or England's Victorian self-certainty, Don Bradman for Australian self-determination, Ayrton Senna for Brazil's sense of martyrdom, Diego Maradona for Argentina's defiance,

Muhammad Ali for America in changing times. Here, Mandela hijacked sport's symbolic power for purposes higher than sport, making a Gandhi-like gesture of self-abnegation – almost self-humiliation – to make as eloquent a statement as sport can come up with. By wearing the shirt he told the world that it was all about Pienaar – which meant that in fact it was all about Mandela – which in turn meant that it was all about the people and the nation he was representing.

A rugby shirt, a bit of sports kit, was now standing for a belief that all harms – even these – could be healed.

Ayyyoh.

~

The women's singles final at Wimbledon is seen as a glorious display of feminism in action. It's also seen as an opportunity for male contempt. Both at the same time. Outside Olympic year this is the most-watched women's sporting event in the calendar. Some discuss only the physical desirability of the contestants, some only their perceived psychological frailties. Sometimes the match is closely contested: at other times it is one-sided, in a way that men's singles matches seldom are. Some put this down to the dominance of serve in men's tennis, which is the result of differentials in muscle mass. Others talk about the greater rigidity of female dominance hierarchies in primates. What offends most of the harsher critics is that women's tennis is in some ways different to men's tennis: proving once again that women fail to be men.

Steffi Graf was playing Arantxa Sanchez Vicario. Graf was a player who had everything, except possibly a backhand; Sanchez Vicario was a hard-scuttling underdog. But she peppered the Graf backhand and won the first set 6–4. Graf took the second 6–1. The match went to 5–5 in the third, with Sanchez Vicario to serve.

This game – this one service game – lasted for 20 minutes, the longest singles game (either sex) in the history of the championships. When it was over the Centre Court stood and clapped throughout the changeover. Comparison: in the men's semifinals, Goran Ivanisevic served a game that lasted 45 seconds. Further comparison: in the French Open final of 1988, Graf beat Natasha Zvereva 6-0, 6-0 in 30 minutes.

A service game can have as few as four points. This had 32. There were 13 deuces and 18 game points, including six break points. It was a perfect example of the contagion of greatness: the brilliance of one player infecting the other and inspiring an equal brilliance, while the strength of one player's mind only makes the opponent's mind grow stronger. Pressure became inspiration. 'Neither of us really played any loose points,' Graf said afterwards. 'Nobody gave up. There was some great tennis. What I couldn't believe is that I stood there and came back, realising she was playing some great tennis.' It was a game that was a serious test of hardness: the sort of test that reveals not champions but great champions.

The Graf backhand was mostly a well-coached slice, a shot designed to keep the ball in play, eventually creating an opportunity on the Graf forehand, which was like a door slamming in a gale. Sanchez Vicario had attacked that backhand all match. The ploy had taken her to the first set, and to this sustained passage of perfect opposition in game 11 of the deciding set.

Graf won it with a blasted backhand drive.

And held serve in the next game to win the championship.

~

The pitch gave nothing; the bowler gave everything. Plan A: bowl fast, try hard. Plan B: bowl faster, try harder. Time and again Devon Malcolm went back to his mark. This time. Surely this time. Then walking back, once again disappointed, those huge and beautiful shoulders unslumped, the crest unfallen. This time, then. Surely this time ... this was, after all, The

Oval, where Malcolm had the previous year bowled the South African side out in a spell of glorious inspiration, taking nine wickets for 57.

Malcolm's morning began with a thrilling edge – but neither Graeme Hick nor Graham Thorpe moved a muscle and the ball fizzed between them. Hick dropped another chance. And, mortifyingly, so did Malcolm himself: muffing a caught-and-bowled chance when Carl Hooper was on one. Hooper made a further 126. This match against West Indies at The Oval was one in which all the odds favoured the batsman. Malcolm ended up with three wickets for 160 as West Indies made 692 all out. It was an innings memorable for Malcolm's glorious struggle. There are times when failure brings glory to those who failed. As a batsman can take pride in a courageous low score when the wicket is swift and dangerous, so a bowler can take pride in a courageous effort across over after over against batsmen in paradise.

What is a nation? A question asked again and again in many different forms by international sport. Hick, a Zimbabwean, had qualified for England by means of seven years' residence. Robin Smith and Allan Lamb, South African émigrés, had both made hefty contributions to the England team. But not everyone felt comfortable with the idea of the England cricket team as the natural destination for deracinated mercenaries.

That's what gave a little traction to Robert Henderson, who extended this sense of unease, so that it covered non-white cricketers, whether born abroad – Malcolm was born in Jamaica – or England. His thesis was that a black player is incapable of giving everything to the national cause. He can never be truly English. His unEnglishness is there for all time, fixed in his unconscious mind, or perhaps in his genes. Henderson had no great familiarity with either psychology or genetics, but he had the strength of his idée fixe. And in an epic piece of misjudgement, David Frith, editor of the magazine *Wisden*

Cricket Monthly, ran a piece in which Henderson expressed his ideas and so brought the issue into the public domain. Here, for all to see, was a theory of apartheid specially tailored for British and English use.

And there's always sympathy for such ideas … ideas that blame an easily identifiable out-group for personal and national failings. This from *Ulysses*; Bloom, the book's hero, is Jewish.

– What is your nation if I may ask? says the citizen.
– Ireland, says Bloom. I was born here. Ireland.
The citizen said nothing only cleared the spit out of his gullet and, gob, he spat a Red bank oyster out of him right in the corner.

A sermon on nationhood and the location of the heart was preached at The Oval in the five-day course of the match, five uninterrupted days in which only 22 wickets fell. In the midst of that draw there was a victory: and a defeat that amounted to a rout.

~

Sport divides. Sport also unites. Both are essential aspects of sport. And here the nation was more or less united in a pleasurable elegiac sadness. It was a death that helped you to appreciate life, not least because the deceased was 30, a fine age, at least for a horse.

He lived in a loosebox behind a car showroom. Second-hand cars, the legend has it, the idea being more picturesque than the truth that new ones were also sold there. And beyond the stable you could come unto these yellow sands: stretching away to infinity along Southport beach. Here Red Rum was trained and here he lived in retirement. Ginger McCain, his trainer, called him 'the old 'oss'.

Red Rum won the Grand National in 1973 and 1974. He

was second in both the following years and won again in 1977. He retired on the eve of the race in 1978. He was beloved for one reason: victory. He was no flashy looker: you could have watched the Grand National runners walk past a dozen times without picking him out as something special. Nor was there anything extravagant about his jumping: he was just very careful and very safe – and at the same time capable of an untiring gallop between fences. A dull horse to interview, perhaps: I just take each fence as it comes, and do my best to keep going in between. I've got a great team and, at the end of the day, the ball's in the back of the net and I'm back in my box eating hay.

Victory. Back then the Grand National was a great deal more dangerous, the obstacles bigger and harder, and falls were more frequent and more damaging. The winner was often unexpected. There was something of the lottery in the race: the craziest pin-picked horse had a chance, and the great spectacle of the race was full of dramatic, often horrific falls. Casualties were routine and equine fatalities taken in stride.

Red Rum did a marvellous thing: he came as close as anything ever could to taking the chance out of a lottery. He ran with a dispassionate certainty that raised the passions of those who watched and especially those who bet. Red Rum bore in his gift free money for all Britain. How could he not be loved?

But he gave more than money. He showed us that the hardest things in life were in fact simple: that the most doubtful venture could be reduced to near-certainty. Red Rum made winners of us all, even those who failed to bet or, worse, bet on the wrong horse.

What happens next? Nobody knows: that is why sport's dramas have their enduring appeal. But when Red Rum ran in the Grand National, the most chance-driven event in the calendar of sport, we all knew what was going to happen next – or at least, we had a damn good idea. Red Rum was a perfect example of sport because in his way he destroyed sport ... at least for a moment or two.

- Another speaker at the physics conference explained that if you can hit a golf ball for 250 yards, you will only be able to hit a golf ball without dimples for 60 yards: back to fluid dynamics and boundary layers again. Oh, and the weight of a bat makes relatively little difference to the distance a cricket ball travels. What matters is bat speed.
- England reached the last four of the Rugby World Cup under Will Carling's captaincy. They lost 45–29 to New Zealand in the semi-finals, with the remarkable Jonah Lomu scoring four tries and doing more or less as he wished. Rugby union became professional that same year, leaving a vast army of Canutes with wet feet.
- South Africa won the World Cup final against New Zealand 15–12, with Joel Stransky scoring the winning drop goal in extra time. The match was remarkable for the way the South Africans were more or less queuing up to tackle Lomu.
- Steffi Graf finished her career with 22 Grand Slam singles titles, Arantxa Sanchez Vicario with four, a remarkable example of the way very small differences between players are made to look vast by results.
- Devon Malcolm finished his career with 128 wickets in 40 Tests. His nine for 57 against South Africa remains the eighth best innings' figures on record.

BOOK 14

1996

In the end, one match, one day or even one moment tells the entire story. Or at least, the entire myth: the sporting myth that endureth forever.

It is Wembley. Old Wembley, in all its gloriously fading grandeur, the dog track forever standing between spectators and players. The occasion was the European Football Championship. England, the home nation, were supposed to win. It was the summer when football was coming home; the nation bathed in warm sun, cold beer and the merry abandonment of objectivity.

After a 1-1 draw against Switzerland, England played Scotland in their qualifying group. The ball fell to Paul Gascoigne, running through as if late for a date with Brigitte Bardot. With his first touch he flipped the ball over the head of the Scotland centre-half Colin Hendry, with his second, having run round Hendry, he volleyed the ball into the goal: and it seemed that glory and triumph would forever belong to England and to Gascoigne . . . just as it did with Italy and Roberto Baggio.

This was a perfect example of one of sport's great illusions, for sport is only ever about now. Sport never reveals what happens next before its time. But in Gascoigne's moment of sporting perfection it seemed that the bad past had been abolished, the good past made safe and the future was all gold. It was a moment when the present was so perfect it seemed to shine with the light of eternity.

Such feelings don't last: but even as they fade they remind us of the player who on that one day defined his sporting life.

The previous year Michael Atherton had done the same thing in a Test match against South Africa: batting for 10 hours and 43 minutes to save the match, scoring 185 runs in 492 balls. Again, it was something that defined him forever: in a period when England lost as a matter of routine, here was a man who gave his soul to the task of not losing.

And there was Eric Cantona, returning from his eight-month ban. He spent the second half of the season scoring the only goal in a series of 1-0 victories – five in all. He also scored in Manchester United's 1-1 draw against Queens Park Rangers, the match when they overtook Newcastle United, who at one point had a 12-point lead. Manchester United won the Premier League for the third time in four seasons. It was the season that defined Cantona and his transformation of Manchester United. As every politician aims to lead the natural and inevitable party of government, so Cantona made Manchester United the natural and inevitable champions of England. And yet Cantona said that of all his great moments in sport 'the one I prefer is when I kicked the hooligan'.

~

He was the man who divided.

For a start he was black, and a lot of people didn't like that.

What's worse, he didn't seem to mind being black. He didn't feel the need to act apologetic. That didn't play well back then.

He also boasted. 'I'm so modest I can admit my own faults and my only fault is I don't realise how great I really am.' That wasn't only boasting; it was also clever. A lot of people didn't like that. It was not only clever, it was irony. A lot of people didn't understand that.

And he said he was pretty. The prettiest. How could a black man be pretty? It was an insult to the white race. And he knew it.

So when he fought for the world heavyweight boxing championship in 1964, people in the crowd shouted to his opponents: kill the nigger! His opponent was Sonny Liston, also black.

In the moment of victory he renounced his 'slave-name' of Cassius Clay. He was now Muhammad Ali. He was a member of the Nation of Islam; one of their movement's core demands was separate states for black and for white people.

He said other things that divided. He said: 'No Viet-Cong ever called me nigger.' He said: 'I ain't got no quarrel with them Viet-Cong.' He refused the draft. As a result – as if the two things were connected – he was stripped of his world title and denied the right to box.

They'd got him. They'd beaten him.

Some liked that. Some liked it very much, but many others did not. These were changing times: there was music in the cafés at night and revolution in the air.

Ali's banishment from boxing cost him more than three years – three years of his prime – and yet he came back and became world champion again. Twice. That was when people who once hated him decided that they'd been rooting for him all the time.

Now, years later, he was once again standing up before the world and billions watched.

The opening ceremony of the Olympic Games is always the hottest ticket of the entire 17 days. It's odd that people prefer choreographed showing off to the greatest sporting action in the world.

And as the ceremony before the Atlanta Olympic Games reached its climax, who to step out and light the Olympic Flame in the Olympic Stadium but Muhammad Ali, gold medal winner in Rome 36 years before?

He was only 54, but those dancing feet were now an old man's bedroom-slipper shuffle. The hand that held the torch trembled, the torch shook violently. But the job was done; the flame was alight as if it had never been extinguished.

The sport of boxing had made Ali what he was: first the greatest, then the martyr, then the avenger, then the symbol of hard-won freedom: and now the parody. The whiff of danger was long gone. Neither his wit not his fists were a threat. Nor even his views.

Now he was powerless it was safe to love him – and so the world united at last – united in the lie that everyone had always loved Muhammad Ali. As if all the harms were now healed.

~

The Olympic Games of Atlanta will be forever recalled as a 'bad' Olympics. Most host cities greet the award of the Games with the feeling that they were lucky to get them: Atlanta knew it was the watching and arriving world that was lucky. The Games were put together with a ferocious parochialism. It was above all a drive to show that the South – the real South – could put on a show as great as any other place in the States. It was suggested, and frequently, that the Games should have gone to Athens: 'Oh no – if the Games was comin' to Georgia, they *had* to come to Atlanta.'

The Games were characterised by the crassest form of com-mercialism and appalling organisation. The public face of the Games was aggressive, confrontational and xenophobic. Security was both rude and ineffective: a bomb killed two people. The president of the International Olympic Committee, Juan Antonio Samaranch, declined to give the city the traditional accolade in his concluding speech: this was clearly not 'the best Olympic Games ever'.

What's forgotten in the justifiable rush to condemn Atlanta is the sport. Once you got inside the arenas – a tough challenge, it has to be said – it was the international governing bodies of the individual sports that put on the show.

And then came the sport.

~

The weight can only ever go up. Never down, not ever. The core principle of weightlifting.

Out they came, these pale giants, out they came with a belly-out swagger: trolls who step from their caves once every four years to spend a brief few minutes in the light. Six lifts, no more: and the weight can only ever go up.

This was the super-heavyweight competition: men for whom there is no weight limit. No need for pre-competition wasting: they strolled blinking into the light, each one concealing his hard-won musculature beneath a comfortable coat of adipose tissue. The winner would have the right to be called the world's strongest man. There are no aesthetic considerations in weight-lifting, and if there is grace, it is in the conception rather than the movement.

Three goes at the snatch, then three more at the clean and jerk, and, with each of the two disciplines, the weights on the bar get heavier all the time. You come in whenever you like. The standard strategy: first a weight you know you can lift, then one you think you can lift and, finally, one you hope you can lift.

You are working at the far limits of what a body can do: no surprise, then, when it goes wrong. Igor Halilov found the weight in rebellion, turning his elbow obscenely the wrong way: instant dislocation, instant withdrawal. Four years: and for that.

All Ronny Weller of Germany had to do was break the world record. So the bar went up: 2.5 kilos beyond the old record: and moments later the giant was dancing about like a vast child, taking off his enormous wooden-soled weightlifter's shoes and hurling them into the audience. Only the last rites left. Andrei Chemerkin of Russia worked out that if he was to beat Weller's combined total – best snatch, best clean and jerk added together – he must beat the newly set world record not once but twice. Not one but two increments. So he caused 5 kilos to be added to the bar. Chemerkin weighed 165.475 kilos; the object he faced weighed 260 kilos. Say, the weight of a small horse.

Empathy.

An essential part of sport, but here stretched to an almost absurd degree. The legs inexorably straightened, the bar pinned cruelly across the chest. Now once more: and from a thousand throats the call was ripped without their owners' will or even knowledge: a roar of effort, strain, anxiety, all his being and all everybody else's being pouring into the muscles, the face wavering and trembling, the entire body about to explode or snap in half: and there was Chemerkin, like a statue, elbows and knees locked, the weight and the body for a long countable second or so under control: and then it fell with the sound of thunder and Chemerkin was dancing the dance of the giants.

~

Eric Cantona's triumph lay in his ability to rise to the small occasion. The best of all have something else. They find their very best at the loftiest level of competition – and then go beyond it. It's perhaps the rarest thing in sport and it sometimes takes the form of complete indifference: as if the athlete has forgotten the importance and the meaning and the significance of the occasion. Champions are not like everybody else: and sport exists to seek out exceptional individuals.

Fu Mingxia showed that quality at the age of 13 at the

Barcelona Games. Four years later, an inch taller at five-foot-two and two stone heavier, at nine stone, she was able to show it again, not just in the platform diving, but now, since she had the power, the springboard as well. She began her set of five dives in the final with an inward dive: turning back towards the board as she flew. Her challengers preferred something less demanding for starters: already the point had been made.

She seemed to have had a fear bypass, in a way that was disturbing, almost unnatural. On the high board, she frequently flicked the fringe of her black-maned boyish haircut against the board on the way down, and yet she had never once hit the board. Her mastery of time and space was that complete, that precise.

The edge was her natural place. What scared others inspired her. And in the fourth round it told. The competitors were tightly bunched until then: you'd have thought that nearly all of them had a chance. But in the fourth round, they began to suffer minute flaws in accuracy: flaws that are magnified and stressed by the nature of the event. An imperceptible small error in takeoff can be detected in the loud and terrible splash as the diver hits the water.

Fu offered a reverse two and a half somersaults piked: soaring high to spring back in and attack the board, threatening it with the black fringe on her way down, before hitting the water with that clean, almost musical thrum. And after that there was no catching her: she became the first female diver to pull off the double – platform and springboard – since Ingrid Kramer of Germany in 1960.

~

He was slow getting out of the blocks. He stumbled on the fourth step. He felt a hamstring twinge in the closing paces. And he was scared. 'I was afraid I wouldn't get that medal. But for me, being afraid is OK. I like to be afraid. I like to be nervous. And I ran like I was nervous.'

There is a strange, wild euphoria that comes over the Olympic athletics stadium – no matter what the Games, no matter what the city, no matter how terrible the organisation – when a truly remarkable performance is completed. Not just victorious, not just very good, but one that seems to be making history, one that seems to be making a mark on time itself. It is not the euphoria of partisanship that you get at a football match; it is not the euphoria you get at the conclusion of a fabulous piece of music: the last 'Amen' of *Messiah*. This euphoria comes from staring in the face of excellence.

The world record for the 200 metres was 19.66. It had been set by Michael Johnson six weeks earlier. Frankie Fredericks of Namibia and Ato Boldon of Trinidad set after that mark and ran phenomenally fast. But Johnson ran impossibly fast. He was *unbelievably* fast: it seemed that nobody in the stadium could really believe that what was happening was real.

But it was. Johnson ran 19.32 seconds: knocking a third of a second off a record in an event in which margins are routinely measured in hundredths.

It was like a cheetah running away from a herd of gazelles. This sport is all about hunter and hunted – but here the master predator ran like a man scared. And in his fear he found perfection and brought it down for everyone to touch.

~

Sport is quantifiable. Or at least, parts of it. So we can measure, at least to an extent, how close we come to perfection. This lays bare an essential truth: that even in victory, sport is about the degree to which we fail. A century in cricket is not perfection, for the batsman failed to hit every ball for six and he got out in the end. It's very good, it's excellent, but it's not perfect. Even when she played Natasha Zvereva in that notorious final, Steffi

Graf lost 13 points. Every round of golf that involves more than 18 strokes has to be regarded as imperfection, and therefore failure.

The cricketer Samuel Beckett (two first-class matches, played in 1925 and 1926) summed up all sports for all time: 'Ever tried. Ever failed. No matter. Try again. Fail again. Fail better.' Once you have grasped that most victories are a form of failure, you have no option but to seek, perhaps in vain, a higher form of failure.

There are exceptions. A clear round in showjumping and cross-country is at least marked as perfection: though in the sport of eventing your dressage score delineates your level of failure. At the Montreal Olympic Games of 1976, Nadia Comaneci had seven scores of ten: the maximum mark. This was, then, official perfection. And at the Sarajevo Winter Olympics of 1984, as we have seen, Jayne Torvill and Christopher Dean were awarded a perfect score of six by all nine judges for the presentation of their immortal *Bolero*, but only for interpretation. They were also marked down for minute technical flaws.

More or less uniquely, Frankie Dettori achieved perfection in racing. No obscure little country meeting either: this day at Ascot was one of the biggest meetings of the season. There were seven races: Dettori won them all. Dettori, a rider of singular elegance and with a natural performer's ability to communicate with crowds – perhaps both attributes came from his mother, a trapeze artist – brought joy to all with his unaffected delight in his own achievements.

It was a day that defined him forever, even in later disappointment, and even in greater achievement. Victory, even at the highest level, is still only victory. This was perfection.

～

Tring left them unmoved. Hemel Hempstead they could tolerate, along with St Albans, Welwyn Garden City and

Knebworth. No doubt Potters Bar was equally acceptable. But Watford was another matter. We hate Watford, the crowd sang. We are the Watford-haters. They were singing these words to stress their love for Luton Town. The Watford-hatees sang their reciprocal and equally visceral loathing for Luton. The spectators swivelled in their seats, facing each other across the corner of the ground, events on the pitch being a distraction at best. This was the Hertfordshire derby and great events excite great passions.

At one stage, in a sublime ecstasy of hatred, a supporter of Luton Town took on the entire police force by himself. It was an impressive effort in its way: he refused to cease struggling and it took six policemen to carry him away.

And perhaps that very day a man from Mars was visiting the earth for the first time, paying a call first at Luton and then at Watford. What radically different thing did he find in each of these towns, differences that provoked such loathing, such desperate wasting of emotion?

The match finished 0–0, more or less fulfilling the ancient jest of Bill Shankly: 'I hope you both lose.' It seemed they both had: the results apparently propelling both clubs towards relegation from the second tier of English football. 'Not much inspiring about that at all,' said the Watford coach Luther Blissett. 'We cut each other's throats,' said Lennie Lawrence, the Luton manager, presumably a metaphor.

When all else fails in sport – purpose, meaning, even basic skills – there is still partisanship. This occasion, awful at practically every level, was nonetheless a matter of deep and powerful passions, the sort of passions that need six policemen to control them.

～

Will anyone ever play 1,000 league games again? Will anyone even want to? But there was Peter Shilton, a goalkeeper who had played 125 times for England, now aged 47 and playing for Leyton Orient against Brighton. Oscar Wilde said that he put his genius into his life and his talent into his work. Shilton put both talent and genius into his own art and had nothing left, nothing whatsoever, when it came to anything else. His life is a tale of marital strife, drinking, financial crashes, purposes mistook. He had 38 creditors and debts of nearly half a million.

It was a life packed with disasters. Goalkeepers, with cosmic unfairness, are usually defined by their disasters: so Shilton is best remembered for his part in Maradona's Hand of God goal, and also for the error that allowed Poland to draw 1-1 with England at Wembley and so qualify for the World Cup finals of 1974 at England's expense.

But the truth of Shilton's sporting life is that it was remarkably free from disasters. He was a master of good sense: in control: commanding. He is remembered as a huge man but he was not: his positioning, his mastery of angle that made him seem twice as big to an advancing forward. He was capable of inspiration but his stock-in-trade was vast controlling calm. In the position that makes doubters of us all, he was a man of certainties. Like Red Rum, he came close to removing chance from a world of uncertainty.

Still hard at it. A man with one vast skill, relentlessly developed, a skill that made him, for a time at least, one of the best in the world at his trade. In his excellence there were hints of tragedy.

- Paul Gascoigne suffered a series of problems with alcoholism and mental health. He last worked in football in 2005, as coach to Kettering Town.
- Andrei Chemerkin competed at the Sydney Olympic Games of 2000, winning the bronze medal. He set seven world records in his career.

- Michael Johnson had already won the 400 metres; the Olympic schedule was altered so that he could attempt the 200 metres–400 metres double. He won gold in the 400 metres in Sydney in 2000. In 1997 he took part in a race of 150 metres against Donovan Bailey, who won the 100 metres in Atlanta. Johnson pulled up with a hamstring problem at 100 metres. Bailey won the US$1.5 million; Johnson taking US$0.5 million. In retirement he does television punditry for the BBC.
- Frankie Dettori rode as first jockey for Sheikh Mohammed until 2012. Shortly after leaving, he tested positive for cocaine and was banned for six months. He made a successful comeback and won the Derby and the Prix de l'Arc de Triomphe in 2015.
- Stan Wawrinka, the tennis player, had the Beckett quote tattooed on his arm.
- Watford and Luton were both relegated that season.
- Peter Shilton retired after playing 1,005 league matches. He works as an after-dinner speaker.

BOOK 15

1997

It was the day sport went dark. Saturday means sport: but that Saturday there was none. No one wanted it. Sport wouldn't have done anybody any harm, but there was an overwhelming and nationwide feeling that sport should not happen. As a closed theatre is said to 'go dark', so sport went dark that day. It wasn't a sacrifice: it was, if anything, a kind of relief.

It was the day of the funeral of Princess Diana. And in the extraordinary outpouring of grief, it seemed that sport must play its part. Sport's sometimes unbearably close relationship with national identity demanded that sport should do something to express the nation's feelings about the death of its princess. The only thing that it could conceivably do was nothing: and so, in the end and not without argument, nothing was what it did.

This national need for darkness was helped by coincidence. It was a football international week, so the Premier League was not in action; England were due to play Moldova in the following week. Most of the rest of professional football called itself off swiftly enough. Scotland were due to play Belarus that Saturday, and the Scottish Football Association resisted cancellation with some vigour, and in the end total lack of success. Three players said they would ask to be dropped if the match went ahead. That and the near-unanimity of public opinion forced them to back down.

Racing, always a royalist enclave, needed no asking to go dark. And just about every other sport did the same thing: kept the doors closed, made complex arrangements about the logistics of cancellation and postponement, and otherwise did nothing.

It wasn't that sport was doing a noble thing. Sport was doing the only possible thing. In the face of the bewildered grief that gripped so much of the nation, the frivolities of sport would have been cosmically inappropriate. No football manager would have complained afterwards that we cut each other's throat.

Few people would wish to see sport cancelled for the death of a former prime minister: that's a mere matter of form, and it doesn't stop you cheering on Scotland – or Moldova – the following Saturday. But this was different. Many people responded with heartbroken grief for someone they had never known.

Sport is many things. But sometimes it's simply not wanted. Any individual is entitled to feel like that: and most of the nation felt the same way.

A need for dark.

~

Barbaric.

Have we sunk to the level of *dumb beasts*?

The world revelled in the shock. This was boxing. This was sport. And yet Mike Tyson used his teeth; used his teeth and bit a piece from the ear of his opponent, Evander Holyfield.

Tyson had turned boxing into uncircumscribed violence, and this was both shocking and unacceptable.

The ultimate achievement in boxing is, as we know, to cause

permanent damage to the brain of your opponent, and that's fine, just fine. But biting: that's disgusting.

It's not violence that shocks, it's escalation. A punch is a matter of routine in rugby, shocking and worthy of punishment in football and it would be an international scandal in cricket. There was scandal enough when Javed Miandad merely squared up to Dennis Lillee.

There is violence of a kind even in chess. The hard stare is one form of violent behaviour. Garry Kasparov used to give a bark of derisive laughter when his opponent made a poor move. In an early, more tobacco-friendly age, cigarette smoke was used as a weapon: Mikhail Botvinnik, a non-smoker, used to train for championship bouts by getting practice opponents to blow smoke in his face.

The fact is that confrontational sports are always about violence, just as dancing is always about sex. Some sports are more violent than others just as some dances are sexier than others.

Tyson knew this. He also knew he was not going to win the sporting side of the contest. How, then, to leave his mark? To let Holyfield know, and remember, that he had been in a fight with Mike Tyson? It was shocking: but it was no more disgusting than boxing normally is. Most people with experience of concussion would sooner lose a little gristle than experience more brain damage.

Tyson was a champion once. Most champions have, in the end, to cope with defeat.

This was Tyson's way.

~

Sport is birdsong.

In a way. Birdsong is a way of resolving disputes about precedence – access to food, territory and females – without recourse to lethal combat. Only when song fails to separate two cock birds do they come to blows. This type of behaviour has evolved thousands of times. Humpback whales posture aggressively, in the manner of bodybuilders, and the clearly weaker male backs down. Puku antelopes will horn the vegetation in a ferocious manner and wear the debris on their heads like a hat: their successful attacking of a bush is usually enough to persuade a real opponent to back down.

Sport developed from such behaviour, sorting out rivalries and dominance hierarchies without much bloodshed. In some sports the athletes don't even touch each other. That doesn't mean that the sports are anything other than ferocious.

Cedric Pioline was beaten long before the final point was played. Pete Sampras won his third men's singles title at Wimbledon by means of total devastation. The final score was 6-4, 6-2, 6-4: as devastating a scoreline as Graf's 6-0, 6-0. And it's about serve, which is a classic expression of dominance. The Wimbledon courts were then truly fast – that is to say, the bounce was low and therefore the points were mostly brief. That favoured the tactic of serve and volley: and in that final Sampras effortlessly passed from champion to something better.

Tennis spells out such things with pedantic clarity; it's a drawn-out business and the most theatrical of all sports. Pioline managed four points against the serve in the first set, three in the second. He had ten in the final set including a break point, but it mattered little by then. Sampras lost only two service games in the course of the entire championship.

Sampras's first serve was of course superb, giving him ace after ace. But his real greatness was in the second serve: less spectacular, less likely to produce an outright winner, but time and again forcing a ball from his opponent for Sampras to volley away.

Many complained that this wasn't beautiful, but such a judgement reflects only the narrowness of the popular idea of beauty. Most people see beauty in sport as something romantic: with Sampras the beauty was classical. Austere, refined, impersonal, intimidating, inspiring more admiration than affection. And not especially prone to bouts of fallibility.

~

How did a nightingale get to have a song with more than 600 sound units and 250 distinct phrases? The answer is evolutionary pressure: as rivals crank up their repertoires, so you must crank up yours or miss out on the great prizes in life. These include the opportunity to breed and pass on your immortal genes.

In ice skating the male competition was about the quad. That is to say, a jump with four complete rotations, landed correctly and cleanly. The triple had been downgraded, given only second-class status. The skater with the triple axel – three and a half rotations – was once the top dog, but no longer. The quad was now the must-have jump: an expression of power, athleticism, accuracy – and dominance. This is a sport in which competitors are not even on the ice at the same time.

Save in the warm-up.

The first quad successfully performed in competition was in 1988. In the decade that followed, the quad made progress from outlier to central part of the repertoire.

There are other factors in men's figure skating, but no one was paying them much mind. The competitors wanted to be known for their quad. Like a great first serve, all things followed from the quad. It was the centre of your being: the thing by which you challenged the world. If you successfully landed a quad, you were at once king of the hill.

The warm-up was the best, and certainly the most dramatic part of the contest. The men skated dangerously close to each other, landing huge jumps bang in the middle of each other's personal space. There was of course no music, so the air was filled with the sounds of the skates: the ripping and slicing of blade on ice and the thump of the landings after these huge jumps.

Three skaters were expected to include quads in their programmes. Ilia Kulik went for his and tripled out; that is to say, he failed to get round the fourth time. The disappointment of his failure overwhelmed the rest of his performance. Alexei Urmanov, an impossibly graceful skater, was forced to pull out with groin strain. That left the field open for Elvis Stojko of Canada, who pulled off the first quadruple–triple combination ever seen in competition: quadruple toe-loop, triple toe-loop, not a step between them.

The top contenders could all perform the quad. The champion was the one who landed it perfectly in competition. There are dizzying skills to be performed in every sport: but of them all, the greatest and the hardest skill is winning.

One player was aged 16 and unseeded. The other was three years older and entering her prime; she had just won the French Open and was seeded four at Wimbledon. All the attention was on her opponent.

Iva Majoli – sometimes called 'Iva the Diva' and not just for the rhyme – had complained that the Women's Tennis Association gave too much of its attention to promoting the marketable kids and failed to cherish its genuine champions. Chance, with typical malice – part of sport's stock-in-trade – gave her Anna Kournikova as an opponent at Wimbledon.

Kournikova could play all right, in the beginning. She was athletic and inventive, a real shot-maker. Her style would have turned heads, had heads not already turned. (Ball boys working at Kournikova matches were told not to stare.) That day she had too much for the passive-aggressive style of Majoli and won 7-6, 6-4 ... but even then she was torn between trading on her looks and trying to win tennis tournaments.

There are a million Kournikova stories and they're all the same. Someone stares at her, unable to conceal his interest.

Kournikova responds contemptuously: 'You could not afford me.' It was her standard line – her only line – and she was using it in her early teens. Innocence, it seems, had passed her by. You could not afford me: effortlessly recalling the famous story attributed to a dozen or more different men: 'We have already established what you are, madam. Now we're haggling over the price.'

Kournikova never won a tournament, yet she was for a while the highest-earning female athlete in the world. So we must accept that for a female athlete, excellence can be a secondary concern – and yet there's another matter. Kournikova had plenty of rivals for the title of world's most beautiful woman, but she, and none other, was famously the most searched-for name on that new-fangled internet thing. It seemed then that sport – or perhaps just her chosen sport – added greatly to the allure.

Kournikova showed that it was now possible to make a fortune out of sport without being near or even terribly close to the top level. McCormack's prophecy was now abundantly true. It was enough to make the highest achievers in her sport despair at the world. And play tennis.

~

Cheap horses know it.

Old racing saw. It means that when you pay good money for good bloodlines, you're not just buying speed. You're also buying an inherited sense of certainty: the idea that when the difference between victory and defeat is down to inches, the better-bred horse will prevail. Because it's in the genes. It's a view that has been proved and disproved a million times over. Racing has always been full of expensive duds and successful chuck-outs: and yet this old saying retains an apparent truth.

When Mike Tyson won, back in his day, it was not just because he was faster and stronger; it was also because he felt he had a right to win. His opponent was a beaten man before the preliminary touch of the gloves. When Pete Sampras took on an opponent on Centre Court, there was a quiet certainty in Sampras that extorted a corresponding deference – however often denied, however well-disguised – in his opponent. Certainly in Cedric Pioline.

The sense of rivalry is pre-human, the idea of stylised non-lethal combat is pre-human, and if the two big ideas behind sport are pre-human, so is that sense of entitlement: the sense of being a winner before a blow is struck.

The notion that such matters are all about propagating your immortal genes didn't wash with Desert Orchid, who was a gelding. But try telling him that. Even in retirement, he carried himself with a swagger, an almost burlesque macho self-confidence. He was leading out the two-year-old fillies at morning exercise, and very congenial he found his work: part of a programme to get him fit for a public appearance. He was to be led out before the crowds at Kempton Park on Boxing Day, before the big race, the King George VI Chase, which Desert Orchid won four times.

But Desert Orchid wasn't Red Rum, and wasn't loved for his certainty. He was loved for his looks: you could always pick him out from a crowded race because he was (a) at the front and (b) clear shining angel-winged white. The least horsey person in the world could recognise him: and empathise with the boldness of his running and jumping – and also with his fallibility. Because he didn't care for races run anti-clockwise; and so the Cheltenham Gold Cup, which should have been his two or three seasons running, was always a touch beyond him, or almost always, for he managed to win it once. The heroes that excite the most love usually have a touch of vulnerability: a flaw, even perhaps a tragic one. We tend to prefer romantic to classical beauty in sport.

But here was Desert Orchid, out on the gallops, a horse that extorted a certain deference from those around him. Without a trace of what horsey people call bad manners, with perfect respect for a human's personal space, he nevertheless carried with him the certainty that he was a pretty special sort of individual and that it was up to the rest of the world to humour him. The world did so with good grace, the memory of those great victories strong in all concerned.

- Mike Tyson's career went on to include debt, drugs, arrests and so forth. In 2015 he announced his support for Donald Trump.
- Anna Kournikova's career contained decreasing quantities of tennis. Injury and other matters increasingly kept her away from competition. In 2003 she pulled out of Wimbledon, but her presence was everywhere in a notorious advertisement for a sports bra that carried the slogan 'only the ball should bounce'. Thus, like Cheshire Cat, Kournikova faded away from tennis, until only the breasts remained. She is now best recalled as a classic example of a person who sold out to her lesser gift.
- Desert Orchid's last public appearance was to his fan club in 2006, aged 27. A few weeks later he died. His ashes are buried near his statue at Kempton Park.

BOOK 16

1998

Inga Lund is another country. They do things differently there.

Irony. Understatement. Overeagerness to apologise. Style and wit tinged with self-mockery. A wacky Creole of a language that combines Latin and Germanic roots. A political tradition that gave fascism a try and decisively rejected it. A certain embarrassment that has its roots in history. A lazy tolerance. Decency and fair play as high moral values.

All these things may help to define England but they have nothing to do with Inga Lund, the nation hymned in drunken triumph in the streets of Marseilles before England's first match in the World Cup. Their opponents were Tunisia.

Most of the England fans had arrived the night before; on the day of the match Marseilles was clearing up the mess. There had been more than 50 arrests and countless minor injuries.

Hard. Well hard. That's us.

As the bus carried a group of England fans towards the Stade Velodrome – an unexpected name for a football stadium – a woman of North African extraction, clad in flowing cottons, struck a vigorous attitude before the bus when it was becalmed at a traffic light. She mimed, with some magnificence, a spit of contempt.

Animals. So said the headlines in the newspapers, though you would never get Desert Orchid behaving in this way. All around the stadium parties of young and shirtless Englishmen, reddened and maddened by sun and by beer, had made their stand. They had drunk themselves beyond speech but not beyond song.

And we're *proud* of it – animals!

And we're *proud* of it – animals!

Whose football team were they celebrating? Whose nation? What part did sport play in all this?

An old boxing story: a boxer was making a loud disturbance at the weigh-in of a fight he was not involved in. Someone shouted: 'Get the gloves on him – that usually quietens him.' So it was with the football. As the singing and the resentment of the singing boiled up towards a climax on an afternoon of good solid Mediterranean warmth, everyone packed into the stadium to watch a dull football match. It featured a competent win from England; 2-0, with goals from Alan Shearer and Paul Scholes. The team lacked spark, but then the manager, Glenn Hoddle, had dropped Paul Gascoigne. At that stage no one was sure if this was a courageous tactical masterstroke or an act of self-important folly.

With exquisite appropriateness the bottles emptied by England supporters were gathered up by helpful North Africans who were not attending the match. They used these to bomb the England supporters on their way back to the buses. The England supporters naturally threw the unbroken ones back, and a high old time was had by all.

The bus, escorted by police motorbikes, made its ponderous way through crowds that jeered and drummed on the sides. It proceeded at funereal pace until at last it got beyond the environs of the Stade Velodrome.

Nobody died.

~

Trench warfare.

That's what they called it, but it was nothing of the kind. It was sport, it was Test match cricket – and, above all, it was a revelation of hardness. True hardness, in the sporting sense of the term.

If you wish to identify a mineral you put it through a Mohs test, in which you measure its resistance to abrasion. Then you can place it on the Mohs Scale of Hardness. Talc is 1, diamond is 10.

Sport is a Mohs test for the human spirit. The dramatic nature of this test is what makes sport compelling to watch and to experience. Perhaps most especially when the test reveals a diamond.

It was Sunday evening and teatime when Mike Atherton gloved a ball from Allan Donald of South Africa to the wicketkeeper, Mark Boucher. Atherton stood there without moving, his face poker-player blank. It was the fourth Test match between England and South Africa at Trent Bridge, and South Africa were 1-0 up. The following passage of play was shown on terrestrial television at the perfect hour. And so, when Atherton was given not out and Donald responded with a spell of violent short-pitched bowling from around the wicket, the nation was captivated by one of sport's classic enactments of the Mohs test.

Donald was all aggression and hard words; Atherton responded with a level stare, the same unmoved expression. Once he gave a small nod, to acknowledge Donald's brilliance – brilliance that was still not enough to get him out. The response was passive-aggressive: my cold to your hot. The facial expressions, invisible to those at the ground, told the true story to the rest of the nation who watched from afar and so were much closer.

One thing became very clear as the contest developed, reached its peak and at last ended, with Atherton not out at the close of play. It was that Atherton loved every second of it. Not in the sense of drinking beer with your mates or meeting a lovely girl or watching the world's funniest film – but in the sense of being tested. This brutal examination of his sporting and moral hardness was something that stimulated him to the core of his being.

Steve Waugh, the Australian captain, had been involved in a similar joust with Donald earlier that year. 'It's the best thing about Test cricket,' he said. 'Having a quick bowler running at you, obviously giving his best. That's what it's all about and I really enjoy it.'

This, then, is the opposite of being a flat-track bully. To succeed when everything is in your favour is hard enough, God knows, but those who succeed when things are at their most difficult are the ones to cherish. And these, inevitably, are those who find sport at its most enthralling when it is most difficult.

Perhaps all sport is a hunt for diamonds.

~

There is perfection in sport and it's not all that hard to find. It comes before the event takes place. It's found in the new morning a few days before the race, when the larks sing high above and every horse is a champion.

Newmarket Heath in spring: sporting perfection unsullied by competition. No victory and no defeat has marred it, not yet. And perhaps – perhaps – defeat never will. The dew wet and splashing around your ankles, the sun saving its warmth for later, the horses almost a mile distant, walking an eternal circle as if taking part in a slow ritual dance. 'Yes,' said Sheikh Mohammed. 'This time is the best.'

Godolphin. He was fed up with trainers telling him how to run his horses so he founded his own racing organisation. And called it Godolphin. The Godolphin Arabian is one of the three founding sires of the breed of horses known as thoroughbred. Racehorses, in short. This was in itself a piece of daring: the Arabs coming to take back their own: for every speedster in the great thoroughbred dynasty that races across the entire world can trace its origins back to one of those three fleet-footed horses of Arabia. 'I know more than a trainer. Trainers would not listen to me.'

His first memory was being on horseback. He was two, his father was riding the horse and he was sitting just in front of the saddle with his father behind him. Horses are to some people walking, breathing symbols of their own wealth and power; when they love their horses it is their own wealth and power that has inspired their passion. But some – even the wealthiest and most powerful of all – love horses for their own marvellous selves. Here unmistakably was one such: a passion for horses and for putting them to the test in sport. Sheikh Mohammed rode regularly in 100-mile endurance races. Around his horses, he was freed for a while from the cares of state and from the dignity of royalty; at that time he was both a prince and minister of defence for United Arab Emirates. He stood there in the same jeans, the same white tee-shirt, the same Godolphin-branded windcheater as everybody else. Just one horseman among many.

But it was simultaneously clear that Sheikh Mohammed was nothing like everybody else. He held out his hand without looking: at once a pair of binoculars was placed in his grasp. As he surveyed the distant circlers the circle broke up, and the horses set off in pairs along the Al Bahathri gallop, the little work-riders crouched oddly motionless over the withers.

But all the same, a filly. A filly in the Derby. Cape Verdi had won the 1,000 Guineas and looked certain to win the Oaks, the one-and-a-half-mile Epsom classic for three-year-old fillies. But Sheikh Mohammed wanted her to run in the Derby, believing she had the speed to beat the colts. The last filly to win the Derby was Fifinella in 1916. Cape Verdi looked great going past. She had the speed, she had the wings. In the cold bright morning light, she was still a champion.

'I have fine memories. I am grateful. But I look always to the next horse, the next *great* horse. Always to move forward. If you are idle, you stand still – you lose, you go backwards.'

He made with his hands a gesture of absolute decision.

'It is the same with running a country.'

~

Too nice. That's England.

And in sport, that's a condemnation. A little too eager to please, so you end up pleasing your opponent. Always ready to apologise: especially if the athlete in question happens to be English. It's been demonstrated – as a piece of anthropological research – that if you deliberately bump into someone at an English train station, you will receive an apology. So a myth has arisen: that a certain type of English athlete – especially one who is a little on the middle-class side – is too nice to win: crippled by Englishness. It's a national archetype, and one we cherish, one that exasperates, one that we take a mild pride in, one that we like to make a quiet joke about.

Petr Korda came into the Wimbledon quarter-finals carrying an injury. He was a little lame. Not moving well. Just a little off his game as a result, and a little goes a long way at elite level. His opponent was the archetypally English Tim Henman.

The previous year, Henman had reached the quarter-finals and given the nation a great emotional ride along the way. These matches tended to be scheduled at teatime, to maximise television viewers. So there were jests, borrowing the phrase from Douglas Adams, about the long dark teatime of the soul.

Henman came from a well-to-do background, and though he learned to put a hint of a glottal stop into his public pronouncements, he was never to be confused with, say, Paul Gascoigne. So inevitably, his defeats, and his regular mid-match wobbles, were put down to the fact that he was too nice.

It's a verdict Korda would contest. Henman took him apart, limp by limp, moving him about the court, playing with unrelenting pace and cadence. He didn't give him a chance and won in three sets. Courtesy is required in sport, because this is an area of play, not an arena of death. Generosity is not.

Lynne Truss once speculated that tennis has a particular attraction for women for exactly that reason: the player is required to inflict continual pain on his opponent – his partner, if you like. He must take satisfaction – if not active pleasure – in his opponent's discomfort. And that, she said, is exactly what women are not supposed to do. Above all, he must take advantage of his opponent's every weakness.

Henman did all this in a mood of cold certainty. And sent the nation dreaming of still greater victory, prizes still more glittering and more opponents ready to be humbled.

～

When you embrace partisanship in its purest form the team or the individual becomes an extension of yourself. That's what gives such zest to the lively hatred of, say, Luton, or for that matter, Watford.

Partisanship will inevitably bring disappointment, but such disappointments come with a subtle additional pleasure. Which is blame. When things go wrong, it has to be somebody's fault. Blame, though seldom recognised as such, is an important part of sport, uniting individuals and communities. More people lose than win in sport, for such is its nature: but sport is endlessly bountiful in providing candidates for blame.

Life is hard. Most of us come to that conclusion at some stage or other. The trick is to accept this and get on with it, making the best of a flawed concept. The great error is to think that life's failure to live up to your childish hopes is somebody's fault. When you blame your spouse for the failures of the universe, you are on a wrong and potentially disastrous track.

But sport lets you off such sanity. In sport you can blame away to your heart's content – after all, you don't have to live with it. It's all play, it's all fantasy. When your sporting hopes fail, you can seek the pleasures of blaming someone for your disappointment. And when the entire nation is disappointed, its population seeks someone to blame with the hunger of a starving man-eater.

When David Beckham started the new football season for Manchester United, everyone who supported any other club was prepared to give him a year of purgatory. Or worse. It was his fault that we – note the pronoun – didn't win the World Cup. He lost it. He deprived us of what was ours by rights.

Beckham was sent off in the course of England's match against Argentina in the round of 16. He took a heavy and illegal tackle from Diego Simeone, the Argentina captain, and lay face down. Simeone, in a classic piece of gamesmanship, the sort of thing that would have had Stephen Potter in ecstasies, then ruffled his hair: a patronising gesture from a tough-as-teak old stager to a pretty little boy. That played well on television. Beckham responded, flat out as he was, with a cross little kick and made contact around the knee. Impossible to do much more than register his presence from such a position, it was nevertheless enough to fling Simeone to the ground in seeming agony. So Beckham was sent off. It was all made much worse by the gloriously futile heroism – always the most vivid kind – as England staged a fightback which narrowly failed. With ghastly inevitability England lost the penalty shoot-out.

So Beckham became a figure of perfect loathing. He was

hated for his pretensions to star quality, and also for his effeminacy. He had been pictured on holiday that year wearing a sarong. A footballer in a frock – perfectly self-cast as national hate-object.

Go abroad. Go anywhere. He was clearly a talented player; many big clubs would love to have him. Whatever you do, don't stay. A fragile little fop like that, with his pretty, decorative talent: he'd surely be destroyed. Football was split between those who wanted him to stay so that he could be destroyed, and those who wanted him to run away so that he could save himself.

But one thing was clear: England had a hate-object who would surely pass the test of time. He was broken.

~

When Florence Griffith Joyner died at the age of 38, it was assumed that her body had collapsed because of the drugs she had used. Not that she ever failed a drugs test. She died after an epileptic seizure. There was no evidence at all to link her death with drugs: it was just that everybody did.

It was a death that gave pleasure to many. It seemed to be a grimly just conclusion to an edifying moral tale. Griffith Joyner could bear symbolic blame for the sins of athletics, for all the sins of sport. Her death provoked a global fit of gloating, and the fact that in law you can't libel the dead gave media commentators a free run at the irresistible subject.

Alas, poor Florence. She tried to please the whole world, and she failed. She was a champion, she was a gold medal winner, she was a setter of world records, she looked spectacular, and she said all the right things. She was a star: and when she died, the world put on its dancing shoes before heading for her grave.

Like a Fellini film her brilliance was rendered absurd by self-adoration, and yet she believed it all without the tiniest shred of irony. If she lived the dream, it was one of those dreams that baffles by its ultimate meaninglessness.

Janis Joplin once said: 'I love being a star more than life itself.' Thus it was that Flo-Jo became just another rock and roll casualty. But at least we will have her records.

- England won the Test match against South Africa by eight wickets; Atherton, perhaps appropriately, finished on 98 not out. That levelled the series at 1-1; England won the deciding match. Re the Mohs test: a few years earlier, David Gower had been invited to condemn the West Indian tactic of fast, short-pitched bowling. 'It's a Test match. It's not Old Reptonians v Lymeswold, one off the mark and jolly good show. You're not expecting life to be made easy for you.'
- Cape Verdi finished unplaced in the Derby. She was still rated the best three-year-old filly of her year. She retired to stud after losing two races as a four-year-old but has produced no great champions.
- Tim Henman was beaten with equal brutality in the semi-finals by the eventual winner. Pete Sampras, neatly demonstrating the difference between very, very good and great.
- David Beckham stayed with Manchester United and played a central role in their treble the following year: Premier League, FA Cup and Champions League.
- Florence Griffith Joyner's records are 10.49 seconds for the 100 metres, 21.34 seconds for the 200 metres. They've still not been seriously challenged. They were wiped off the official records in 2017 when the IAAF decided to abandon all records set before 2005.

BOOK 17

1999

Quixall Crossett had run 87 races.

And lost them all.

He was second twice, mind. 'He always quickens up towards the end of a race,' said Ted Caine.

Caine was a permit trainer: done it for 20 years, bar a year out. He and his wife Joy ran High Crossett Farm on the North York Moors. They currently had four horses, but Quixall was the star.

Every few weeks they'd enter Quixall in a race, always for amateurs or apprentices, and Quixall would have a trudge round, giving a nice day out to the amateur or a good schooling run to the apprentice, and Quixall would lose and everyone would go home happy.

Caine did the training, and the feeding and the work-riding and the mucking out. 'We just do bits round the farm.' The Caines bred him themselves; the stallion's fee was £50. Though Quixall was becoming in a small way a celebrity. He got fan mail: people sent him Polos, or a couple of pound coins: 'Ask Mr Caine to buy you some carrots.' All this amused the Caines, but they insisted that he really wasn't the worst racehorse in Britain. 'People like to say that, but he isn't.'

It was about quiet, understated love for horses, for sport, for trying and for failing. All that's perfectly understandable. What's not is that Caine stopped training for a year.

'Oh, that was when our son was killed. I didn't feel like training then, but I took out a licence again the following year.' Their son Malcolm was killed in an accident on the farm. Malcolm, who was going to take over the place. It was Joy who found his body.

And in an instant it was clear what this was really all about, why Quixall was still running with 87 defeats behind him.

If you have horses you're not allowed to give up. You have to feed them, water them, exercise them, muck them out, check them last thing at night, hearing the sound of their munching from the blackness of the box and then feeling their sweet breath on your cheek.

And it's sport, too. Competition, facing the world. Doing your best. Sport may not matter, but it can certainly make life more enjoyable. And sport can also make life slightly less difficult to endure.

Somebody died.

The Caines and Quixall Crossett were undefeated.

~

Juan Antonio Samaranch was undefeated. He was still president of the International Olympic Committee, even though it was proved beyond doubt that members of the IOC had been taking bribes from cities eager to host the Olympic Games. Six members had been expelled for accepting bribes in the form of scholarships from Salt Lake City, as part of its victorious campaign to hold the Winter Games of 2002. Three more were under investigation.

Samaranch held an incomprehensibly vast press conference and announced that these people had done great harm to the Olympic movement. And that was it. He was still His Excellency. He was still the president. He still flew in private jets, still swept about the place in incomprehensibly vast cars, still slept in presidential suites, loving not their luxury but the aura of importance they conferred on him. He was still treated with deference by real heads of state, blind to the fact that they were humouring him because they wanted something. He was the phoney leader, His Excellency the President of Nowhere. He posed as an apostle for a greater future of the globe and still believed that he was to be given the Nobel Peace Prize, some coup for a former follower of General Franco. ('He had no choice,' as his biographer David Miller inaccurately wrote.)

His achievement was to bring multinational companies into the Olympic movement, which in turn brought a lot of money into the Games, a process that started at the Los Angeles Games of 1984. The payback was corruption. Perhaps Samaranch was not corrupt himself, in the sense of squirrelling the stuff away for his own use. But he blind-eyed that process in others, and no doubt did so to secure his own power-base. If a corrupt person relies on you for his money, you can, if you like, call it loyalty.

What Samaranch prized above all else was being a president. He loved to play the part of a head of state, without any of those tedious encumbrances like running a country, as Sheikh Mohammed did. He couldn't see that he was nothing more than a man in charge of a rather good circus. He was a Barnum, a showman dressed up not in top hat and a whip but in a sober suit and an expression like his own passport photograph.

His number one tactic was to exploit the idea that sport is by definition virtuous, and that the Olympic Games are more virtuous than anything else in sport. If this illusion was destroyed by Ben Johnson in Seoul, Samaranch still clung to it. Myths are tenacious and resistant to truth, and they are forever exploited by people in search of power or money or both. Under Samaranch everybody involved in sport was conspicuously virtuous, and you could be associated with such virtues at a very reasonable price. So for years, real politicians, McDonald's and Coca-Cola humoured the phoney president for what they could get.

Goodness, what beautiful pearls, someone once said to Mae West. 'Goodness had nothing to do with it,' she replied.

Goodness, what beautiful sport.

~

Edward Wightman was the last person in England to be burned at the stake for heresy. He was executed on 11 April 1612, having, among other things, denied the doctrine of the Trinity and the divinity of Christ.

Glenn Hoddle, manager of the England football team, was not actually burned at the stake, but all the same, he became perhaps the first major public figure to lose his job for heresy since Archbishop Thomas Cranmer.

Hoddle had taken up religion. Under the influence of a faith healer, Eileen Drewery, he abandoned orthodoxy and started to make it up as he went along, mixing Christianity with a spot of Hinduism and a dash of Buddhism and a merry sprinkling of New Agery. Thus he took on reincarnation and the notion that disabled people were paying for sins committed in an earlier existence. He had expressed these beliefs on the radio and no one had paid much attention, bar the odd rolling of the eyes. But when he repeated them to a newspaper reporter, the newspaper sensed their shock value, homed in on them and went big.

Hoddle was invited to deny them in a gloriously sycophantic interview on BBC television. 'I never said them things.' No one asked the obvious question: 'But is this what you believe?'

Hoddle's denial failed to stand up, and the public turned as one against him. He was manager of the England football team, so he represented us. But he expressed views that didn't represent us. We are supposed to be living in a secular age: here the subtle, secret and enduring power of religion was made plain. It's not right for a man to believe such things; certainly not a man who does stuff in our name – like managing the football team that represents us. That was the instant consensus.

Would it have been different if Hoddle's England team had won the World Cup the previous year, instead of losing to Argentina? Would it have been different if Hoddle had been less happy to blame David Beckham? Would it have been different if Hoddle had not made money from his World Cup diary, in which he told tales out of school and lost the trust of his players? Would it have been different if the qualifying matches for the European Championship were going better (defeat in Sweden, goalless draw at home against Bulgaria)? Almost certainly yes. This is sport, after all. Sport encourages us to be inconsistent and emotional. One of the greatest pleasures of sport is that it lets us off rational thought.

Perhaps it was the memory of Hoddle as a player that gave the affair its sinister edge. Everybody recalled the sight of Hoddle bossing a game, with immense elegance of movement, making 50-yard passes that dropped perfectly into the stride of the goal-bound forward, so that at times it seemed as if an angel had dropped down to earth to show us how football is played in the vaults of heaven – so what glorious virtues must his soul have accrued in previous lives, to live on earth with a body as beautiful and as capable as that?

Hoddle's views also went against an emerging and encouraging orthodoxy, one that says disabled people are all right, that the able-bodied must deal with the problems of the less fortunate, and do so without distaste. They must put up with any slight inconvenience this may cause, and do so with a cheery understanding. And if it was easy to fall short even of this ideal, Hoddle's public dismissal of this new orthodoxy was troubling.

You can't say that. You can't say that and continue to represent us. You can't say that because it's heresy.

Alas poor Glenda.

~

There are rare occasions in sport when all save the partisan are united in joy. They tend to come from a swirling combination of beauty and the underdog victory, and together they create a kind of sporting perfection.

The Rugby Union World Cup was held in England, and New Zealand were favourites. They were shatteringly efficient and they still had Jonah Lomu as their unstoppable finisher. In their semi-final, deep into the second half, they were leading France 24-10. New Zealand looked infallible. They were a machine – or at least, that was the illusion they fostered.

It was then the game went mad. But slowly, slowly. Christophe Lamaison hadn't played in the tournament before that day, only making it this time because of an injury to Thomas Castaignède. He had already scored France's try, finishing after a wild wriggling run from Richard Dourthe. Now he got to kicking, landing two drop goals and two penalties. And it was then that France were taken over by a mad frenzy, a *folie à quinze* – and New Zealand found themselves crazily caught up in it, somehow caught in a need to humour the French madness.

Everything that France tried came off. Christophe Dominici miraculously gathered a wild kick at full speed to score; Dourthe picked up a bouncing, tantalising kick-ahead for another try; Philippe Bernat-Salles came fizzing through to score one more to make it certain.

It was like being drunk, at the stage when the drinker becomes almost too wonderful for this world, when everything you fear has become insignificant and everything you desire is yours for the asking. All you need to do is reach out. Twickenham was as ever full of Englishmen, at a time when England were rowing with the French about cattle imports, and yet Twickenham was filled with a joy imported by the French. It was an occasion that burst the banks of partisanship, filling hearts and minds with the gloriously improbable joys of sport: banishing reality and making life accord to the deepest and most secret fantasies of us all: fantasies in which we too can bend reality to our own needs, overcome every obstacle, beat the book and romp home a winner at a million to one.

~

There are occasions when sport touches something very close to perfection – and hardly anybody notices. These occasions may not be beautiful in any obvious way. Generally, the loveable underdog loses and people walk away from perfection disappointed.

It's not hard to spot this kind of perfection, but it tends to involve an awful lot of time: far more time – and for that matter thought – than normal people give to sport, perhaps more than sport is worth. Hours and hours of watching sport, days and months and years of watching and thinking about sport: such things give you a different view of sport to those who turn to sport to add savour to already enjoyable lives. And so the men's singles final at Wimbledon brought perfection – and was a deep disappointment. People had been looking forward to a golden triumph for the golden couple: Steffi Graf to win the women's singles title and her fiancé, Andre Agassi, winning the men's. Agassi was in the form of his life after winning the French Open, completing a glorious self-rescue from a ranking of 173 in the world.

Lindsay Davenport unexpectedly beat Graf in the women's final. And in the men's, Pete Sampras beat Agassi in straight sets. The score was 6-3, 6-4, 7-5. Agassi played brilliantly throughout. He played without weakness of character or of performance. He played so well that he forced Sampras to play the greatest three sets of power tennis, of fast-court tennis, of serve-and-volley tennis that the world has ever seen. The triumph of the French at Twickenham some months later made you want to stand up and cheer; the victory of Sampras made you want to sit very quiet and still and marvel at the man who could do such things.

It was an occasion that gave little scope to partisanship, for Sampras, like the All Blacks, tended to inspire admiration rather than affection. There was no drama. This was just pure sport, ratcheted up to a point beyond mere excellence, to a point where it almost attained some mystic level: perhaps reminiscent of those things sought by Eugen Herrigel in what remains the finest book on sports psychology ever written, *Zen in the Art of Archery*.

Sampras closed things out with a second-serve ace. He was asked in the press conference afterwards: 'What was going through your mind on that last point, Pete?'

A slightly baffled pause.

'There was absolutely nothing going on in my mind at that time.'

~

The last Test match of the summer took place, as always, at The Oval. England lost the match and with it the series against New Zealand, back then the weakest of the Test match countries. The defeat put England at the bottom of the Test match rankings. The crowd booed the new captain, Nasser Hussain, as he stood on the balcony to be interviewed after the match. The defeat was considered a national disgrace. The front page of the *Sun* the following day carried the headline: The Death of English Cricket.

~

Peta Beckett.

Robert Slade.

Polly Phillipps.

Simon Long.

Peter McLean.

Eventers. They all died in separate incidents in the course of the same year.

National Hunt jockeys ride with very short stirrup leathers, so they can throw their weight forward to aid forward speed. When they are involved in a fall, they tend to get catapulted off ... clear of their own horses and, with luck, clear of the others. Injuries are frequent, fatalities are rare.

Eventers ride long. That's because they need lateral control of their horses when they aim for very precise and narrow spots in the fences before them. When there's a fall, they tend to stay with the horse. When a horse falls on top of a rider, the rider can die.

Some responded to this terrible succession of deaths by seeking someone to blame: someone negligent, uncaring, stupid. Others looked for solutions: adjustment of the time allowed, redesign of jumps, jumps that collapse when you hit them.

Eventing is not violent. No one caused these accidents, or sought those deaths. The riders were not pursuing some mad death-wish: rather, they sought the complex joys of the horsey life, of which risk is an inevitable part.

These were not wasted lives. Sport is trivial, but these were not lives lost in pursuing something with no meaning. The riders were involved in the pursuit of excellence, and it was in their nature to make this pursuit on the back of a horse. They looked for sporting fulfilment knowing the dangers involved. They died because something went terribly wrong – not, as in boxing, because something had gone terribly right. Their deaths don't invalidate their lives or their sport.

- Quixall Crossett retired after 103 consecutive defeats.
- Juan Antonio Samaranch was cleared of any wrongdoing by an IOC investigation. He did not seek re-election, standing down in 2001 after 21 years as president. He campaigned for Madrid's bid to hold the Games of 2012 and 2016, both unsuccessfully. He died in 2010.
- Glenn Hoddle had spells managing Southampton, Tottenham Hotspur and Wolverhampton Wanderers. In 2008 he founded the Glenn Hoddle Academy in Spain, now based in Buckinghamshire.
- Australia beat France 35-12 in the Rugby Union World Cup final.

BOOK 18

2000

They've gone on from The Mortimer pub to Casanova's Chinese Restaurant and now they're discussing the great lover himself.

'Why should he be considered a great man because he had a lot of women? Most men would have ended by being bored to death.'

'That is why he was a great man,' said Moreland. 'It wasn't the number of women he had; it was the fact that he didn't get bored.'

This from Anthony Powell's *A Dance to the Music of Time*. And it's true for Steve Redgrave: and is the key to his greatness.

The rowing lake at the Sydney Olympic Games, the day still a little cool for this breakfast-time race. The air of fragility that surrounded Redgrave's boat: lacking the monstrous certainty of 1996. Redgrave had been ill, diagnosed with diabetes. The four had suffered traumatic defeat that year.

Unless you stand exactly on the finish line you can't judge a close finish in this sport, and the race was very tight indeed.

The British boat had led from the start and opened up a decent gap, but that gap was vanishing with every stroke. From most angles the finish was deeply ambiguous: it seemed that the pursuing Italians had done enough in the last great smashing strokes of the race.

So why were a small group at the finish cheering and waving Union Jacks? And yes, the cheering was spreading: a slow, glorious, joyous, hilarious realisation among the many British supporters there that day. The impossible victory had taken place before disbelieving eyes. 'It was never in doubt from 250 metres,' Redgrave said.

So, a gold medal. His fifth in five Games: one at every Games since 1984. After the victory in Atlanta four years earlier he had announced to the television cameras: 'Anyone who sees me in a boat again has my permission to shoot me.'

Then he found the old instincts stirring. And the truth was, he was not bored at all. Not with training, not with pain, not with self-deprivation, not with water, not with racing, not with cracking that blade into the water and moving a boat at impossible speed.

The old process had him as enthralled as ever, and neither age nor illness was enough to stop him striving, or for that matter, succeeding. It was clear that the demands required to win again and again and again can only be met by truly exceptional people. It wasn't that he failed to get bored because there was nothing else in his life: it was because there was nothing as good, as big, as meaningful. 'Nothing will ever give me the same satisfaction as what I do here,' said Sugar Ray Leonard, marching proudly to humiliation. Not only did Leonard and Redgrave have exceptional natures, they both had a need to prove that their nature was exceptional. The stuff that would send normal people walking away only made them want more. And find more. And – sometimes – win more.

It was not a lack in himself that made such a search necessary. Rather, it was the need to get the most, the very last drop, from the talents that he possessed: talent for moving a boat, talent to work at such a thing with undying enthusiasm, talent to convert all that into victory on the one day that counted.

And it seemed on that day that he had become the essence of every sport: or, rather, of every victory. That need to win, and to do so again and again and again, was never sated: a quality we might call Redgrave. Just as Napoleon was said to ask of his generals: 'But has he luck?' – so anyone seeking athletes committed to the pursuit of victory must ask of each and every one: 'But has he Redgrave?'

~

There is often a moment of validation in a young person's life: a moment when you know you can do it, you're all right, you're accepted in the grown-up world. It's not the end of ambition, far from it: rather, you now know, with some certainty and for the first time, that your ambitions are realistic. For a singer it might be the moment when a member of the choir is asked to sing a solo. For a journalist, it might be the first piece accepted by a national newspaper. It's a moment when doubts about your own fundamental adequacy can be laid to rest.

For Venus Williams all it took was victory in the women's singles at Wimbledon.

It's all very well your father telling you that you're going to be a champion and a very great one. Until you have that moment of validation – a moment that's for you and you alone – you never really believe such a thing. These things are many millions of times harder when you come from a disadvantaged background. And, of course, when your skin happens to be black and your sport of choice is . . . well, the Wimbledon dress code for players says it all. Predominantly white.

Things are always harder for the older child. Many great

athletes have reached that status because they spent their child-hood trying to beat a big brother. Often these second sibs go on to succeed where the older ones fall short.

The two sisters had been promising too much for rather too long: the breakthrough to the top was overdue when the younger sister, Serena, won the US Open the previous year. They had compensated, and overcompensated, for the difficulties of their upbringing with an attitude of defiance. They had also taken the prevailing tactic of power tennis and added to it a dimension of their own: more power.

Venus and Serena. Such names! Mars and Turbulena, more like.

Venus met Lindsay Davenport in the final, took the first set decisively and was serving for the match at 5-4 when she double-faulted twice. In tennis, psychological flaws are given dramatic force by the nature of the action, by the way that some points are more equal than others.

It came to a tie-break, with the advantage shifting to Davenport: but Venus won it with some style, taking it 7-3.

She had gone into the final like a twitchy adolescent, bluster and strut covering up self-doubt. She came out of it a person fully validated in the world she had chosen. The difficult part was done. The sisters had taken control.

~

If ever a man had cause to hate the sport of eventing, it was Vere Phillipps. A few months ago it had killed his wife Polly: Polly the courageous, the joyous, with cataracts of blonde hair, and all ready to take the next big step, the one that goes from very promising to serious achiever. Polly was one of the five eventers killed the previous year.

Phillipps's response was to take up the sport of eventing. Many thought he was mad: as if Ayrton Senna's girlfriend decided to take over his racing car in the fullness of her grief.

'Think of it this way – I will never again have the chance to ride two horses that Polly has trained.'

Phillipps was a serious professional horseman, the man you went to if you wanted to buy a serious jumping horse. He bought them up, brought them on and sold them when they were ready. It was not that much of a stretch, then – at least, not until you came to dressage, the discipline that takes place on the flat. He was learning this new branch of equestrianism with sheer grinding willpower: and his aim was to ride in the year's second four-star – highest level – event, Burghley.

'These horses are going to event and they're going to carry brown and yellow. They're going to carry Polly's colours. I'm not just having a go, you know. I won't compete at Burghley unless I can make the top ten. I'm certainly not trying to die.'

In the house, everywhere you looked, there were pictures of a woman on a horse leaping some fabulous obstacle: a woman with colossal amounts of blonde hair escaping from beneath her riding helmet. Pictures that burned themselves into your mind, or perhaps that was the force of the emanation from the mind of Vere Phillipps.

One more time he tried to explain.

'It keeps Polly alive.'

~

Sport can take any amount of disaster. It can take cheating, bad vibes, reckless behaviour, terrible injuries and even death. It can take sledging and abuse, bad blood, any amount of disgusting behaviour. It can take drugs, it can take lies, it can take cover-ups, it can take conspiracy. It can lose dignity, it can lose moral force, it can lose self-importance. The one thing sport can never lose is uncertainty. Once you know what happens next, sport ceases to be sport.

The fixing of results is not a crime against sport. It is the destruction of sport.

The door opens a crack and you think that perhaps that's all: a small chink of light that won't really help anybody to see. But the door opens a little wider, and then wider again, until then you know that in the end it will swing wide open and nothing can be concealed any longer.

Hansie Cronje had led the South African cricket team back into the world after the years of apartheid had ended. He came across as the perfect man for the job: as if the essential Afrikaner decency he represented was a necessary part of the healing of harms. Fine man. Upright. Christian. Moral. Gave bottom, gave confidence, gave meaning to the South Africa cricket team as they made their first tentative steps into the world.

But now he admitted he had been 'dishonest'. He had taken between US$10,000 and US$15,000 from bookmakers. The information, he said, was not for fixing, it was for forecasting. He smoked but he didn't inhale.

So how much do you trust a man who said he was dishonest in one way but not in another way? Can you believe that the cricket matches he had been involved with had all been true and real? When we watched matches that involved him, all of us caught up in the passion of sport – which is always based on the fact that you don't know, that nobody ever knows what happens next – could we trust they were real?

We already knew that Cronje was not entirely real: that he was a stinking Tartuffe of a cricketer. But were the matches real? Was the next match going to be real? Once we ask that, we have lost the sport. Lost it entirely, lost it forever.

～

I want people to recognise me.

From half a mile away.

Words of the Russian gymnast, Svetlana Khorkina.

I realise that I am not just Svetlana, but in a sense the person-ification of gymnastics.

It's all right to be a diva in, say, ballet, when you know Odette will marry the prince. Much harder to be a diva in sport, when you don't know what happens next.

Khorkina was head and shoulders above her rivals at the Sydney Olympic Games. Quite literally: she stood five-foot-five inches, six or seven inches taller than most, and three inches taller than Svetlana Boginskaya. The taller you are, the harder this is: a simple issue of biomechanics. If you have a problem understanding this, try to visualise George Foreman performing a somersault.

So if you are substantially taller than the rest, every somersault is twice as difficult. The payback is that it looks twice as beautiful. And perhaps Khorkina was all the more beautiful because she had to work so close to failure. The combat sports are measured in weight divisions: it would be fair for gymnastics to be divided into height categories: events that featured six-foot-tall gymnasts would add a new dimension to the sport.

Khorkina left the dangerous kind of gymnastics – which is called artistic gymnastics – for a year. She was pushed into rhythmic gymnastics, the stuff performed on the floor with a ribbon on a stick, or a ball or other props. You don't fly. It's gymnastics with the heat off. Khorkina stuck it for a year and went back to flying, knowing she had chosen a discipline in which everything was stacked against her, with the exception of her own talent.

In the team competition she had a fall from the asymmetric bars which cost Russia the gold medal. In the individual all-around competition, she was leading after a glorious routine on the floor. But she had a fall on the vault and then an error on the bars, and after that she sat apart with her sorrow, looking like Anna Karenina on the train.

But in the individual apparatus competition she stayed on the bars, completed a routine of memorable beauty and at last won her gold medal. After the hugs and the kisses she went back to the bars, seized the lower one and rested her face in her hands and wept. Thousands – millions – perhaps billions – wept with her.

∼

Sport is instant mythology and its participants become instant archetypes. There is always a temptation, then, to jump the gun: to turn athletes into living symbols of glory before glory has actually been achieved. And that complicates matters, because this is sport and not art. And nobody knows what happens next.

In an act that was simultaneously glorious and cruel, the Sydney Games recruited Australia's greatest athlete and most spectacular gold medal hope and cast her for the opening ceremony. Not just the opening ceremony but the central part of it. So there was Cathy Freeman, her glorious athlete's body clad in shining Lycra, revealing far more than it concealed of that honed, ready-to-race physique: standing with the Olympic torch raised above her head in the centre of an artificial cataract, lighting the flame.

This, then, was what Australia wanted to be: young, athletic and glorious and with glories still to come, but at the same time utterly at peace with its past.

For Freeman was from the Aboriginal people of Australia: Australia's eternal reproach, a perpetual reminder that God's Own Country is built on the land taken from the people who lived there first. The Australian government had refused to acknowledge the problem of the 'stolen generation' of children taken from their parents to be educated in an approved European fashion; it had consistently turned down land claims from Aboriginal people; it had refused anything in the nature of a 'national apology' to Aboriginal people. And yet at the same time it wanted forgiveness: to be a country of genuine freedom and justice in which glorious young people could achieve great things. No matter what their ancestry.

The one potential flaw in all this symbolism was that Freeman had a race to run: the 400 metres, which is perhaps the cruellest event in track and field, for this is the one in which the anaerobic disciplines of the sprinter collide with the aerobic – oxygen-craving – demands of the distance runner in the last 100 metres of the race.

She did it.

She finished the race and collapsed face down on the track, staying down for what seemed an hour, apparently in agonies of sheer relief. Perhaps no athlete in history has been so put upon – so greatly required to win for reasons far beyond the personal – but she did it and she wept.

~

There are people around whom suspicion accrues naturally. There are others for whom it is a kind of blasphemy. Hansie Cronje was a classic example of this. So was Marion Jones, who won the 100 metres in Sydney with the fastest times since Florence Griffith Joyner. She ran with such grace, her smile was so sweet, her bearing so modest. If Redgrave was Britain's star of the Games and Freeman was Australia's, Jones was the star for America and the world: an embodiment of natural talents honed to perfection, and presented by a person of genuine charm and worth.

It was a blow, then, when her husband and mentor, J.J. Hunter, a shot putter, tested positive for drugs. This was old news but it had been suppressed: and the ancient rule is that when you hush things up, they are invariably five times as damaging when they eventually burst free. Hunter wept and swore by everything that he had absolutely no idea why his body contained one thousand times the permitted limit for nandrolone.

Hunter was in the first category of suspicious people. It was hard to reconcile this with Jones, but you had to ask: did the two have different kinds of cereal on the breakfast table?

There was knee-jerk cynicism for Hunter; for Jones, an almost childish need for reassurance that she was all right, that she was real, that she could be believed, that the sport she was delivering was in fact sport.

~

Sometimes we like sport best when it represents a glorious antithesis: a straightforward duel in which one participant represents one way of approaching life and the other its opposite. Cavalier v Roundhead; flaky artist v conscientious labourer; youthful promise v old master; good big 'un v good little 'un; patrician favourite v the tough of the track. You pick one or the other according to temperament or local allegiance; reserving, perhaps, the right to change sides at any point.

The last duel between Bonfire and Gigolo was just such an encounter. It took place in the individual final of the dressage event in Sydney: the almost perfect competence of Gigolo, ridden by Isabell Werth, and the flamboyance and extravagance of Bonfire, ridden by Anky van Grunsven. These ladies wore top hats, swallow-tailed coats and pearl earrings, with fine gold hairnets over their fine gold hair, and they duelled without quarter.

Dressage, a discipline based on the manoeuvres needed by cavalry horses in combat, is an extreme form of gravity defiance, and it stands comparison with gymnastics. But in dressage the humans sit perfectly still, or at least appear to, while the horses dance, strut, skip, evade lances and at times stand with perfect unflinching motionlessness.

Expressive paces. That's what people talk about in dressage. In dressage, the movement of the top horses is spectacularly elevated, so that every stride in trot seems to launch the rider towards the moon. Four years ago in Atlanta, the expressive paces of Bonfire won the crowd, while the more conservative Gigolo won the gold. Judges are like that: always easier to punish a fault than reward a virtue. It's always twice as hard for the maverick.

But in this last duel Bonfire transcended himself: giving every possible hint of expression to every pace while failing to make an error of overenthusiasm. Balanced on a knife-edge of possibility, the great horse danced his way to something pretty close to perfection. The marks came up: Bonfire had won, four points clear, and the crowd responded with joy. Van Grunsven did as a good horsey person must in such circumstances: she gave her most dazzling smile and pointed. At the horse.

That's one of the things about sport: the cynics never get it all their own way.

- Steve Redgrave did retire this time.
- Vere Phillipps rode Coral Cove at Burghley, putting in the third-fastest time over the cross-country course and finishing 12th, one place above William Fox-Pitt, one of the world's leading eventers. He then went back to his horse-dealing business. He later remarried.
- Hansie Cronje was found guilty of match-fixing and banned from cricket for life. He died in a plane crash in 2002. A few years later he was voted the 11th greatest South African of all time.
- Svetlana Khorkina stayed in training for the next Olympic Games in Athens, where she won bronze in the team event and silver in the all-around. She retired the following year. She produced an autobiography, *Somersaults in High Heels*. She later married Oleg Kochnev, a former general 23 years her senior.
- Cathy Freeman retired from athletics in 2003. Later she established the Cathy Freeman Foundation to aid indigenous people. She was married in 2009.
- Marion Jones consistently denied using performance-

enhancing drugs but finally, when evidence became overwhelming, admitted that she had used drugs and lied about them for most of her career. She was later stripped of the medals she won in Sydney.

~

BOOK 19

2001

How tall the mast! So tall they had to open Tower Bridge to let it through. And how small the boat: surely intended for some quite other mast. Yellow and squat, it sat placidly on the waters of the Thames just downstream of the Tower, in the manner of a celluloid duck.

Step on board, climb down below. A tiny cockpit, pictures of loved ones still roughly taped up, untasted sweets and treats still in the locker, toothbrush still ready for use by a sink in which you could perhaps wash one hand at a time. A padded bench where Ellen MacArthur could curl up and catnap.

She had just completed the Vendee Globe, the race for single-handed circumnavigators, and she had come second, finishing the course in 94 days, 4 hours, 25 minutes and 40 seconds: down the Atlantic, full lap of the Southern Ocean and back up again. She had gone through storms with waves higher even than the mast. She had climbed up every inch of that mast to fix the sail-raising machines. She had gone through everything that the ocean could throw at her, but it wasn't about adventure at all. Or survival.

It was about speed.

She wasn't out there seeing if she could do it, she was there seeing if she could win it. She didn't deny herself sleep and accept all the other privations in order to survive: she did that to conjure an extra half-a-knot of speed from *Kingfisher*.

She loved to sail. She had always loved to sail, to see what a boat could do, but more than anything else she was a racer and what she loved, what she excelled at, was pushing her boat to the very limits of its capacity.

She spent those 94 and a bit days seeking and finding that little bit more from her boat, and when she became a national heroine she was largely misunderstood. Her video diary was broadcast on television, and in its course, she wept from self-pity. She learned about despair without despairing. She was seen as immensely brave, being female and standing just five-foot-two, but she wasn't being brave at all. She was racing. So you get on with it, don't you?

Soon, *Kingfisher* was to be given a proper overhaul: 'It'll be hard, but I have to see it as a chance for her to put her feet up.' Not an atom of jest in this statement.

'On the last night I was checking the sails every 20 minutes. The moon was so bright I didn't need a torch. And I went out once and found a whole school of dolphins swimming alongside in the moonlight.'

And all at once her eyes went misty. She continued, in a voice with a choke in it.

'It's not hard to see why it was hard to get off that boat.'

Later she got back on that boat, photo-op, sponsors to please. Shooting Tower Bridge, its roadway raised in double-salute, in the bows a small figure dwarfed by that sky-reaching mast, left arm wrapped easily about the forestay, right arm raised, fist clenched.

Not a person you meet every day.
Which of us is mad? Which sane?

~

In snooker, more than any other sport, the neurotic is cherished, beloved, indulged and admired. In this sport more robust and — if you like — more manly talents get far less love, far less acclaim.

Ronnie O'Sullivan was the third in a line of unstable, delicate geniuses who have taken snooker to unexpected levels of perfection. The problem they shared was winning. Alex Higgins won the World Championship just twice, overcoming his own unquiet nature on both occasions. Jimmy White was forever runner-up. And O'Sullivan, going back to the Crucible for the World Championships at the age of 25, had yet to win. He was the best player — at least when it came to playing snooker shots — but many wondered if he would ever put together the results needed to win the greatest championship of them all.

Steve Davis, who won the World Championship six times, loved the game to distraction. 'Of course it's all right to talk during sex,' he once said. 'So long as it's about snooker.'

But O'Sullivan often hated snooker. He first retired from the game at the age of 18, and he had been retiring and unretiring with dismaying regularity ever since. He seemed a living embodiment of the difference between a talent for playing a game and a talent for winning games.

There were times when O'Sullivan played very close to perfection. In the final of the tournament against John Higgins he put together four frames of such voluptuous kinetic beauty that it left you dizzy: the rapture in action. But he couldn't do that every single time, and that failure dismayed him. He knew he could do it sometimes. So why didn't he do it every time?

Like all these geniuses, like many other sporting geniuses, sport was the thing he found easy. It was the stuff that came in between sporting events that tried him. He could play snooker like God: but his talent for life was more elusive. And yet, at times, even that was all fine by him. He talked with admiration of John McEnroe and Eric Cantona. 'I like mad people,' he said. 'Anyone who is a bit normal, I think is boring.'

Those four perfect frames were followed by a passage of uncertainty. Perhaps some observers thought that this period of self-doubt revealed his neuroses, but that was very wrong. It was the perfection that revealed O'Sullivan's strange and troubled nature. Was it marvellous, marvellous beyond belief, to live through such a passage of sport? But the problem with touching perfection is that it makes everything else in sport and life seem drab, pointless, worthless ...

~

He'd surely be the last man to get served at the bar. A couple of years ago, the stewards had denied him entry to the winner's enclosure at Cheltenham – even though he'd just trained the winner of the Gold Cup. It wasn't just that he was young, only 31 now. It was the meek way he carried himself. So unassertive you hardly noticed he was there.

This was Aidan O'Brien, who was running Ballydoyle on behalf of ruthless billionaire racing interests, knowing that if ever he started failing to deliver winners he'd be out of the place without a moment's pause for regret. He had just trained Galileo, winner of the Derby, and Imagine, winner of the Oaks, and for most trainers that would be glory enough for a lifetime. For O'Brien, it was routine. Not something to get worked up about. The horse did the running. But he was pleased, you know, pleased for the horse.

Sport is by definition about uncertainties, and the uncertainty is doubled in the horsey sports because horses can't speak. So if you're a trainer, it's all about your capacity to understand. Some guess. Some guess very well. One or two actually know.

'It's about not harming the horses, mentally, or physically,'

O'Brien said. Painfully shy in interviews involving eye contact, but his subtle, quiet, utterly confident self gradually reveals itself when he is talking the horsey talk in his own acres at Ballydoyle. And right now he was talking of the great hurdler Istabraq: 'If you tune his mind up too early before a race he will slowly destruct his body ... you have to be very careful as you tune his mind up. He has that much adrenalin in his body, he can't last long in that stage.'

But who knows when enough is enough? Who knows when to stop before it is too much? That's all down to the trainer: and the strange processes of tuning in: tuning in across the boundary of species and getting hundreds of tiny decisions right in a single day, millions in a year. Here was a special nature: was there a little madness in it? How do you know when a horse is right on the limit?

'I don't really know ... you *know* ... and he knows ...'

Behind all the diffidence was the most colossal self-belief. It was O'Brien's job to know.

~

There is Good Goran, a damn good tennis player. Then there is Bad Goran, sometimes known as Crazy Goran, whose racket-smashing rages and violent mood swings had so often got in the way of victory. Then there is the Third Goran. 'He is real emergency situation. He is 911 guy. Ace, ace, thank you every much.'

Goran Ivanisevic had been discussing his own nature at Wimbledon. He was no longer high enough up the rankings – he'd sunk as low as 125th – to get an automatic invitation, but he came in as a wildcard, because he is a player much loved. He would, it was thought, add drama to the occasion. And wildness.

He did. Especially as Pete Sampras went out in the fourth round to a young player – one said to be quite promising – named Roger Federer. Ivanisevic elaborated, weaving this fantasy of his doubly divided self. 'When it's a question of surviving, then you can't have three Gorans there – you have to have one if you want to survive. But probably mixture between bad one, good one and this 911 emergency one. He's a special one. It's tough to describe. That one is the brain one. He is the one there, emergency one, like all the emergency. When it's tough, he comes in, steps in. Sometimes he cannot help, because Crazy Goran is too crazy to help him or good one is too good to do something. He has a tough job.'

These complexities always kept Ivanisevic a notch below top-rank. His was not the kind of madness you find in champions. He lacked the singularity of nature that permits no compro-mise and allows, at least for a while, sustained and perfect self-confidence. Ivanisevic was almost joyously fallible. It was a trait that made for drama and made him widely beloved but it meant that the record of Sampras would be forever beyond him.

All the same, he got to the final, beating Tim Henman in a patriotic orgy that lasted three days with rain delays. This was the year the top players fell one by one, leaving the title open to someone of the second rank. It was Henman's year, in short: but alas, he failed to embrace his destiny.

Ivanisevic did instead. He won the final, which took place on a Monday after the rain. He beat Pat Rafter in five sets of ebb and flow. At 8-7 in the final set and serving, he muffed three match points: no chance here of Sampras's second-serve ace. No chance that nothing whatsoever was going through Ivanisevic's mind. He was double-faulting, crying dementedly for a return of the one lucky ball among the six on court, living and dying, rising and falling, losing and winning almost on alternate points.

But finally he won the last point of the match, to great joy. Some said this was the greatest men's final they could remem-ber. It was the most dramatic, but it was not the best. That took place two years earlier.

So this Wimbledon offered two of the ways we enjoy sport. The semi-final with Henman was about partisanship, the final was about drama. For the third and highest level you had to look back two years. Or forward, you can always look forward . . .

~

The events of 11 September did not stop sport. It just made sport look silly. This was not an outpouring of grief, as there was with the death of Princess Diana, for grief is an aspect of a personal relationship, no matter how one-sided. Instead there was the sense of bewilderment: and the weight of the realisation that the world had changed forever. It was not just the terrible nature of the events: it was the eerie question of what would happen next that preoccupied us all. At base was the certainty that no good could come from this. The world was a worse place than it was last week.

The weekend routine of sport came round far too quickly. But even before it arrived, they had agreed to postpone the Ryder Cup, the biennial golf match between the United States and Europe – scheduled for a few weeks later – for a year. They don't really get international sport in America: for the most part they look inward on their quartet of endemic sports. But it was clear at once that the forthcoming golf event needed to be stopped before it became an embarrassment.

In Europe the sport continued: an embarrassment to itself, in defiance of the needs and wants of most people. The events generally included somewhat sheepish ceremonies, minutes of silence and black armbands. Then they went right ahead: there were, after all, financial considerations and contractual obligations.

'We are in a state of concern and wonderment,' Murray Walker said, as commentator for the British television coverage of the Italian Grand Prix, 'as to what is going to happen about pit stops.'

'Disaster,' said Martin Brundle, Walker's co-commentator, 'for Rubens Barrichello.' The petrol-pump attendant had picked up the wrong hose and cost Barrichello six or seven seconds. Disaster indeed.

On Sky's football coverage, Richard Keys claimed that football was 'playing its part in bringing back some kind of normality'. But no one was really ready for normality.

It's what we do – we're footballers. Such was the mood in the game, embarrassed but oddly defiant. But being in professional sport is not like being a dustman. You're not needed every week, and there are times when you're not wanted at all. But at least there was the consolation of the 'off' button.

~

One kick to save the world . . . and David Beckham struck it clean. It was perfect. The world was safe, Beckham was safe: because of that kick, in the 93rd minute of a qualifying match against Greece, England were now going to the World Cup finals in Japan and South Korea the following year.

England weren't going. The match was almost at an end. And then they were going. Because of one kick.

One kick from David Beckham, the daft little fop, the villain who had got himself sent off against Argentina three years earlier and been hanged in effigy in his sarong. He was now captain, he was now leader, he was now saviour. At once everything was possible.

Beckham played the entire match in a frenzy, apparently trying to fill all four midfield positions at once. He had a series of chances to score from free kicks just outside the penalty area and blew every one of them. So he might have turned down that last one: after all, Teddy Sheringham offered to take it. But no. This one's mine. And it was – and yet it wasn't, because it was also everybody's.

That's because he was playing for England. He was not just

playing great sport for his club, he was – so it seemed – playing great sport for us all. So it was our goal. That draw – the match ended 2-2 – was our victory. It was joy beyond analysis: for analysis would only have spoiled it, proving only that England were no worse than the 32nd best national team in the world.

Better to savour the saviour and salute the salvation of the world: the single kick that saved us all. And of course we knew it was nonsense, of course we knew it was pretend, of course we knew it was all make-believe, of course we knew it didn't solve any of the problems that the events of 11 September had set. But for a moment it gave us a glorious tale of redemption. What could we do but cheer?

- Ronnie O'Sullivan has five World Championships at the time of writing.
- Aidan O'Brien continued a career of almost unbroken success. The Coolmore operation that backed him became the most powerful force in racing, taking over from Godolphin.
- The Wimbledon victory was Goran Ivanisevic's only Grand Slam singles title. He retired for the last time in 2004.

BOOK 20

2002

There is only one sport.

That's because all sports are the same: you do something silly with immense seriousness, and somebody wins and somebody loses. It follows that all sports are equally compelling, equally enjoyable, equally futile.

It's only familiarity and the soap opera cast of characters that make a difference between one sporting encounter and another. Forget that and you have but a single sport. Any argument against is silenced by the Winter Olympics in general and, in particular, the women's curling at the Salt Lake City Games.

In slow motion, Rhona Martin and her team slid beneath the nation's guard . . . or behind the nation's guard stone, if you prefer. The slow build-up became oddly compelling, and, on the night of the final, people tuned in to watch in millions – and stayed watching as a very tight match against Switzerland went to the last stone. Five million people in Britain watching curling at one o'clock in the morning.

The last stone of the last end, the tenth, was launched by Martin: a lump of polished granite rendered weightless by its friction-free passage along the ice, Martin calling out instructions to the gracefully progressing stone, two other team members sweeping clean its passage as it moved with agonising slowness towards the house, the gathering of the other stones. A red-tagged stone of Switzerland was in the dominant position, the winning position, the gold medal position – but Martin had the final say.

One stone to save the world.

And it was as if the stone, tagged yellow, tagged gold if you prefer, was travelling on a long predetermined course as it entered the house, slithering past the guards, and ever so gently, ever so subtly nudging aside the Swiss stone to take its place, nestling there at the house's heart. It was Britain's first gold medal at the Winter Games since Torvill and Dean and *Bolero* in 1984.

Partisanship had drawn in millions and the intense pursuit of victory kept them there. Victory made the experience and the tale part of our lives: a dream of victory that took place when sleep seemed a wiser option. There are no such things as good sports and bad sports: there is only sport.

~

Paula Radcliffe was an athlete doomed to finish fourth. But only after leading every step of the way until the last 100 metres. She was one of those tragic figures of sport, embracing gallant failure and futile heroism. Then one fine spring morning in London she emerged from the chrysalis of failure and took wing.

She left the track and its maximum distance of ten kilometres and entered the London Marathon, four times longer. She ran the first half of the race very fast and established a decisive lead. She then did something still more remarkable: she accelerated. She ran the second half of the race quicker than the first: what runners call a negative split.

What was hard had become easy. Where exhaustion should have cut in she found exhilaration. Here was Paula Unbound: enraptured: newly revealed as a person ruthless and uncompromising in seizing the victory that was her right. It was a poignant thing to witness: who does not cherish the idea of moving from disappointment to world-conquering success in a single bright morning of inspiration? Who would not relish the joy of knowing that all life's previous failures were, had the world but known it, vital preparation for today's glory? She finished the course in 2 hours 18 minutes 55 seconds, the fastest time for a women-only race and the second fastest time in history. All London was Paula that day.

~

David Beckham spent four years at war with time: seeking to undo the act of folly by which England lost to Argentina in the World Cup of 1998. It was not an error of sport he had to overcome, a failure of technique or strength or skill. It was the failure of his own nature. Beckham was revealed as a man of perfect technique and unstable temperament. He had been made captain of England; he scored the goal against Greece that got England to the World Cup finals in Japan and South Korea. And so, with one of sport's great plonking ham-fisted bits of inadvertent drama, England were drawn in the same group as Argentina.

The match took place in the horrible indoor stadium at Sapporo. England looked sharp, purposeful, gaining confidence as the match advanced, particularly as Argentina were terrified by the pace of Michael Owen. Owen hit the post – and then, a little later, he was brought down in the penalty area by Mauricio Pochettino. Penalty.

Who to take it but Beckham? Who to taunt him, even as he placed the ball on the spot, but Diego Simeone, the hair-ruffling opponent Beckham had so disastrously kicked in St Etienne four years earlier?

This was one of sport's classic binary situations. Score the goal and you find redemption, fulfilment, revenge, a reckoning, and emergence from the chrysalis of failure. Fail and it's all the same as before, but a billion times worse.

Not a great penalty, as it happened. The goalkeeper, Pablo Cavallero, might have stuck out his left hand without moving and saved it. He almost did: but he had already committed his weight to the right, just as Gordon Banks might have told him not to, and so he had disastrously wrong-footed himself. Or had Beckham done that for him, by giving the eyes to the place he was not hitting the ball? Either way the ball struck the net, not terribly hard but in an earth-shaking and life-changing way for Beckham. Once again he had one kick to save the world: once again the world was saved and Beckham with it.

And now there were whispers that England might win the World Cup: that here was the best team England had taken to a World Cup finals since 1970. This was a team that could rise to an occasion: and that is the sort of team that wins in tournament football.

~

Work in progress.

That was James Joyce's codename for *Finnegans Wake*, chosen for his love of secrets. It required 17 years of progress, but it got there in the end: the undisputed mad masterpiece of modernism. But in modern sport, the phrase 'work in progress' means not very good, but we're hoping for improvement. And if you're a work in progress – well, you don't have to deliver. You can beat Denmark 3-0 in the round of 16 and have the supporters performing a conga all round the stands, but when you play Brazil in the quarter-finals you're not expected to win, because this is, after all, a work in progress.

They were the Golden Generation, and the deadline for

delivery was always two years off. Or four years off, when the next World Cup comes around.

There's a standard negative in the language Bahasa Melayu, or Malay: *belum*. It means 'not yet'. Do you speak Malay? *Belum*. It's a lovely word that seems to open the way for a boundless future of high achievement. Has the Golden Generation won the World Cup? *Belum*.

England scored first, Michael Owen again, from a fine pass from Emile Heskey. Brazil equalised, Ronaldinho setting up Rivaldo with an almost grotesque shimmy.

From directly behind his shoulder blades, in a straight line from Ronaldinho to ball to far post, you could see from the set of him what was intended. A free kick: too far out for a direct shot ... except it wasn't: a great loopy, swirly effort that made an ass of poor David Seaman, the England goalkeeper. He was prepared for every eventuality except the stuff that lay beyond his limited imagining. Ronaldinho's free kick was simply too far out.

Ronaldinho was sent off for a tackle in the 57th minute, giving England more than half an hour against ten men. But, alas, they were already beaten. The soaring imagination of Ronaldinho's free kick had undone them: they were not worthy. And besides, next time round they'd be *really* good.

~

Mike Brearley, the former England cricket captain, once said that the result of every sporting event tends to be seen as (a) inevitable and (b) morally appropriate. Destroying the profession of sportswriting in a line.

We love the narrative nature of sport, and it is our tendency to turn any sporting event into a story, preferably a 19th-century psychological novel. Our preference is that the good end happily and the bad unhappily: that is what sport means.

It follows that we frequently underestimate the importance of physical abilities as we construct our narrative. We operate on a notion that, at elite level, most contestants have roughly the same degree of skill, but the winners are psychologically stronger – and if they happen to be from our nation or our favoured club, it's proof that they are morally superior.

But we are not made equal, and nor are elite athletes made equal. Ian Thorpe of Australia was perhaps the optimum build for an aquatic human: six-foot-five, with immensely long limbs, colossal power and – a detail that charmed far beyond its relevance – size 17 feet. He weighed 16 stone 5 pounds, heavy for a swimmer, but he had the flexibility to exploit the added power the weight gave him. He also had something still rarer: a complete affinity for the water. As Mark Todd rode a horse, so Thorpe rode the water. He seemed like a new species of humankind: *Homo aquaticus*.

It was a joy to watch him swim at the Commonwealth Games in Manchester. With many great performers there is an illusion that they are moving in slow motion while everyone else is at normal speed. With Thorpe, that was no illusion. He was making 29 strokes for every length of the pool while everyone else was in the mid- to high thirties. In a tight finish – on the rare occasions there was such a thing – he seemed to get more languid as the race came to a conclusion. He set a world record in his first race at the Games: for the 400 metres freestyle, 3 minutes 40.08 seconds.

It was another of these fleeting, tantalising glimpses of perfection.

Perhaps that is part of sport's eternal allure: you can, occasionally, and sometimes for seconds at a time, understand what perfection means.

~

Natalie du Toit had a body that was marvellously well put together for swimming. Then, as she was on her way to training, her motorbike was hit by a car and she lost half her left leg.

The Manchester Games were revolutionary. They included events for disabled athletes and the medals won were identical to those won by the athletes in the usual events. Du Toit won gold medals in the 50 metres and 100 metres disability races. She also reached the final of the able-bodied 800 metres.

At longer distances, leg power is less important than it is at the sprints. The rhythm slows, so that a swimmer kicks only once for every arm stroke, rather than kicking the water into Guinness, in the manner of Ian Thorpe. It follows, then, that an amputee has a better chance against able-bodied competitors at longer distances . . . That's the biomechanics of it: but that doesn't mean it was not a quite extraordinary achievement. It was also a drastic change of emphasis for people who watch sport and are accustomed to seeing bodies closer to perfection than most. It took, it seemed, only the smallest adjustment: du Toit was cheered mightily and where once people might have felt distaste they devoured inspiration.

'Swimming was my life and still is,' du Toit said. 'The water is a gift that gives me back my leg.'

~

Oh yes, those champions with adamantine minds, teak hard, Kohinoor hard . . . compare and contrast with the figure slumped on the chair, someone who was losing, it seemed, rather more than a tennis match. He kept reading and rereading the same piece of paper. Gill Allen, hyper-alert photographer, caught it in an over-the-shoulder shot. It was addressed to: 'My husband – 7-time Wimbledon champion'. It was full of motivational messages: 'Remember this. You truly are the best tennis player ever to pick up a tennis racket.' Words inscribed in neat capitals by Bridgette Sampras. What terrible scenes of doubt had played out between them that she needed to compose this touching epistle? Doubts revealed first in privacy to the person he was closest to in the world; and then revealed to half the population on earth.

For Sampras lost. No matter how many times he read the letter, he lost. He lost in five sets. He lost to George Bastl, ranked 145. The photographed letter remained unprinted: it was, after all, a piece of private correspondence.

Here was Icarus after the wax on his wings melted; here was Samson newly barbered; here was Superman encountering green kryptonite. Here was a champion tasting life as an ordinary man: and learning that being a champion destroys the pleasures of ordinariness.

A broken champion. It was the day of perfect trauma, not something you see an athlete recover from.

A few weeks later, Sampras reached the final of the US Open in New York, the year's last Grand Slam tournament. He played Andre Agassi and he won. That was his 14th Grand Slam title. He had been given back himself. And so he gave permission for the newspaper to print the photograph of his letter. Weakness could be admitted in this moment of strength. Privacy was set aside in this final detonation of brilliance.

～

The Ryder Cup is as unfair as the penalty shootout. Both put unfamiliar demands on a player, demands for which he is likely to be unsuited as well as unprepared. Tournament golf is about being alone, with responsibility for no one and a world in which all the world is your enemy, even your closest friend. It's a hard and difficult world though it suits some.

But the Ryder Cup is all about taking responsibility for others, being a leader, being a follower, taking one for the team and doing it right so that others might prosper.

There was a just-audible gasp as Tiger Woods took his putt on the tenth on the first day of the Ryder Cup – taking place at last, postponed for a year after the events of 11 September 2001 – at The Belfry in England. He was playing a foursomes match: that is to say, two players a side with one ball between them. Wood's partner was Paul Azinger, but Woods didn't seem to have noticed. He just continued playing poorly. Every nuance of body language was that of a person who wished to be somewhere else. And the match swung on that hole. Woods left his putt short: and that is a significant sin in this format – nothing less than a complete giveaway that you're not playing for the team. Woods was not making the stroke with his partner's needs in mind. Tiger was as happy as a wet cat.

And yet there, playing for Europe, was Colin Montgomerie, who always fell short in the high and lonely demands of tournament golf. But he was almost unbeatable in the Ryder Cup. In the cosiness of the team he could find all the good things in his game that he often mislaid when he was alone. His features in competition were memorably described as 'like a bulldog licking piss off a nettle'. And yet here he was sunny, outgoing, and generous: Monty Unbound, even enraptured. If it were possible to have a temperament transplant, and Woods and Montgomerie made a swap, would Montgomerie have won eight major titles, as Woods had at that stage? And would Woods, for all his talent at striking a ball, have none?

In the context of a team event, Woods was Icarus Unwinged. Even if he was the greatest golfer ever to pick up a golf club.

Sport treats its champions like this.

It is infinitely more cruel to the rest.

- Brazil won the World Cup, beating Germany 2-0 in the final. Ronaldo, Brazil's star forward, scored both goals. Diego Simeone went on to manage Atletico Madrid with some success, and Mauricio Pochettino became manager of Tottenham Hotspur.
- Ian Thorpe won five Olympic gold medals and 11 World Championship gold medals in his career. He retired and

unretired several times. In 2014 he came out as gay. He has suffered from depression and drink problems.
- Natalie du Toit swam in the 10km 'marathon' open water event at the 2008 Olympic Games and finished 16th.
- Pete Sampras stayed retired.

~

BOOK 21

2003

Winning is the hardest thing in sport. That's why sport is structured to create events of ever-increasing intensity: each one harder to win than the one before.

It's not just that the opposition gets better. Sporting events are designed so that, with each advance, each participant has the opportunity to play worse. Great sporting occasions are designed to inhibit: to flood the athlete with fear: to suppress the skills that the athlete has spent a lifetime acquiring.

Sport is like walking the kerbstone with the gutter growing deeper and further away at every step. At first it's easy. But by the time the drop from kerbstone to gutter is 10,000 feet, it's a little harder. There is a Zen parable of the monk who escapes a ravening tiger by leaping off a cliff and grabbing a plant to save himself. It's a strawberry plant. He looks thousands of feet down: at the bottom of the ravine stands another tiger. The monk plucks a fruit and eats it. 'What a delicious strawberry!'

Pete Sampras saw only the nature of the tennis ball he held

in his hand as he prepared for that second-serve ace. David Beckham saw only the ball's aerodynamic potential as he prepared for that Earth-saving free kick. The moment of perfect present: that's what athletes seek when sport reaches its points of greatest intensity. Seek, and seldom find.

England were the best rugby union team in the northern hemisphere and perhaps in the world. Yet on three of the previous four occasions, in their final match of the season, the one that would have given them a perfect record – the infinitely desired Grand Slam – they fell at the last, beaten by Celtic opposition that was statistically inferior.

England went to Dublin to play Ireland, and once again they needed only this last win to complete a Grand Slam. They needed this with something not far from desperation. That's because the World Cup was taking place in the autumn and they were already favourites to win it. It was their year. If they could make it so.

Jonny Wilkinson, the fly half, tackled like a rat trap that day, and kicked for goal with astonishing precision. But his tactical kicking was awful. There was a paralysing sense of fear about England, for all the discipline of their defence. They made good attacking positions but then committed offences and got penalised. Again and again.

Sometimes in a match there is a point when everything suddenly becomes easy. When all at once you have no idea what all the fuss was about. When suddenly you realise that the kerbstone is six inches wide and anyone can walk along it. It was in the second half that the England forwards set up a perfect situation, Mike Tindall came in at speed, smashed through two tackles and scored. All at once England were flat-track bullies. They won 42-6.

Losing, they said, was 'unthinkable'. So they thought about it all the time. Losing was 'too awful to contemplate', so they contemplated it for all they were worth. Staring at tigers, staring at the terrible drop to the cruel rocks so far below.

And then in an instant it was all right.

Delicious strawberries.

~

Who wants to be ordinary?

A long glower around the room. He had them transfixed. A big man with a big voice and big belly. And a presence.

Who wants to be average?

Sydney is regarded as the Olympic Games at which Great Britain retook their place as an elite sporting nation. Not in swimming they didn't. Swimming was as dire as ever. For the first time since 1936, Britain didn't win a swimming medal of any colour at the Games. So they hired Bill Sweetenham. He was now three years in the job and taking warm-weather training for the endurance swimmers in Cyprus.

Come on, guys, this is a no-compromise workout. You're being kind to yourselves!

A swimmer finished the last 150 metres of the set he was working on and set his best time of the day. Bad mistake. The mistake of a man who didn't know his coach. 'You were saving yourself! You were holding back!'

A last harangue, Sweetenham, huge on the poolside, seven goggle-eyed faces looking up at him from below ground level. He more or less blotted out the sun.

'Compromise is not something I consider,' he explained. Unnecessarily.

There is an extent to which all coaches are actors. Sweetenham loved to be the purveyor of brutal wisdom. Part of his mission was coaching the coaches: to create a culture of uncompromising pursuit of excellence. 'So you want them to have a soft workout this morning and soft workout in the afternoon and then we give them a morning off? And then maybe a soft workout tomorrow afternoon?'

Such a schedule is fine ... if you want to be ordinary.

Exceptional people must do more. Must want to do more. Or at least accept the principle and do more.

So when does the relationship between coach and athlete become abusive? At what point does a no-compromise coach become a bully? Or is the coach not a bully at all: merely the vector through which the supremely bullying nature of elite sport is transmitted? If you want to win a gold medal, you must take on an impossible life. There are ways of ensuring that the athlete does, indeed, do all that's possible to seek a place at the very top, and for some, it is in a relationship with a dominant coach. Every great athlete needs, at some level, to take on some kind of brutality in life, whether that is imposed from the outside or from within. Talent is rarely enough in any sport, and hardly at all in the heartland Olympic sports.

You don't have to accept that. You can always walk away. And be ordinary.

~

The comic side of all this was that this was the year they wanted to make tennis more beautiful by means of legislation. At least, that was the intention of a loose band of ex-champions. They were concerned that the advancing technologies of racket construction were spoiling the game: lighter rackets and huge sweet spot made the game easier in terms of technique and therefore more amenable to sheer power. They were concerned that elite tennis was becoming a bashing contest. Losing its tactical nuances. Losing its sense of touch. Losing its beauty.

There comes a time when any rising athlete has to stop being promising, abandoning that comforting state in which you are constantly admired and praised for all the things you haven't done yet. In 2001, Roger Federer was promising, and he beat Pete Sampras in the fourth round at Wimbledon. The following year, still promising, he went out in the first round, beaten in straight sets by Mario Ancic.

The year after that he went to Wimbledon and was never promising again. It was a rare example of promise kept. And even if that single tournament had been all he ever did in sport, it would be recalled as a masterpiece. It contained beauty of a kind few of those ex-champions could have matched. And there was also a serene certainty about it all. He had to win. Even the annual British glorying in the adventures of Tim Henman was set aside, for Federer was taking sport into another dimension entirely. Federer pushed tennis way beyond partisanship and way beyond mere drama, soaring to unprecedented heights of excellence: and, in doing so, he created a new kind of partisanship. This was a constituency of his own, and it was one that cheered for the nation of excellence.

Tennis had never looked like this before. It was as if Federer issued instructions to the ball, and the ball carried them out slavishly. Even when he hit the ball to a ball boy, often with an almost horizontal racket, it was a thing of beauty, the ball nestling in the ball boy's hands sweet as an alighting dove. In action Federer created a startling illusion: it was as if the court he was aiming at was twice the size of the one he was hitting from. The ball seldom seemed to land far from him, and yet there were vast Serengetis of space for him to aim at on the other side of the net.

Before the tournament began, people had been tipping Andy Roddick to take over from Pete Sampras as Wimbledon's unstoppable master of serve. He managed only four aces against Federer in their semi-final. In the final against another big server, Mark Philippoussis, Federer did that thing that great players can do: and raised his game. At the end of the first set and the beginning of the second, Federer delivered a genius-storm, a passage of the rapture, winning the tie-break and then breaking Philippoussis twice in succession. That settled it.

And if there was opportunity to wonder how Federer might follow this quite extraordinary achievement – for he was only

21 – there was still greater meaning to be found in what he did that day. The experience of something so close to sporting perfection is radically different from glorious partisanship or brilliant drama. The Centre Court applauded Federer all right, but not to purge their feelings, as they did for Henman or, two years previously, for Goran Ivanisevic. It was so that Federer might know that his crowd understood how good he was: to show him they genuinely appreciated the rich, rare stuff he was offering. Most people probably wanted to leave at the end in awed, head-wagging, shoulder-shrugging, gape-mouthed silence.

It was not to be confused with a religious experience: but all the same, it was not unlike a religious experience. There was a sense of greatness that did not diminish the onlooker: rather, it lent a little greatness to all those who shared the moment.

～

There is a famous photograph of the England football team, taken in Berlin on 14 May 1938. The entire team is performing a Nazi salute. It was 'to the eternal shame of every player and Britain as a whole', said Sir Stanley Matthews afterwards; and he was one of the saluters. The instructions to salute came in spite of the players' desperate wish to refuse. Ultimately they came from the prime minister, Neville Chamberlain.

Now the England cricket team were scheduled to play a match in Harare against Zimbabwe as part of the World Cup. And no one wanted to issue any instructions whatsoever.

The match was likely to require the England captain, Nasser Hussain, to shake hands with the Zimbabwe president, Robert Mugabe. Such an act would look like England's symbolic acceptance of Mugabe's policies of torture and genocide: a parental blessing from the mother country to its turbulent offspring. Sport is good at symbolism, remember, better than almost anything else in the world.

The International Cricket Council said that there was no problem with this. This was their money-making tournament and they had no interest in political problems. Or morality. The England and Wales Cricket Board declared that they were as entitled to trade with Zimbabwe as anyone else: as if the England cricket team was a soft drinks company. They said they would only refuse to go if the government ordered them not to – provided the government gave them £10 million. Which was not going to happen. So many people passed the buck that, in the end, a major decision on international politics was left to someone who happened to be quite good at cricket. 'A few years ago I was a kid playing for Ilford second XI,' Hussain said. 'Now I'm expected to make a political judgement on whether I should lead the England cricket team to Zimbabwe and perhaps shake the president by the hand.'

Sport is a process of heaping increasingly unfair demands on those who take part: here the principle was carried to a genuinely unhinged level. In such circumstances you can't suddenly become an expert on post-colonial politics, or take a quick doctorate in ethical philosophy. All you can do is rely on such decency and courage as you possess. Hussain chose not to go. England forfeited the match. England went out of the competition at the group stage, partly because of this decision, and partly because of some poor cricket. Hussain resigned as one-day captain at the end of the tour. It was a hopeless mess, caused by a seemingly endless round of buck-passing.

But there is no photograph of the England cricket captain shaking hands with Robert Mugabe in Harare.

～

How hard can it be to claim your own? There was fear in England's narrow victory – 28–17 – over Wales in the quarter-finals of the Rugby World Cup in Brisbane, settled in the end by a brief genius-storm from Jason Robinson. The semi-final against France took place in a time of high wind and horizontal rain, and so it was all about who had the most reliable kicker. So that was all right then: Jonny Wilkinson scored all England's points – five penalties and three drop goals – as England won 24-7.

The final in Sydney was a puzzler. Partly it was England's reluctance to put the game beyond Australia's reach; partly it was a bizarre performance by the referee, André Watson, whose ambition seemed to be to make the game as close as possible, with only passing regard for the actual laws of the game.

It was close all right. It went to extra time; it went to the last minute of extra time. In the course of the match England had set up two drop goal chances for Wilkinson and he missed both. The score was tied at 17-17 in the last minute when England gained possession from an ill-advised kick from Mat Rogers. Martin Johnson, the England captain, called the play: zigzag. To set up yet another drop goal attempt. Matt Dawson, the England scrum half, made a scuttling run as Australia dropped back, anticipating a pass to Wilkinson; he picked up damn near 20 yards. With Dawson, by definition the team's best passer, at the bottom of the ruck, Johnson had the wit to pick up the ball and run into contact, gaining a good centimetre or so. Dawson, wriggling free, collected the ball from the ruck and sent a pass whizzing to Wilkinson. And it was a good one.

One kick to save the world.

He took it on his wrong foot, his right.

There was a truly terrible children's serial imported from Australia in the 1960s. It was called *The Magic Boomerang*: when this boomerang flies through the air, all time stands still!

So it was that night as the ball went end-over-ending into the black Australian sky. Everything seemed suspended, including the ball itself, in that impossible fragment of eternity. In the stadium where Cathy Freeman had almost literally run her heart out for Australia, the ball hung there like an oval moon. In that moment of stillness – no one on the field was able to do anything either to help the ball's flight or to impede it – all fates were settled one way or the other. Then came the bile-taste of defeat for Australia; and for England, a sense not so much of joy but of relief, of the vomit-inducing kind that's almost worse than defeat. Relief of the kind that Freeman herself has endured.

~

Great sporting events, especially those with a nationalistic tinge, tend to unite the nation in question. Some would say, unite them in a bad way, in hatred of foreigners, ugly resentment of the success of others and gloating triumphalism in rare victory. Inga Lund is a country many would deny in the face of all the crowing cocks of history.

Two weeks after the final of the Rugby World Cup the England team took an open-topped bus ride through London. Three-quarters of a million people came out to greet them. These were not rugby people, there aren't enough of them. The crowd was everybody who had been caught up in the story that had led to that impossible climax on that Sydney night. It had been the most wonderful tale: it needed an epilogue in which the homecoming heroes could be celebrated.

I won't have sex except with Jonny. Jonny, I want your babies. Johno, show us your bum. A selection of banners. They climbed bus stops to give a wave. They mounted pillar-boxes. They stood in gangs on the roofs of bus shelters. They hung from windows; they clambered from windows onto ledges and rooftops. They were all people who'd had their hearts lifted as individuals and as members of a nation, and they were out there in freezing weather to celebrate. They were white, black and brown of skin, male and female, children, teenagers, old codgers and everyone in between. It wasn't even terribly boozy: just a chance to say hurray. Hurray and thanks. It was a day of joy unstinted and unambiguous and uncomplicated and, above all, shared.

Sport can do this.

- Bill Sweetenham left the Great Britain job in 2007 for family reasons. His vindication came the following year.
- In Zimbabwe's opening World Cup match, the former captain, Andrew Flower, and Henry Olonga, the first black African to represent Zimbabwe, wore black armbands. They made a statement: 'We cannot in good conscience take the field and ignore the fact that some of our compatriots are starving, unemployed and oppressed.' They beat Namibia in a rain-affected match. Zimbabwe reached the Super Sixes stage of the tournament, which is more than England did (Zimbabwe were helped by England's forfeiture of the points from their scheduled match) but they failed to make the semi-finals. Australia beat India in the final.
- Robert Mugabe was ousted in 2017 after 37 years in power.

~

BOOK 22

2004

Athletes have two great vices: the future and the past. Their virtue is the present: the rare moments in a sporting career when they're actually playing.

At all other times they are committed to the future: always preparing for this or that event, and, often enough, the event itself is the preparation for one still greater.

Eventually, and almost always with appalling reluctance, they retire. Then, often after a painful – to all concerned – series of unretirements and re-retirements, they are forced to admit that their meaningful life is over. For an athlete, the age of 35 is not *nel mezzo del cammin*. It's the end of the road. At this point their relentlessly future-gazing eyes swivel through 180 degrees and the past acquires a meaning and a relevance that the future can never threaten.

But the truth is only ever in the action. In the eternal now of sport.

~

All his sporting life was a decline from that week, that one week in Portugal when he was 18. Nothing would ever top it. Wayne Rooney was never a man given to introspection, but perhaps even he sensed it.

At the time everyone talked about what he might go on to achieve: what lay ahead. That feeling of infinite possibility was part of the glory of that fine, warm week when even the Atlantic looked inviting. But it was what happened in the now that counted: the impossible things taking place before our eyes.

It all began so badly, too: and perhaps that was what made it all so splendid, at least for a while. England were leading 1-0 against France in their first match of the European Championship, but in the closing minutes Zinedine Zidane scored twice. So when England played Switzerland they needed cheering up.

Rooney was right on the edge of control; perhaps a little beyond, for his strength was also his weakness, as always in sport. He had been booked once and looked as if he was going to get booked again. He was playing with naive recklessness and outrageous physicality: a playful young bull released onto a field full of old bullocks.

It was his youthfulness that made it joyful: the glorious impetuousness of it all. He was able to use collisions with other players as a kind of Newton's cradle: rebounding off defenders while impossibly still in balance, the ball still impossibly under control, his pace still impossibly rapid.

He didn't look like a footballer. He looked like a fan, a kid who had invaded the pitch for a bet.

He scored England's first goal against Switzerland with a header, which was followed by an ungainly monster cartwheel, a boy who had no idea what dignity meant nor why anyone should bother with such a thing. England made heavy weather, even though Switzerland had a man sent off: it was a classic example of England's angst-ridden tournament football. But with 15 minutes to go, Rooney made an edge-of-control charge through the defence and smacked the ball against the post. It rebounded, hit the goalkeeper, and re-rebounded into the goal.

A few days later, England were playing Croatia in Lisbon. England went a goal down, equalised, and then Rooney gave them the lead with a galumphing net-buster. Croatia had to press for a goal, and Rooney caught them on the break for his fourth goal in two games.

Nothing would ever be quite as good again.

~

Andrew Strauss scored a century on his Test debut for England against New Zealand at Lord's. He came in because the captain, Michael Vaughan, wrenched a knee. So who would be dropped when Vaughan was fit again? Probably for the next Test?

In the second innings, England were chasing 283, Strauss was on course for his second century in the same match – until he was run out by England's former captain, Nasser Hussain. All the same, the incomparable beauty of promise dominated the match.

What could Hussain do? He scored a century himself, making the second 50 in 45 balls, reaching his hundred and, moments later, hitting the winning runs. He then retired from cricket.

Perfect.

He had taken on the England captaincy when England cricket fell to the bottom of the world rankings with that defeat against New Zealand in 1999. Since then England had risen, were once again a serious force in world cricket. Hussain's anger, his hatred of those who gave anything but their best, had transformed England from worst to almost-best. He was aided by the coach, Duncan Fletcher, with whom he struck up an invaluable alliance, and by the institution of central contracts for

England players, freeing them from the relentless will-sapping, body-crushing routines of county cricket. All these things mattered – but Hussain's anger was at the heart of England's revival.

He was booed on the balcony of The Oval after his first series as England captain. He was cheered unendingly at Lord's when he completed his last innings for England. It wasn't true that nothing became him in his England career like the leaving of it: but, certainly, he brought things to an end with panache.

Now the future was for Strauss and the others. They could take on Australia – due in England the following year – without Hussain. He had rejected self-pity after that unfortunate run-out; he had rejected self-pity after he had been booed. Both times he responded with the stubborn anger that was the remaking of his team. His team was now – well, really rather promising.

And somebody else's.

~

It is the most shattering experience of a young man's life, when one morning he awakes and quite reasonably says to himself, I will never ... play ... the Dane ...

That's Uncle Monty in *Withnail and I* – and it's a common human experience. Not as good as you hoped. Some realise this when kicking a ball against a garage door.

There is failure on every step of the stairway save the very last. Best defend yourself by never trying the last flight, best stay on the landing of the nearly-greats. Or the landing below, where you find all the damn good pros. Stay at lower level because the knives of failure cut sharpest and cleanest when the summit is in sight, and deepest of all when it seems that one more step will do. It's like the character in Henry James: 'Osmond, in his way, was admirable; he had the advantage of an ingrained habit. It was not that of succeeding, but it was something almost as good – that of not attempting.'

Almost all sporting careers end in failure, even if, like Steve Redgrave, Pete Sampras and Nasser Hussain, you time your exit with perfection. So it was that David Beckham attempted to lead England to their first major international trophy since 1966, and in the quarter-final England failed, and England failed because Beckham failed.

One kick. One kick to save the world.

And this time he missed.

It was a penalty shootout following England's match against Portugal, home nation in the European Football Championship. England's hopes were already soaring gloriously skywards, thanks to Wayne Rooney.

Beckham chose to lead the way, to set the tone, the example. And did so. I'll take the first one, lads. I'll show you how it's done. Alas, his penalty soared skywards: his nerve lost at the moment the overwhelming question was asked. England never recovered from Beckham's miss and Portugal won the shootout 6-5. The Portugal goalkeeper, Ricardo, saved a shot from Darius Vassell and then scored a penalty himself: a little self-certainty on an evening of self-doubt.

Beckham had set out to be the greatest footballer in the world. So do we all, so do we all, but he carried that ambition deeper into maturity than most of us, and there were times when it seemed perfectly feasible. He was good enough, his team-mates were good enough – surely Beckham would take the doubters with him and bring home the glory.

People who dare great things – even in the little world of sport – suffer in ways beyond the imagining of those with smaller hopes.

The great Portuguese writer Fernando Pessoa wrote in *The Book of Disquiet*: 'I've had great ambitions and boundless dreams, but so had the delivery boy or the seamstress. What distinguishes certain of us is our capacity for fulfilling them.'

Every book that attempts to tell the truth about sport is a book of disquiet.

~

Simon Worrall, journalist and very decent club tennis player, had an assignment to write about some child prodigy of the game. He was mid-forties, the girl was 11. He was pretty fit. He had more shots, more power, more nous, and a man's weight of serve. He played a full set of tennis against her and lost. So far as he remembers, he played better tennis. It was just that the girl declined to lose.

'I don't want to get better,' she was saying six years later. 'I want to compete. I fight and I really want to win.'

She was ten when she went from Russia to stay by herself at Nick Bollettieri's tennis academy in Florida, youngest in her dorm by six or seven years. It was horrible. 'I never cried.'

In the final of Wimbledon Maria Sharapova, aged 17, took on Serena Williams and won 6-1, 6-4.

Sometimes inexperience is an asset. Sometimes naiveté is a strength. She stepped out onto Centre Court against the most fearsome player in the history of women's tennis, and when the ball came to her, she gave it a wallop. 'To tell the truth I didn't have a big tactic going into the match. I was just there to play my game and figure out a way to win and figure out what I needed to do to get used to her game.'

So play as if you were playing Simon Worrall: wallop the ball when it comes to you, don't lose, and remember to win the last point of the match.

For Sharapova, as for Wayne Rooney, the truth was in the action. They showed the same contradiction between the classic teenage body language of uncertainty and bluster, and sport of astonishing self-certainty. And with both, it was as if a new age had opened up before us. Surely we were watching the greatest talent the world had ever seen in this or any other sport. What could possibly go wrong?

We are seduced by such thoughts, even while knowing that they are a betrayal of the moment, a betrayal of sport's essential now. Few of us realised, or even stopped to wonder, if this year might be the summit of two great careers: that their greatest talents might be for beginning rather than sustaining.

Sport reflects our normal lives in many ways, that's why we are forever watching the stuff. But there are very few worlds in which you can achieve the highest thing of which you are capable before your 19th birthday.

Rooney, Sharapova: boundlessly gifted. Cruelly, severely, almost cripplingly gifted.

~

Paula Radcliffe arose from a lifetime of disappointments to become a glorious unchained queen, taking on the marathon and making it her own. She followed that first run at the London Marathon with another still better. As she did in her first, she ran away from the field; as she did in her first she ran a huge negative split. This time she set a world record: 2 hours 15 minutes 25 seconds.

By the time she reached the Olympic Games in Athens she was a lay-down certainty for the gold medal: the marathon queen taking her own in a race that started at Marathon – where else? – and finished at the gorgeous marble horseshoe stadium that was built for the first modern Olympic Games of 1896. It seemed that every circumstance had conspired to bring about her success.

How awful it was. She suffered a physical breakdown with 18 miles to go. The eating part of marathon running is a difficult thing and Radcliffe got it drastically wrong; no doubt the tensions of the occasion made it worse. She was brought to a halt by vicious stomach cramps and ended up sitting on the kerbstone weeping as if her heart had broken. Sport had promised her everything she wanted and then snatched it away at the last moment.

But it was more than that. It was as if she believed that without victory she could not be loved. That her life, her nature, her being could only be validated by an Olympic gold medal. Without such a thing she was nothing.

She faced the press with courage and honesty ... and found herself surrounded by males who spoke to her in their softest, most cooing voices, with downward-looking eyes, soft arm-pats, gentle cupping of the elbow and a general agreement that asking a difficult question would be like mocking the sufferings of a wounded bird.

It was like being part of a bereavement.

Radcliffe didn't run as if victory was the most important thing in the world, she ran because it actually was.

Was that why she lost?

~

There's a devastating line in Kipling's extraordinary book about his schooldays, *Stalky & Co*. Unlike practically every other school story ever written, *Stalky* is explicitly concerned with what happens next: where all this education will lead the boys who are outwitting the teachers, playing pranks, smoking hard, dealing out mayhem and playing the fool with pistols. The teachers – sorry, masters – are conferring and one declares that Winton is 'a first-class type; absolutely first-class'.

'Ha-ardly,' said the Reverend John. 'First-class of the second class, I admit. The very best type of second class ...'

That was Kelly Holmes. First-class of the second class. Absolutely splendid athlete, no doubt about that. One of life's minor medal-winners. She was now 34 and had spent her racing life dealing with injuries and racing gallantly home just behind the winner: bronze at the Olympic Games four years ago (she had led with 50 metres to go), silver and bronze in the World Championships of 1995, silver in the World Championships of 2003.

The final of the 800 metres took place on the day of Paula Radcliffe's tear-drenched press conference. And as the race got towards the business end, Holmes found herself alongside Maria Mutola, her long-standing rival, who always beat her. That's the way life was supposed to be: and everybody accepted that.

But suddenly Holmes was going past her. It was the sun rising in the west, it was the world rotating backwards, it was the stars stopping in their courses, it was water flowing uphill, it was a moment that required a radical rethink about the kind of person you happen to be and the kind of world you happen to live in.

Holmes swept past the finish ahead of all the rest – and was still unable to believe what was happening. She was bewildered. The sort of thing that doesn't happen was clearly happening, and she lacked the equipment to cope.

Athletes normally know when they've won a tight finish. This was tight all right, but not that tight. Holmes crossed the finish line and raised her arms: and at once her face flooded with disbelief. She lowered her arms in slow motion, staring at the electronic scoreboard, waiting for the result to come up and confirm that, once again, a minor medal was hers.

But it didn't.

She had won and eventually even she believed it. A few days later she was in the final of the 1500 metres and she won as if victory was her inalienable right, going wide round the last bend and running away from the field in the straight. She had pulled off the double that Sebastian Coe never managed. It was reckoned to be the greatest feat of middle-distance running in British history. Saving the best till last, but not as policy. It was more a question of never giving up, and finally running a major championship when free of injury.

First-class type; absolutely first-class.

~

Should you aim for victory, then? Or should you aim higher? For pure excellence? Should you seek to redefine the possibilities of sport? Or confine your attentions to the winning of gold medals?

And while you're pondering these questions, what should the sport itself do? Should it encourage the risk-takers, the barrier-busters, the redefiners? Or should it reward those who fulfil the brief and do so without error?

Gymnastics has always attracted risk-takers, but had always rewarded those whose priority was avoidance of error. The scoring was essentially negative: a maximum of ten marks, from which marks are deducted for error. It encouraged an approach based on the virtues of not making mistakes.

The entire sport changed in a quarter of an hour in Athens. The standard in the men's competition had been set by Paul Hamm of the United States, who had already won the all-around competition by elevating competence to something not far from brilliance ... but there was a restless feeling that this wasn't quite right. People came to the gymnastics to see humans fly. They didn't want the best of fliers penalised for their daring.

Alexei Nemov of Russia took his turn on the high bar in the individual apparatus final. High bar demands greater height, greater flight and greater risk than any other piece of apparatus. He performed a routine full of flying elements. It involved six separate release moves; four of them in succession, movements in which the gymnast is travelling through space under his own power, unattached to anything.

The mark was shocking. Gasp-making. Impossible to believe: 9.725, placing Nemov third with several other gymnasts to come. There was an outbreak of anger at the judges, at the sport itself. Sport is an artificial world in which we can control a good deal of what goes on: here the wrong notions were being encouraged. This was a kind of blasphemy against gymnastics, against sport. It wasn't a partisan-type protest. It happened because the notion of excellence was being betrayed.

Nemov's mark was adjusted to 9.762, still not enough for a medal. Nemov eventually stepped up and asked the protesters to keep quiet. And the sport carried on.

Knowing that it had to change forever.

- Maria Sharapova never mounted a sustained challenge to the dominance of Serena Williams, but she collected five Grand Slam singles titles. She was for 11 successive years the world's highest-paid female athlete, so sporting greatness is not everything in sport. At the Australian Open of 2016 she failed a drugs test and was banned for two years.
- Paula Radcliffe won the New York Marathon a few weeks after the Olympic Games, and the London Marathon in 2005. She took time off and had a daughter, Isla. She returned to sport and won the New York Marathon in 2007 and 2008. She finished down the field in the marathon at the Beijing Olympic Games of 2008. Her world record for the marathon was annulled in 2017, when it was decided that no record set before 2005 was acceptable.
- Kelly Holmes retired from athletics in 2005.
- Gymnastics abandoned the old perfect ten and went for open-ended marking, in which the more successfully completed moves a gymnast pulls off, the higher the mark.

BOOK 23

2005

That willing suspension of disbelief for the moment that constitutes poetic faith.

That's Coleridge. And sport.

You suspend your disbelief in sport's importance. That means that you reactivate your lost innocence, accepting – for the moment – that these things are what they seem: amazing, revealing, meaning-packed, contested by people who have a right to haunt your imagination.

You don't cease to be a grown-up when you watch sport, but you suspend a certain worldly wisdom, a certain hard-earned grasp of the essential realities. You accept sport on its own terms; at least for the moment.

That's not being wilfully stupid any more than accepting the adventures of the Ancient Mariner makes you stupid. You can't understand with arms-folded cynicism. You must submit to its spell.

That's why Britain in general and London in particular was

filled with innocent joy on 6 July, when it was announced, to epic surprise, that London – and not the favourites, Paris – were to hold the Olympic Games of 2012.

For most people it was a joyous prospect: hurray for sport and, as Brendan Behan unforgettably wrote, fugh the begrudgers. The idea of the 100 metres final taking place in London, or the gymnastics – or, well, everything, the whole lot, 200-odd countries and 10,000-odd athletes all there in pursuit of glory and medals and excellence and beauty and wonder – and all in our place, breathing our air.

It was a day when, it seemed, the city and the nation danced for joy.

~

The end of the world at half-time.

Joy beyond measure less than two hours later.

Sport can do this.

But what do they think now, those Liverpool supporters who walked out of the stadium at half-time and set off into the Istanbul night in search of a beer good enough to wash away despair? Liverpool had fallen behind in the first minute of the Champions League final against Milan, and by half-time they were 3-0 down. They knew there was no coming back from that.

How do they cope with the fact that they were there – but they weren't there?

For Liverpool did come back. In a mad second half inspired by their captain Steven Gerrard they surfed a wave of excitement that at first seemed nothing more than a spirited defiance of reality. Gerrard scored the first goal with a header, Vladimir Smicer got another with a rather improbable long-range effort, and then Gerrard was brought down in the box. Xabi Alonso took the penalty; it was saved but he put away the rebound.

Extra time. No more goals. So penalties.

It's not destiny. It just seems like it. Is that what the players thought as they went through the strange ritual of the penalty competition? Or did it only seem like destiny afterwards, when the uncertainties of sport are remembered as if everything was preordained: both inevitable and morally appropriate.

For it did feel as if the match had been decided by forces more powerful than the footballers on the pitch. After all, Liverpool were seriously outgunned and mostly outplayed. Milan, it seemed, were fighting a hostile destiny rather than a second-class football team (the very best sort of second class, naturally). So it was that Serginho missed the first penalty for Milan, put off by the mischievous posturing of the Liverpool goalkeeper, Jerzy Dudek.

The goalkeeper's fear of the penalty is a myth. For a goalkeeper it's the one situation in which there is no fear, or very little. If a goal is scored, well, that's what's supposed to happen. If the goalkeeper makes a save, it's gloriously beyond the call of duty. A penalty competition makes the goalkeeper the underdog in each individual kick – concealing the fact that he is ultimately in the position of strength.

Dudek saved the second penalty, from Andrea Pirlo, and then, with the score 3–2 in Liverpool's favour, he saved from Andriy Shevchenko. Shevchenko put it straight down the middle, Dudek managed to reach back and get a decent hand on it even while he was diving away.

It was called the Miracle of Istanbul. It was no miracle, just sport, just football – but the Mildly Improbable Incident of Istanbul wouldn't have had the same ring to it.

Instead, it was as if Superman had made the earth rotate backwards to rescue what was dead and buried. The euphoria of the occasion was available to all those who had suspended their disbelief.

~

That moment of commitment. That moment when you take the first step on a great adventure ... the hand sliding along the back of the sofa, or blinking in the sun at the top of aircraft steps, or putting your foot into the stirrup iron and taking your weight from the ground ...

What will happen next?

This is not wishing your life away. This is savouring the beginning of something that might be wonderful and might equally well be the worst humiliation of your life.

You could sense this all along Wellington Road to the Nursery, the walk from St John's Wood station to Lord's: an excitement that was so much greater because it was shared – and because it was so liberally mixed with fear.

England had a cricket team. A very decent cricket team. First-class – well, certainly first-class of the second class. England had a chance in an Ashes series. For the first time in 18 years there was a belief that England might beat Australia in a Test series. It was almost too good to be believed: it imparted a dizzying sense of euphoria and terror.

Absurd that it should mean so much, but it bloody well did.

If we can just make a contest of it. If we can just win a few sessions, if we can just make the Australians take us seriously. If we can make them – however briefly – feel inadequate. Second class. Not quite good enough.

The problems included Shane Warne, the great leg-spin bowler, and Glenn McGrath, the equally great seamer. Australia had been the best in the world for years, mostly for those two reasons. The fact that England had for years been seriously woeful was not a factor in Australia's rise to the top. But under Nasser Hussain England had shed that woefulness and now, with Michael Vaughan in charge, they were a little closer to believing that they might – well, make a contest of it. Win a session or two. That's all I ask, people said again and again as they marched towards Lord's.

Then came the second ball of the series.

It was delivered by Steve Harmison of England to Justin Langer. It was short, but not drastically so. And it leapt. It leapt savagely. It struck the Australian batsman Justin Langer on the elbow and he went down like a skittle; a brutal and painful blow.

There was a sudden gasping hush.

And in that instant 13 players out in the middle, nine more back in the dressing room, several thousand people in the ground and millions watching on television all felt the same thing.

Bloody hell.

This is serious. This is serious cricket and England have a serious chance.

There was a pause of gratifying length while the physio attended to Langer and got him back up again. The series had already changed. We-just-might had become we-bloody-well-could.

Intoxication.

~

Andy Roddick came onto Centre Court in the Wimbledon final with a game plan: to blow Roger Federer off court. He played with speed and power. And by the time the first set was over he had the uncanny feeling that he was doing exactly – but exactly – what Federer wanted. He had a spooky notion that a driving, aggressive, all-power game backed by the finest serve in the tournament was precisely what Federer had asked the waiter to bring. As if each violent, precisely struck serve was the very thing that Federer wanted most. Roddick was broken twice, lost the first set 6-2.

So Roddick raised his game. Terrific. That's what top tennis players do. Broke Federer's serve. Right back in the match now. He had taken Federer's best and had now found his own A-game.

So Federer raised his game. Again. Because that's what

Federer did – and he had more raises than anyone else. You keep raising your game till it's the ultimate expression of your capabilities – and Federer will then find one more raise. He broke back, and took the tie-breaker emphatically.

Rain delay. Roddick came out with intent – and, in a classic seventh-game break, Federer took command and won the final in straight sets: 6-2, 7-6, 6-4.

You could, if you wished, have found that boring. But people didn't, not really, even though it was a match without the usual agonies of alternating advantage. People found it hard to see the point of Pete Sampras six years ago when he beat Andre Agassi by the same margin, but very few doubted the value of watching Federer. Federer's perfection was acceptable where Sampras's was not.

With Sampras the beauty was subtle, the tactics and execution were obvious. With Federer, it was exactly the other way round.

~

It's all about who wants it most.

That's what they say. They say it even when there are only two athletes or teams in the contest, and they mean who wants it more.

But in the true grammar of sport it's often about who wants it less: or who, at least, can forget the circumstances of the occasion and play the ball.

Perhaps that was Tim Henman's ultimate failure: he wanted it more. And the wanting got in the way of having. And doing.

But there's no shame in failure in sport. Most people fail, at least to some degree. The shame is not giving the best of what you have – or worse, in not attempting. And Henman always did both those things. He never stinted himself. He gave everything his talent and his nature permitted. Could he have won, should he have won, in that Wimbledon when it rained and he lost in the semi-final to the eventual winner, Goran

Ivanisevic, in three days of locker-room waiting with occasional outbreaks of tennis?

Maybe – but, if so, the only task was to forgive him.

It was a small indoor tournament in Basel. He was now 31, and facing an opponent aged 18. A lanky, promising lad with a prickly nature, a touch on the ball that might remind you at times of Roger Federer, and a knack of taking on big names without anxiety. Playing the ball, not the name, as you're supposed to. But as so few promising teenagers can.

Andy Murray, of course.

For once, though, Murray let the situation get in between himself and the match. That was in the second set: perhaps something told him it wasn't fitting to beat Henman in straight sets. But he shaded the tie-breaker in the third, winning 6-2, 5-7, 7-6.

The thrill of promise: that treacherous thrill of promise. Henman had been cheered and cheered again, and we thought there would be no one to follow him. But here was another talent that might be almost as good. Or perhaps . . . never mind. In that match in Basel there was the thrilling, fearful sense of commitment: as if we were setting off on a new adventure. This was not the impudent savouring of imaginary future triumphs but the scintillating taste of possibilities: the start of an adventure that would bring disappointments for sure, but might, just might, bring something more. And even if it didn't, it would be a journey worth taking.

'I've passed on the baton,' Henman said afterwards, in his agreeable way. 'Or is it the torch? Anyway, whatever it is I've passed it on.'

~

Well, it was a great journey and a great summer and, if it's to end in disappointment, we had a good run for it, and if the disappointment feels both cruel and crushing, that's only because we all cared too much. If we get crushed to death by the pitiless wheels of the Juggernaut's chariot, we have only ourselves to blame. Only our adoration of the idol put us in so vulnerable a position.

The first Test that began to promisingly with the blow to Justin Langer's elbow ended in defeat, and a classic England batting collapse. But then England established a position of dominance, one compromised only by their inability to deal the killing stroke when required. Modesty Blaise, in the greatest thriller sequence of them all, talks about 'stab-fright' and 'trigger-freeze': the inability to commit at precisely the time when commitment is required.

England established a position from which winning the second Test was a formality and almost contrived to lose it, winning at the last gasp: that phrase no metaphor but a more or less literal description of the nation's mood as they watched the nightmare almost but not quite coming to pass on that endless Sunday morning.

The third Test saw England draw – but the Australians were the ones celebrating, and their celebration gave England fresh heart. They scrambled a victory in the fourth Test, requiring the unlikely intervention of a Matthew Hoggard cover drive to close things out. And so to the last: The Oval. Win or draw and England regain the Ashes, winning an Ashes series for the first time in 18 years. Lose and –

– but no. Impossible to think of such a thing. Except of course it wasn't.

That last day. The crowds emerging from Vauxhall station and walking down the Harleyford Road, looking anxiously at the sky. They were looking for rain. They were *hoping* for rain. Just about everyone following the cricket in England – and that summer it was millions – would have settled for a day of solid rain, including – perhaps especially – those who had paid their admission money. They would have sat through downpours and drizzle eating damp sandwiches and drinking rain-diluted beer in plastic glasses and done so rejoicing if not a ball had been bowled, for that would give England victory in the series.

It really seemed as if life and death depended on such a thing.

And it began to go wrong. Hopelessly, inexorably wrong: disaster materialising in front of the crowd in slow motion, like an imagined monster slowly becoming real.

England began the day on 34 for one in their second innings, Australia still to bat again. All – all! – England had to do was to bat for 98 overs. Soon they were 133 for five. Glenn McGrath took two in two balls, the hat-trick ball went straight through Kevin Pietersen and there was an appeal like the Hound of the Baskervilles howling for its prey. The umpire, Billy Bowden, somehow gave the correct decision: not out, came off his shoulder.

But Shane Warne got him out: a catch to Matthew Hayden – no! Dropped it! So now it was the turn of Brett Lee, bowling at frightening pace in the murk. In a few more immortal words of Brendan Behan, Pietersen was bitched, bollixed and bewildered. And he gave a catch that fizzed through to Warne at first slip: reverse the hands and take it, easy, a great slipper like Warne doesn't miss those.

But he did.

Lunch.

What happened next? Here's the version from Michael Vaughan, the England captain; the first voice is Pietersen's.

'Skip, what do you want me to do?' He looked at me in a very sheepish way. He had been battered by the short stuff before lunch and was a little rattled. I took a breath and asked him two very simple questions. Kev, what sort of cricket have we played all series? When do you play your best?

He paused and then just said: 'I like to attack.'

So I just laughed and said, 'There you go. You go out after lunch and try and take them on. If Brett bounces you again you must attack it and try and score. One hour of you and the Ashes are ours . . . and by the way . . . fuckin' enjoy it!'

Pietersen came out after lunch and went for Lee in a manner that was wild, reckless and deranged. Had he failed he'd have been the man who lost England the Ashes.

But he didn't.

In 13 balls from Lee he scored 35. He also scored heavily off Shaun Tait. But McGrath and Warne he played with circumspection. For all its madness this was an innings of thoughtfulness and intelligence. By the time he was out for 158 there was no more time for Australia to win. A draw was now inevitable. England had surely won the Ashes.

They made a tee-shirt to commemorate the occasion. It said: Now I Can Die Happy. It scarcely seemed an exaggeration. That afternoon, partisanship, drama and excellence combined in a way that the country hadn't seen since 1966.

~

But don't let's miss out on the glorious bathos of the end. England were all out for 335, the light fading fast and little time left. But regulations are regulations. Australia came out to bat needing 342 runs in about half an hour. After four fierce deliveries from Steve Harmison the umpires took the players off for bad light. For 16 minutes the playing area stood empty, the sky above one vast dark cloud, one that brought vast leaping solar flares of joy to the watching crowd. Or did we still believe that, somehow, this marvellous thing might be snatched from us at the very last? Eventually, like temple handmaids performing an obscure but necessary ritual, the umpires came out again. Each one removed the bails from a set of stumps.

Match over. Match drawn. Series won.

England have the Ashes.

The Ashes is or are a tiny and truly absurd trophy, one that never leaves the Lord's Museum. England reclaimed something that Australia had never held in any physical sense. The trophy that wasn't even a trophy was surrendered, having never even been held. It existed mainly in the minds of the millions who followed the series: and they made it, for that summer, not only real but the most important thing in the world.

Eighteen years.

～

It was a lovely morning. And for once the papers were full of good news, nothing but good news, the best. London went to work in sunshine.

'Trust me,' said a piece in *The Times*. 'Seven years of whinging, rows, misery, scandals, spin, claptrap, disasters, backstabbing and sulking will be followed by the greatest celebration of life that London has seen, that Britain has seen, that the world has seen.'

London was to stage the Olympic Games. And the buses and the tubes and trains and streets were full of people talking to each other for once – and, if not, it was a chance for a good old think – and about good things for once.

I wonder if I could get tickets for the 100 metres final.

Gymnastics, I have to see the gymnastics: especially women's floor and the men's high bar.

There'll be all those free events, won't there? Triathlon in Hyde Park, cycle racing round Surrey, marathon all over town.

I'd like to get into those really funky sports. Handball, for example.

Is it right that they're holding the archery at Lord's? Can't resist that.

Yes, but what about beach volleyball on Horse Guards Parade? Surely that was what gave London the edge in the final vote.

Wonder if we'll win lots of medals? We must do, surely.

Rowing's always a good place to start. Isn't that going on at Eton?

Yes, but the horses will be right in the middle of London: Greenwich Park, they'll be practically jumping into the Thames for the water jump.

It'll be one great big street party, won't it?

God, I hope nothing goes wrong. Like that lunatic in Atlanta, the anti-abortionist with his pipe bomb.

But we're good at dealing with that stuff these days, aren't we?

And really it's the sport that matters, isn't it? That and the joy.

Yes, you're right. Sport and joy.

Bring it on, eh?

At 8.50 that morning, three bombs were detonated, one near Liverpool Street station, another near Edgware Road station and a third near Russell Square. An hour later, a fourth exploded on a double-decker bus near King's Cross. There were 52 people killed and more than 770 injured.

Why?

No one ever got to the bottom of that, but no one ever does. Terrorists create terror. There's nothing else to it. And to target a city in a joy adds to the terror very considerably.

Sport, it seemed, had become a matter of life and death.

And perhaps that horrible day there was a feeling that if that's the case – well, better vote for life, then.

~

There are no what-happened-next notes for this chapter. All these are stories that will and must be picked up later.

~

BOOK 24

2006

He was incapable of doing wrong, incapable of failure. Nothing could go wrong. A setback was only an opportunity for still greater glory.

It was easy.

Andrew Flintoff was now captain, albeit a stand-in, of the England cricket team. England went to India where they hadn't won a match for 21 years. They drew the first Test and lost the second by nine wickets. They were seen as a rag-tag outfit, with the leading fast bowler Steve Harmison and the captain Michael Vaughan injured. The Test defeat reinforced that impression. Flintoff was a man short of options and out of his depth.

And then this.

In the third Test in Mumbai the Indian captain Rahul Dravid won the toss and asked England to bat. It didn't work. England made 400, with Andrew Strauss scoring 128. There are times when disadvantages work the other way: in Harmison's absence, Jimmy Anderson led the attack, took four for 40 and England had the advantage. They struggled with the bat in the second innings, but Flintoff scored his second 50 of the match. It took him three and a half hours, and on a long, almost static day of cricket it was impossible to know whether England were batting with masterly restraint or poking gingerly at the chance of a cricketing lifetime. The answer to such things comes with the result, for sport delights in such simplicities. So India had a chance, yes, and more than a chance as they batted on that final day and they reached 75 for three.

And 100 all out.

Gaudy, glorious, impossible times, times when it all goes right. Flintoff bowled like a man possessed, taking three for 14 in 11 overs. It was a personal triumph but, above all, a personal triumph of leadership. Flintoff's band of new bugs, afterthoughts and selectorial punts came good and won a supremely unlikely victory which moved them up to second in the world rankings.

He'd been asked about captaincy after the Ashes victory the previous year. 'If I was ever to do the job,' he said, 'I'd have to do it as one of the lads.'

Wince-making, yes?

Many thought that making Flintoff captain, even on a temporary basis, was certain disaster. It would destroy his own ferocious abilities by means of responsibility, in exchange for the vast tactical nous he clearly did not possess. And yet here was Flintoff conjuring one of the rarest kinds of victory, and all of it dedicated to the one-for-all spirit of laddishness. He got the big one, too. Dravid looked as if he could bat for a week without error, but he touched one from Flintoff to the wicketkeeper and set India's collapse in motion. Shaun Udal, brought into the team at 37, produced a beauty to dismiss Sachin Tendulkar.

Flintoff was a man who could do no wrong.

~

And here was another.

A dramatic personal superstructure is prima facie evidence of inferior performance, but not in this case. True, he was dressed for tennis in the manner of Natty Bumppo or first assistant to the pirate chief, but as soon as you saw him striking tennis balls all this stuff fell into place: an essential extension of his sporting ability.

Rafael Nadal was now 20. He had won his first Grand Slam title in Paris the previous year and was back to defend it in calf-length trousers and feel-my-pecs vest, headband barely containing a ferocious black haircut.

There was a sense of ownership in that swagger, and that was what made the swagger important. Nadal's statement of outrageous physicality might have been designed – perhaps it was – to impose itself on the mind of a single opponent.

Roger Federer.

Well, who else? Here was Nadal in the first round of the French Open, striding in as champion and winning his first match against Robin Soderling for the loss of eight games. Already it was clear that we had not just a tennis player and not just a champion. We had a rivalry.

Nadal's overstressed masculinity made Federer's style look no less exquisite ... but perhaps the teeniest bit wimpish. Nadal took on a clay court with an explosion of power: as if an animal rather than an artist had been turned loose. The power and depth of shot, combined with relentless topspin, were there to intimidate. The physical appearance – physical presence – was all part of the package.

Tennis is a dispute about ownership of place, in which a trespasser can be quickly despatched by the rightful owner. Here was Nadal establishing rights of ownership.

He already had a winning record over Federer, 5-1 up, after beating Federer in Rome just 16 days previously. He had done so by making tennis a thing of physical splendour. True, Federer made tennis seem like a game of metaphysical splendour, but in Nadal he found a man and technique capable of putting his nose out of joint.

So we had a perfect contrast, and that is the making of those eternal rivalries of the kind that tennis goes in for rather more than other sports: repeating duels creating the shape of the sporting routine. Borg–McEnroe, Evert–Navratilova: we now had Federer–Nadal.

And already the greatest champion of them all was coming second.

~

This was not a fixture for martial metaphors. A group match at the World Cup finals, held in Germany.

It offered the sort of clodhopping irony that only sport can produce. It seemed to be embarrassing for everyone involved. A rivalry that dare not speak its name.

Germany v Poland.

Must we?

But there was no way of getting out of it. And then it became clear why Germany had bid for the World Cup.

So that German people could cheer for Germany and not feel embarrassed. Even when they played Poland.

It's all right. History is only history. The people who did those terrible things were dead or in their dotage. For most people, it was no longer 'that time'. It was 'that period in history'. The country was democratic, prosperous and unified. It was surely all right to cheer. This wasn't a rally: this was a football match. It was patriotism, but that's OK. Isn't it? Because it wasn't nationalism.

If you're a nationalist, you believe that your country is better than all the others, and therefore has rights over all the others. A patriot is different. A patriot can have a sense of irony. Resignation. Acceptance of national flaws. A certain cynicism. Perspective. Balance. Sanity. Acceptance of national setbacks.

Generosity to other nations, to people from other nations. All that sort of thing. You can still cheer for your national football team: but you know it won't go to your head.

We can deal with such stuff these days. Trust us.

The local derby was played with all the intensity you'd expect. Poland were unrecognisable from the side that had lost 2-0 to Ecuador. And certainly, the two best forwards on the pitch were born in Poland. The trouble is, they were both German: they both moved across the border as children: Miroslav Klose and Lukas Podolski.

As so often in fraught matches, the two sides cancelled each other out, or perhaps no individual had what was necessary to seize control. At 90 minutes, the match was scoreless. A minute later, Oliver Neuville scored for Germany.

Much cheering.

Football, you see.

～

All about who wants it less.

Four years ago Felipe Scolari – Felipao or Big Phil – won the World Cup as manager of Brazil. This time round he was managing Portugal. He said: 'My priority is to ensure that players feel more amateur than professional. Thirty to 40 years ago, the effort was the other way. Now there is so much professionalism, we have to revert to returning players to like the game, love it, do it with joy.'

That's a notion that covers two things at once. The first is that modern defences are more likely to be unlocked by a quarter-second of inspiration than by drilled, thousand-times-practised routines. The second is that matches are more likely to be lost by a player overwhelmed by the nature of the occasion than by one playing the ball with innocent confidence.

But who can play a penalty shootout with love, with joy?

～

By this time it was clear that club football was now at a higher standard than international football. The evolving game was consistently producing sustained, controlled performances by the world's leading clubs, performances beyond anything that could be hoped for from what were essentially scratch sides. This was coached football v pick-up football – but pick-up football was more important.

More important in non-football terms. That's because non-football people get caught up in international football tournaments. Sporting agnostics turn to football and the team's progress becomes a thing shared: triumph, anguish, anger, exasperation and above all hope. And we participate in millions.

Wayne Rooney crashed to earth like a stricken oak a few weeks before the tournament, suffering a broken metatarsal, just like David Beckham four years previously. It felt like the most terrible curse, and millions of people in England were eaten up with concern about a single small bone.

The England squad responded with a single small German word throughout much of the competition, and it was not *freude*. It was *angst*: and the theme of the tournament was the *Ode to Angst*: a symphony played to the tune of who wants it more. Or less.

England scrambled a victory in their first match against Paraguay and were struggling goalless against Trinidad and Tobago – till Rooney made his long-delayed return. He came off the bench with half an hour to go and seemed to bring joy and swagger to the game. That was his gift. More: that was the England game plan: take the tone from Rooney. And with Rooney on the pitch, England won 2-0. They drew 2-2 with Sweden in the third match to reach the round of 16.

They played Ecuador, and again it was a performance of massive anxiety. But David Beckham, ill, at one moment vomiting on the pitch, saved the day: a free kick on the hour from

30 yards, curling in a perfect, glorious and beautiful arc: and at once England were unbeatable.

Hope.

That's the best thing about tournament football, about international football: that shared feeling of hope. Surrounded by caveats and gallows humour, of course: but it might be all right. After all, it was only Portugal. England had a chance, a real serious chance of making the semi-finals for the first time since 1990.

Back then England had been inspired by Paul Gascoigne: and surely Rooney was an equally inspirational figure, a player capable of cracking a game open by the force of his presence and his will.

Only three matches and England have won the World Cup.

You didn't even have to believe it. Hope is not a matter of faith. It's the thing that keeps us alive, that's all. And here, savoured for a mere football match, was hope. It was there for all, and for the simple pleasure of hoping.

Who knows what we can do? Who knows what Rooney is capable of? He's back. England are marching forward. Hope, which is not the same as optimism, was sparkling in the air.

How wonderful it was.

~

If the fielding side permits the cricket ball to strike a temporarily discarded helmet, they are fined five runs. If a fielding side alters the condition of the cricket ball, they are also fined five runs.

The first of these is a clumsy, foolish or unfortunate error. The second is an offence against the higher morality of cricket, sport and life. It follows that to make an error in judgement about the former is a small matter. To make an error about the second is not.

Try explaining that. Try explaining that to, say, the man from Mars, when he has finished his visits to Watford and Luton.

You're not allowed to change the condition of the ball in a manner that helps the bowler to take wickets. Except you can a bit. You can polish it. You can spit on it. You can put sweat on it. You can clean dirt from the seam with your fingernail: all that's absolutely fine. But you can't put lip salve on it. You can't lift the seam with your fingernail. You can't deliberately abrade one side of the ball, even though you can deliberately shine the other.

Do one set of things to the ball and you're just a cricketer. Do the other and, in the words of Stalky & Co., you're frab-jously immoral.

In all sports there is confusion between legality and morality. It's not immoral for a footballer to be offside, but, at least in British circles, it's immoral for a footballer to pretend to be fouled. It's considered rather worse to commit a knowingly dangerous foul. In athletics, it's considered immoral to take illegal drugs, but right and proper to take legal dietary supplements. It's legal in some circumstances to take forbidden drugs under medical supervision.

International sport is by definition political. As soon as a flag mounts the flagstaff there's politics. And in some international encounters, like this one, there are also questions about reli-gion. And race.

Should a match official bear all this stuff in mind when making decisions? Or is it always and only about the laws and the rules of the game?

The fact is that Darrell Hair had no evidence that the Pakistan players were altering the condition of the cricket ball when they played England at The Oval. He just had a hunch. A feeling. He felt it in his water. And also, he had a taste for controversy, having no-balled the Sri Lankan spinner Muttiah Muralitharan. So he signalled that Pakistan were to be fined five runs and that the ball should be changed to one of England's liking.

You can accuse a woman of being a tease and cause little more than bad vibes. To call her a whore raises the situation to another level. If you wish to do that in public, you'd better have some pretty solid evidence. And Hair didn't.

The Pakistanis accepted the deduction, but in the tea interval they got together and a great unhappiness developed. They didn't come out to play on time. So Hair declared that they had forfeited the match: victory to England. After a while, Pakistan cooled down a little and were ready to continue. England were happy to do so. So were the team's two governing bodies. And so, for that matter, were the crowd and the television audience.

But Hair had declared the match over and so the match was over.

～

Steve Harmison declared the series over and so the series was over.

Unusual, that. For it was the first ball of the series.

England had gone to Australia with the highest hopes in the world, led by the unstoppable Andrew Flintoff. At last, England would travel to Australia and take them on. And surely win.

Till that first ball. Bowled in the horrible industrial stadium in Brisbane, the Gabba.

It flew straight to second slip – never went near a bat – where it was taken with the greatest nonchalance by Flintoff.

Doubt. Doubt as individuals, doubt as a team, doubt (if you like) as a nation.

～

The recovery from defeat in Brisbane was glorious, inspiring, all the stuff that partisanship brings you. In Adelaide in the second Test, England batted first and reached 551 for six when Andrew Flintoff declared. Paul Collingwood had made 206, Kevin Pietersen 158. Shane Warne returned figures of 167 for one. He was reduced to bowling round the wicket, wide of leg stump, containment his only goal, and Pietersen declared that Warne had been mastered.

Australia managed 513 in reply – a draw, then, for all money.

England 69 for one. A genuine recovery, then. Time to start thinking about Perth and the third Test.

Then the house fell down.

Shane Warne's imperious appeal persuaded Steve Bucknor to give Andrew Strauss out, caught off his pad, no bat involved – and with that moment of help, Warne took over. It was majestic, wonderful, appalling. Pietersen was bowled round his legs trying to sweep; the ball hit the outside of off stump. Mastered. The rest followed: England were out for 129 and Australia knocked off the rest with 19 balls to spare.

Tharn.

A word in *Watership Down*. It describes what happens to a rabbit in the headlights, and that was England's response to Warne, to the Australian team, to Australia itself. Had they attempted to score a few runs as they processed on and off the field, the task would have been beyond Australia, but they did no such thing. It was a wonderful victory. It was an equally wonderful defeat.

England supporters left white-faced, suffering from a kind of disaster-shock, as if they had been caught in an earthquake. To move from despair to hope to triumph to anxiety to despair, all in the space of a few days, was too much. This was a genuinely traumatic experience: for many the worst wound of a sporting lifetime, the more severe because of the greater hope involved.

And that surely is why we allow partisanship to play so great a part in sport. Where else but in sport would we get the opportunity to feel so bad, while knowing all along that it mattered not a jot?

England supporters felt wonderful the year before when England won the Ashes. Now they were paying the price for that exaltation. Willingly. Gladly.

And for all the anguish of Adelaide, and however much it felt like it, nobody died.

Sport had given England supporters the privilege of feeling

extremes of emotion without any risk whatsoever. It was an emotional stake that would never leave you bankrupt. All those who cheered for England, at the grounds or watching television or following events in other ways, were part of a great myth that was being written by us and for us – and yet at the end of it everybody went back to real life without so much as a scratch.

For many, this was the most intense experience of their sporting lives.

A privilege indeed.

- England were knocked out of the football World Cup in the quarter-finals, losing to Portugal on penalties. Wayne Rooney was sent off in the 62nd minute. The score was 0-0 after extra time. England scored only once in the penalty competition, losing 3-1.
- England won the series against Pakistan 3-0. In 2008 the International Cricket Council changed the result of The Oval match to a draw. The following year they changed it back to an England win.
- England lost the series to Australia 5-0.

~

BOOK 25

2007

Hatred.

It's part of sport.

You can hate the opposition. If you all hate the English, clap your hands. Stand up – if you hate Luton, stand up.

But the sweetest hatred is the one that comes when you turn on your own.

Sven-Goran Eriksson was welcomed as England's new football manager in 2002: the man to lead England to a glorious future. He was welcomed with intemperate, even incontinent hope. In 2006 he left the job to volleys of hatred: the man who betrayed the Golden Generation. But for his criminal ineptitude, England would have won at least three tournaments. Three successive quarter-final appearances were not success but failure.

He was replaced by Steve McClaren. After that, Eriksson didn't seem too bad. In the qualifying tournament for the 2008 European Championship, England had a goalless draw at home against Macedonia and lost 2-0 away to Croatia. This was followed by another goalless draw in Israel. Not good, it has to be said. It was already clear that McClaren was a man out of his depth. A decent man over-promoted. It happens.

Fat lot of good his decency did him. He became the first England manager to suffer prolonged and consistent abuse in the course of a 3-0 away victory. The place was Barcelona. The team was Andorra.

The television images brought us an almost orgiastic scene of hatred. This was not the hatred that comes from fear: this was hatred lovingly nurtured, for the deep pleasure of hating. This was the profound joy of destroying something of your own: turning out to watch the England football team and seeking to inflict on it the maximum pain and humiliation.

This hatred was sanctified by feelings of honour. The people shouting the abuse genuinely felt that they were doing the right thing, the noble thing. England deserved better: therefore they turned against those who represented England. And, in particular, the man in charge.

It's never been wholly clear what a football manager actually does. But his function has always been obvious: he's there to blame. He's there so that someone can be hated in times of defeat. Like the temporary kings of ancient times, he is there to be sacrificed when the crops fail. When the playing fields no longer yield a harvest of victory, he must give himself up to his own.

The fields were barren. Steve Barleycorn must die. There is joy in the distant past, and joy, too, in the unreachable future. But for the present, the only truth was hatred. It was therefore necessary to create a self-fulfilling prophecy of failure.

Only failure can license hatred, only failure can trigger change, only failure can create belief in the golden future of glory.

So failure became the most desired thing in sport.

~

It was a beautiful day.

It was a beautiful match.

It was a beautiful and necessary defeat for England.

And no hatred. That's what made it so beautiful.

They played 'God Save the Queen'. The England team sang it and so did 7,000 or so England supporters. And nobody booed.

And this was Croke Park. Croke Park, of all the places in the world to play the national anthem of England. Croke Park, home of the Gaelic Athletic Association, the only sporting organisation founded on avowedly political grounds, and anti-British grounds at that. When the GAA was founded in 1884, you could have nothing to do with the organisation if you played football, if you played rugby, if you were a policeman.

Croke Park was the site of the Bloody Sunday massacre of 1920, when British soldiers killed 14 Irish people who had turned up to watch a bit of sport.

God save our gracious queen . . .

Not a boo, not a catcall, and why should there be? And after the singing a brief, spontaneous moment of silence . . . which was followed by a brief round of applause. Not for the anthem, God forbid, but for the silence. For the fact that there was nothing left to boo, no reason to catcall.

Then two more anthems: 'The Soldier's Song' and 'Ireland's Call'. The team opposing England was not officially a nation: a united Ireland that has no political reality.

But bugger the politics and fugh the begrudgers: this was sport and time now for a crashing, bashing, smashing game of rugby. Ireland won by a distance, as it happened: 43–13. And that's all that mattered: just the sport, the beautiful day, the craic, and afterwards the bars, green shoulders and white shoulders rubbing hard at bars as their owners sought the black drinks and the gold.

That's the end of eight hundred years of shite.

Overheard in one of those bars.

Sport didn't heal those harms, though perhaps it played some small part. But sport had the symbolic vocabulary to spell out the healing of the harms in letters of fire.

No hatred. No shite. Just your lot v my lot and a bloody good drink after.

Back to *Ulysses*. 'But it's no use,' Bloom says. 'Force, hatred, history, all that. That's not life for men and women, insult and hatred. And everybody knows it's the very opposite of that that is really life.'

God save our gracious sport.

And fugh the begrudgers.

~

Sport requires certain decisions about self-presentation: how you show yourself to your audience and how your audience responds. It's a process that's complicated – or simplified – by the fact that in competition an athlete is emotionally stark naked in front of us. Little room for artifice or evasion in the ferocious scrutiny of contest.

Tennis is a duel between individuals, and that makes it more like a *comédie de caractère* than most sports. The requirement to appear before the media after every match adds to that impression.

Tennis is by tradition a sport of privilege. In America it's the country club: those sports that require generous space, plenty of upkeep and a chance to socialise: tennis and of course golf. A long way from the Cadillac Hotel, as always. And traditionally with black servants. It follows that audiences prefer the sort of tennis players who fit into this vision of life. Who accept the rules and the conventions and so can be admired and, as their careers progress, loved. Some are loved almost at once, like Roger Federer; others can be loathed, like John McEnroe, until time and fallibility and familiarity work a strange magic and turn the hate into love.

It happened with Martina Navratilova, whose brilliance and athleticism were initially forbidding. But it never really happened with the Williams sisters.

Oh, non-white players have been beloved by the Wimbledon crowd before and since, but these were players who fitted in, who made a point of fitting in. Arthur Ashe, Evonne Goolagong, they were easy to like, easy to love.

But the Williams sisters never asked for approval. They never sought such a thing. They showed no humility. They were unapologetically themselves at all times. There was Venus, now 27 and three times a Wimbledon singles champion, unapologetically herself and playing Maria Sharapova in the round of 16. Venus stood very tall, as always, an immense arm span, a great deal of skin exposed and every square inch of it black. She played without elegance and without charm: with muscularity, with power, with a determination to seize control of time and place.

My space. My changeover. I'll serve when I'm ready, and you'll serve when I'm ready. Not endearing, not supposed to be. But damned impressive, especially if you happen to be on the wrong side of the net. Sharapova, number two seed that year, won only four games in that match and the route opened up to the finals for Venus.

She played Marion Bartoli in the final and did so on a court and time of her own choosing, or so it seemed. So often in tennis it seems an equal contest until you reach the moment when it actually matters. Bartoli served at 4–5 in the first set and was broken. Double-faulting twice, but both the Williams sisters had the power to force errors from their opponents without touching the ball. Their oppressive presence on the court, their oppressive ownership of those enormous points: it was all too much.

Bartoli, a very decent player, gave it the lot in the first game of the second set, and it was the best period of the match for both players and for spectators. Venus won the game – and that was it. Bartoli won one more game in the match.

Not much affection for Venus that day on Centre Court, but respect. And perhaps respect is all the more satisfying when it is forced from the begrudgers.

~

Never wonder why a team that has created brilliance and victory and joy can shift – sometimes gradually, sometimes with impossibly violent speed – into self-destruction and despair. It happens again and again and yet every time it happens it's reckoned to be a mystery. It's often presented as something like the break-up of a happy marriage: one of those eternal contradictions of human life.

But it's not. In sport, everyone you come up against in the way of business is actively working for your destruction. It's their job to drive you to despair, just as it's your job to push your opponents in the general direction of disaster and horror.

Andrew Flintoff chose to despair on a pedalo.

England had begun the Cricket World Cup with a defeat by New Zealand, and a consoling drink turned into the kind of drunken despair that's cunningly disguised as hilarity.

It wasn't about New Zealand. It wasn't even about the World Cup. It was about Adelaide, when England lost from 551 for six declared, the declaration coming from the stand-in captain Andrew Flintoff. It came from the fact that Australia won that Test series 5-0. It came from the surrender of the Ashes. It came from the horrible contrast between the celebration of victory in the Ashes in 2005 and the terrible losses of the following year, and on into the January just gone. It came from the resulting loss of confidence in the head coach, Duncan Fletcher, and a general acceptance of the fact that the great team that brought such joy had gone wrong. Its mechanism had gone. This was supposed to be Flintoff's fault. This was supposed to be Fletcher's fault.

But it was nothing of the kind. It was Australia's fault. They destroyed the England cricket team. In their hearts all England supporters knew it. Which is why it was unforgivable.

Michael Vaughan had returned from injury and was back as captain. He remembers the way that drunken night – in which he played no part – spoiled the rest of the World Cup campaign.

The criticism of England was based on a false premise: that the players were not fulfilling their responsibilities to their country. That they were behaving foolishly, frivolously, without thought for what victory might mean for England. Nothing of the kind. Vaughan said: 'We just started taking it all too seriously . . . everyone was too tense, too desperate.'

After the night of drunkenness England wanted it more than ever, needed it more than ever, and disaster followed with dreary inevitability. The team as a unit, including the coaching staff, had reached the end of its useful life. Vaughan looked back on those matches of desperate, unavailing effort.

'There was no escape.'

The mechanism's gone.

~

Jonny Wilkinson became sport's Job.

He had every reason to despair, but he didn't.

After his drop kick won England the rugby union World Cup of 2003 he suffered a series of injuries and illnesses: an operation on the nerves of his neck, a blood clot in his bicep, damaged knee ligaments, persistent groin trouble, a lacerated kidney, shoulder injuries and appendicitis.

These troubles stopped him from playing rugby for most of the three years that followed the World Cup. He did rehab for three years and did so without losing hope.

He then came back to an England team that had lost all the old stagers and all the old certainties, along with the coach Clive Woodward. Somehow, this raggle-taggle team bluffed and fought and lucked their way to the semi-finals of the World Cup in France. And took on France. In Paris.

One of the strange things about Wilkinson is that he never let his own poor form put him off. He never let his own mistakes affect him. To do so would have been self-indulgent: an unseemly concentration on self. He was a team man, perhaps more than anyone else has ever been a team man. For him, the collective was all, the individual nothing.

He had missed penalties, he had missed a drop goal attempt and France were leading 9-8 with five minutes to go.

You could never accuse Wilkinson of playing without seriousness, of playing in a carefree fashion. He always wanted it more – but not for himself. And so when England won a penalty with five minutes to go, it wasn't about him. Even though it was.

He kicked it to give England the lead. And then, with France seeking the single score that would restore their lead and give them victory and a place in the final, the ball came to Wilkinson again. Wilkinson back in the pocket, the position of privilege, the position of responsibility.

Drop kick.

Left foot, this time, his favoured kicking foot.

As if no time had passed at all in those four years, the ball was end-over-ending, was magic-boomeranging through the posts.

Ah, those sporting moments when the live action seems already to be in slow motion, the way the actual events seem to take place for the first time as an action replay, so certain does the outcome seem to be.

The greatest sporting courage comes not from the untried but from those who have suffered and learned the taste of despair . . . and play on.

This was a moment of perfect sporting courage and for a moment a drab tournament seemed lit up with the flames of eternity.

~

Olympic Way, which is more usually called Wembley Way, runs between Wembley Stadium and Wembley Park tube station. It takes a little more than five minutes to walk its length on a non-match day. The night the England football team lost to Croatia it took two hours. It rained throughout with dismal determination. That was why the trains had stopped working. Their mechanism had gone.

Many thousands of people stood along the slow length of that road contemplating the meaning of defeat. It was a defeat that meant England would not qualify for the European Championship. It meant that the manager, Steve McClaren, would be sacked in the morning; he had declined to resign overnight.

It could hardly have gone more wrong.

McClaren dropped the regular goalkeeper, Paul Robinson; he also dropped David Beckham. Within eight minutes of the start, Robinson's replacement, Scott Carson, who was 22, fumbled a 25-yarder from Niko Kranjcar and the ball slithered into the net. At half-time, England were 2-0 down, and McClaren brought on Beckham from the bench. England pulled one back from a penalty and then Beckham set up an equaliser for Peter Crouch with a finely judged cross. Was it after all, and impossibly, going to be all right?

It was Mladen Petric of Croatia who scored the winner. It was a left-footer, neatly enough struck, but it hit the net not with the force of individual brilliance but with the still greater force of inevitability. As if it was already an action replay.

England had lost patience with Sven-Goran Eriksson, McClaren's predecessor. In striving for something greater, England failed in a still greater manner. But not by daring more greatly. Not by flying too close to the sun. They failed because they assumed, despite all the weight of sporting history, that England had a right to be counted among the very best football teams in the world. They thought it would be – well, not easy, but at least within the bounds of possibility.

Perhaps all football is fantasy football. The game is run by hard-headed men of fantasy: perpetually amazed when their team falls short. And that's truer of the England national team than it is of any other football team in creation.

The rain fell. The police looked down from the watchtowers of their horses, rain beading on the horses' visors, and running from the rain-sheets spread across their backs, while the crowd shuffled another ten paces towards the station and then halted. The sun would rise the following morning. Another new dawn for the England football team.

Heigh-ho.

The Jubilee line, the Metropolitan line, were at least ten steps closer than they were before. Now to wait again. Was the rain getting a little easier?

It was not.

- France beat Ireland on points difference to win the Six Nations tournament. England were third.
- The England cricket team reached the Super 8 stage of the World Cup, but then lost four of their matches and failed to reach the semi-finals.
- England lost the rugby union World Cup final, going down 15-6 to South Africa.
- Steve McClaren was sacked by the FA and replaced by the Italian Fabio Capello.

BOOK 26

2008

Not a duel, not a duello. A three-way shootout: a triello. Like *The Good, the Bad and the Ugly.*

The early skirmishing in Beijing, inside the Bird's Nest stadium, the smog-heavy sky above. Below the level of the roof, inside the great bowl, dragonflies and red-rumped swallows.

The first round.

The three. Asafa Powell, Jamaican, shaven-headed, carried himself like a star, conscious of his destiny as a superman. Ran his heat in the 100 metres with tremendous early pace, slowing up almost ostentatiously towards the end.

Tyson Gay from the United States, looking edgy. Nothing wrong with that: this is an event in which overwrought nerves can be an asset.

The third was narrow favourite. Another Jamaican. Poor starter, but there was always such a lot of him to get going. Once he was up he was fast: and only 41 strides from beginning to end, world record holder, 9.72 seconds. But he didn't even think that the 100 metres was his best event.

Bolt.

Usain Bolt.

Later that same Friday, the quarter-finals.

Gay finished second and didn't look like a man saving himself. 'I felt good and relaxed,' he said afterwards. Lying, probably.

Powell finished in 10.02 seconds in full control and easing up.

Bolt hurried. For the first 50 metres he hurried. After that he looked about him with mild interest as he jogged home in first place.

Beautiful. Outrageous.

What's next?

~

The Champions League final between Chelsea and Manchester United took place in Moscow. To offset the carbon from 40,000 fans travelling five hours from England would require Uefa to restore an area of tropical forest equivalent to 547 Luzhniki Stadiums. Not that they did anything of the sort.

This surely is not real. It didn't feel real. It didn't feel as if it mattered. It was hard to suspend disbelief in this sporting occasion. Sport had gone too far. Sport was getting silly, in the manner of Monty Python.

The match continued in a manner that seemed absurd, detached, without point. Cristiano Ronaldo scored for Manchester United with a header; Frank Lampard equalised.

Extra time.

Penalties.

The penalty-taker has an opportunity to give a bravura performance of himself. He has time to think, to prepare, to perform. Spontaneity, the footballer's stock-in-trade, is removed. This is no longer a playing field: it is a stage, for strutting and fretting on; it is a circus ring, roll of drums, absolute silence ladies and gentlemen, please. It needs only the lady with sequins and fishnet tights to cavort and gesture as The Great Ronaldo places the ball on the spot and takes his run-up.

Tricks. Tricks within tricks. Tricks within tricks within tricks. Ronaldo, the great trickster, was once described as setting a new world record for stepovers in a single match, reaching 524, beating the previous record of seven . . .

He placed a huge stutter in his run-up, for he was the greatest and all other players were beneath him.

Petr Cech saved it.

So Chelsea were going to win. Don't worry, Dad's here. The leader, the legend. John Terry's penalty. One kick to win the greatest prize in club football for Chelsea. Terry, the man with the athlete's body who was fined £60 for parking his Bentley in a parking bay reserved for the disabled.

One kick to save the world.

To define a career. To justify a life.

Missed. To be precise, fell over. Leaning back as he went into the shot. At this precise moment his technique deserted him. Hit the outside of the post. Gone.

Nicolas Anelka was a classic vanity signing. Every manager thinks he will be the one to crack it, to get the best from a considerable but elusive talent. Anelka's penalty was saved without apparent difficulty by Edwin van der Sar. It was a penalty that, like Anelka, seemed short of commitment; just as Terry's effort had too much. Who wants it more? Who wants it less?

Manchester United won the penalty competition 6-5 and thus the Champions League.

Not a great night for football; not a great night for sport. Now to try and get home.

In the bushes that surrounded the stadium a thrush nightingale sang with heart-breaking beauty.

~

Partisanship. Drama. Excellence. And, yes, beauty and even perfection. You can have too much of such things.

Sport brought them in such lavish quantities that it became unbearable. No longer pleasant, no longer even watchable.

Does that happen in art? Not in the highest art, for there is some kind of detachment, some feeling of the creator removed from the immediate action, invisible, refined out of existence, indifferent, paring his fingernails.

But sport is by definition uncontrolled and spontaneous. It follows that it often disappoints; it also follows that there are times when its gifts are too many.

The action took place over 4 hours and 48 minutes. The match took a great deal longer: the start was delayed 35 minutes by rain, there was an 80-minute rain delay in the third set and a 30-minute rain delay in the fourth. The match finished as it was getting dark, too dark to see: a quarter past nine in the evening.

Facts? Rafael Nadal beat Roger Federer 6-4, 6-4, 6-7, 6-7, 9-7. Federer saved two championship points in the fourth set, but it was Nadal's day. Or night.

Centre Court is a temple of love. The crowd there loves to love. It makes favourites who can do no wrong, pantomime villains who can do no right but who, by a mysterious process peculiar to Wimbledon, slowly become love-objects, but only when the time is right.

Federer had always been loved, even though one year he turned up in a cardigan with gold buttons. Nadal should have been the villain then, but that could never work. His nature and his style of play were too engaging. The two men had already established a rivalry based on decency and respect: and between them they had won 14 of the previous 16 Grand Slam titles. It was their time. It was their game. Centre Court was their place.

Partisanship brought pain as hopes were raised and dashed and dashed and raised. Drama brought more pain as the advantage switched one way and then the other, with the weather enforcing its own capricious timing onto events. And excellence … the most beautiful shot-maker of all time taking on the greatest hustler of all time. Styles make fights, the boxing people say, and this was a classic contest of different kinds of excellence, which forced each player to find something more and then, impossibly, more again. Raise your level and I'll raise mine, even if that means you'll raise yours again … that process continued until excellence itself became a kind of torture.

At seven games all in the fifth set, you'd have taken a draw. Begged for a draw, if only to stop these impossibly wonderful performers provoking each other to such terrifying peaks of excellence. We don't need a winner, we've seen enough. Let's have peace, let's share the damn title, shake hands, embrace and for God's sake all go home satisfied, satisfied almost as never before at a sporting event.

But no, it had to go on into the darkness.

There's a famous papyrus in the British Museum, from the *Book of the Dead*, in which the jackal-headed god Anubis weighs the soul of Ani against a feather. In this context the feather-weight weight of a feather can sometimes be too much.

In this tennis match, the difference between Federer and Nadal – two of the greatest players that ever played the game – was a feather.

Neither man was diminished by this match. It was just that sometimes a feather can be too much. And sometimes sport itself is too much.

~

Who wants to be ordinary?

The affirmative answer demands years, even a lifetime.

And, also, a second.

And, perhaps crucially, the ability to recognise that second for what it is.

Bill Sweetenham, who had asked the overwhelming question to British swimmers, had left British Swimming the previous year, returning to Australia for family reasons. At least something of his harsh message remained.

The 400 metres freestyle race for women at the Olympic Games in Beijing was to be decided between two swimmers: Katie Hoff, of the United States, and Federica Pellegrini of Italy. In the crucial moment of the race, with the two favourites each waiting for the other to make the first move, a third swimmer reached a decision in the light of the indecision of others. And made her move. She was a swimmer accustomed to endure and once she had made her move she was uncatchable.

Rebecca Adlington won a gold medal for Britain. In the press box above the pool, a statuesque lady of a certain age got to her feet and watched in unbelieving silence as the deed was done. This was Anita Lonsbrough, the last female British swimmer to win an Olympic gold medal – 48 years previously.

'Too long!' said Lonsbrough. 'Too long!'

A joy mixed with sadness, at losing her uniqueness, at the fact that it had taken so long, all but half a century, to happen. Past and future met with the utmost delicacy, a rare thing in sport.

And then joy. Not a rare thing at all, not in sport, not at any rate for spectators. But rare enough for the individuals who take part. For those with the highest goals of all, it comes once a lifetime, if that: and here was pure, ecstatic, unbelieving joy, of the kind that lights up faces, making them beautiful for all time. That was Adlington, under the cruel lights of the Olympic pool: filled with joy and beautiful for all time.

~

The cameras never leave your face. Not if you're a serial champion. They catch you in air-punching triumph. They catch you in smiles. They catch you in shock, or in relief. They catch you receiving congratulations and dealing with them graciously or not graciously. They catch you in moments that look like prayers and sometimes are. They catch you in moments of stern resolve, and, occasionally, in something not far from panic. These close-ups reveal what the champions never tell you in words: that it's not easy being a champion. Being ordinary – it's so much more comfortable.

Michael Phelps had just won his fourth gold medal of the Beijing Olympic Games, in the 200 metres butterfly: two more and he would equal his haul from Athens four years earlier. Four more – that was his target – and he would beat Mark Spitz's haul of gold medals from the Munich Games of 1972, which had been seen ever since as an impossible, for-all-time, never-to-be-repeated – still less beaten – achievement.

Phelps won well, he won convincingly, but it was not the display of perfect dominance that had been anticipated. He finished, stood, removed his cap – two caps, one on top of the other – and his goggles and tossed them onto the side of the pool in an oddly dismissive way, all without a smile. You could see all this on the big screen above the pool. And a look of utter soul-weariness swept over his face. Physical weariness too, of course, but here for a moment was a weariness that went beyond anything that could ever be brought on by mere physical exercise. Enough, he seemed to be saying. Enough. This is too much.

He was by then 54 minutes away from the final of the 4 × 200 metres freestyle relay, in which he was supposed to anchor the United States to yet another gold medal.

It was all cruelly upside down, that meet: heats in the evening, finals in the morning, just after breakfast – all to catch East Coast primetime, of course. It was horribly unnatural: the athletes forced to work against the circadian rhythms of their own bodies.

Phelps was on course, yes. But such a long way still to go.

The swim in the 200 metres butterfly was, if anything, a trifle disappointing. He had set a world record but not by much. He had beaten his rivals, but not by a great distance. He was the best, but he didn't look like the best ever. It was all oddly flat: just part of this great traipse from gold to gold.

The reason emerged later. Round about the second turn, with 100 metres to go, his goggles had filled with water. He had to swim blind. He couldn't see the pool walls; he couldn't see the stripe on the pool bottom. He had to work by counting strokes. All of a sudden it was a test of swimmer's craft.

He completed the race in front, with the great butterfly swimmer's pouncing lunge at the wall, like a water creature rising up to grab some land-dwelling prey.

He triumphed, but without any sense of triumph. He had got away with one. He was too weary, too shocked even to show relief. After all, he had another race in less than an hour.

Perhaps for a second, Michael Phelps wanted to be ordinary.

But only for a second.

~

Is it about the individual? Or the collective?

A question that lies at the heart of sport – and it has a million answers.

Sink self and give all to the common good? Or is the common good best served by a brilliant individual effort, like Kevin Pietersen at The Oval? When is it taking responsibility? And when is it showing off?

The greatest quarterback in the world can't do a thing without the protection of the offensive linemen. The world's greatest batsman will never win a Test match unless the bowlers take 20 wickets. Tiger Woods never understood that the Ryder Cup was about being a team; Colin Montgomerie could only function at his best when he was doing it for others. All in the way these things take you. Many of those who take part in the individual sports feel that they are doing it for others. Tim Henman felt the world, or least all of Britain, on his shoulders as he went through his four-set martyrdoms at Wimbledon. Track and field athletes take part in individual races feeling a responsibility for their coaching team.

China is the land of the crowd and, to a Westerner at least, the Chinese understanding of the relationship between individual and collective is forever difficult, elusive and perhaps even frightening.

It came down to the rings.

The gymnastics apparatus, the rings, is a place where pain and beauty meet. It's not especially dangerous, when compared to apparatus with more flight elements, but it hurts more. It requires immense strength expressed in the line of beauty: perhaps above all in the position known as the crucifix, which needs no additional information save that the strongest will release the hand grips and extend the fingers through the rings to show how great their strength and how perfect their balance, their stillness.

China had dominated the qualifying process at the gymnastics and were supposed to be a lay-down certainty for team gold. But they had a poor floor exercise and a pommel that was OK at best: three gymnasts in each team on each bit of apparatus, and all three scores count. No discards. No room for error. And China were fifth.

It was then that Yang Wei took control. It's all right. Dad's here. And he performed a routine on rings that changed everything. Belief was restored. And in the vault – one vault each – China flew to the top and it was all over.

A couple of days later, Yang went for the individual all-around competition: all six pieces of apparatus, one gymnast. Yang had always had a problem with individual glory. He was known as the silver collector, after coming second in the Sydney Games and in the 2003 World Championships. In Athens four years earlier, he had fallen off the high bar and finished seventh. He was now 28, at the peak of his powers . . . and he stepped off the mat during the floor exercise, incurring penalties, and then performed another poor pommel routine.

Once again the rings.

Was he doing it for himself or for the home nation that he represented? Who can say? But it was a performance of marvellous, elegant strength, strength expressed as beauty – and he was away from the rest, a fine vault followed by a brilliant parallel bars, every handstand perfectly vertical, no hint of the hollow back that can mar a performance even among the greatest gymnasts.

He could have fallen off the high bar and still won, and in fact he had two gross errors, and in this moment of anticlimax he achieved his triumph. For himself, for his team, for his nation.

Whatever.

~

Yelena Isinbayeva was never greatly distracted by considerations of the collective. She accepted, with becoming modesty, that it was all – pole vault, track and field programme, Olympic Games, city of Beijing, nation of China, the world – about her.

At least for one evening. And so it was.

'Pole-vaulting is like limitless happiness,' she said.

Pole-vaulting for women was a young discipline. It had made its Olympic debut just eight years earlier. Sometimes in a young sport an individual can establish a personal fiefdom, and this is what had happened here.

Pole vault is a protracted event, unfolding in slow motion, so contestants need a lot of kit. Not just their poles: stuff to keep warm and comfortable during the considerable downtime that the event always offers, the times when the other jumpers jump.

Isinbayeva brought a bed. She knew she was going to do a lot of lying down.

You come in at the height you choose, bearing in mind that the bar can only ever go up. It's about coming in at a height you know you can clear, without wasting energy on jumps far below your capabilities. It can go wrong: it did for the great male pole-vaulter, Sergey Bubka, who broke the world record 35 times. He failed to record a jump – no-heighted, in the jargon – at the Olympic Games of 1992 and did it again in 2000.

Isinbayeva made no such error. She waited in her bed while the lesser jumpers fought it out for the minor medals and then she emerged and cleared her first height first off. A little later, she took her second jump. It was enough to win the competition.

And then it began.

She had the bar set to 4.95 metres, failed twice – and then cleared, to set a new Olympic record.

She was reckoned to be the only female vaulter who could teach the men something about technique. She had been a gymnast until she grew too tall when she was 15. The L-phase, at which the bending pole and the vaulter's body make two opposed letter Ls, was a thing of perfection: the classic translation of forward speed into height.

Isinbayeva was the only woman to have cleared five metres. She had broken the world record twice in the previous month. She now had the bar set to 5.05 metres. Failed twice – and then cleared it to set a new world record.

Baron de Coubertin, founder of the modern Olympic Games, had declared that the function of women at the Games was to crown the victors with laurels. Here was another notion of the eternal feminine: strong, victorious, soaring to the sky.

- Rebecca Adlington won a second gold medal in Beijing in the 800 metres freestyle. At the London Olympic Games in 2012, she won bronze medals in the 400 metres and 800 metres. She then retired.

- Michael Phelps completed his haul of eight gold medals at the Beijing Games. He won four more golds at the London Games, retired, unretired and won five more golds at the Rio Games of 2016. His final total was 28 Olympic medals, 23 of them gold. He also set 39 world records.
- Yelena Isinbayeva took bronze at the London Olympic Games. She was unable to compete at the Rio Games of 2016, because Russia had been banned from track and field after a culture of state-sponsored drug-taking had been exposed. She then retired. She finished with two Olympic Gold medals, the first in Athens in 2004. She set 28 world records, and still holds the indoor record at 5.01 metres and the outdoor record at 5.06 metres, set in Zurich in 2009.

BOOK 27

2009

Fake blood from a joke shop.

As a symbol of sport it can hardly be bettered.

At what point does the intense pursuit of victory become cheating? When does the idea of victory at all costs – or even at high cost – become immoral? When does the pursuit of victory start to destroy the meaning, function and purpose of sport?

The answer to such questions lies in the joke shop. When sport becomes farce.

There is a limit to the number of tactical substitutions you can make in rugby union (they prefer the term 'replacement' lest you confuse their game – perish *la pensée* – with association football). But there is no limit to the number of replacements you can make when players suffer blood injuries. They must be patched up, for the health and safety of all concerned, and, of course, it's hardly fair to penalise a team whose player has been bloodied.

Say you lose your best kicker to some non-blood injury. Say he's called Nick Evans, and you want him back on the pitch.

You want him back because your team, Harlequins, are trailing 6–5 in the quarter-final of the Heineken Cup. But you can't get him back on because you've already used up your legal number of tactical replacements.

Tom Williams came off the pitch with his mouth dripping with blood, and Evans trotted innocently onto the pitch again. Didn't kick the winning goal, as it happens, but worth a try, eh?

The blood that Williams was spitting was fake. It came from a phial purchased, yes, at a joke shop. The ruse was uncovered. The censure began. First the director of rugby, Dean Richards, was suspended for three years. The club was fined £260,000. Williams was suspended for a year. The physio, Steph Brennan, was suspended for two years. The club doctor, Wendy Chapman, was warned by the General Medical Council; she had cut Williams's mouth in an attempt to cover up the fakery.

In the aftermath, Richards was accused of running the club as a personal fiefdom and establishing a culture of bullying. It's hardly unusual for a head coach to run a sporting organisation in a despotic fashion: Bill Sweetenham, Brian Clough, Sir Alex Ferguson: the list is endless. On the whole it's sport – clarification: elite sport – that makes unreasonable demands. Every individual has a choice of whether or not to submit to its demands. Whether or not to be ordinary.

A bully is not just someone who rules by fear. A bully is not just someone with a great deal of power, or even someone with a great relish for power.

No. A bully abuses power. A sporting bully loves power even more than victory. A bully causes distress, dismay and hurt for the simple pleasure of it. A bully leads his charges into wrong-doing. Bullying is an abuse of power, an abuse of the individuals in your care, and, above all, an abuse of trust. It is abuse – and not power – that defines a bully.

～

Those Rooney moments. Those moments when it seems that you've been granted a privileged vista of the future, and that future is all gold.

My God, I think we've got one here.

The real thing. With the right stuff. Not a rough pebble. Not a glister of paste.

A diamond.

Cut and polished and already perfect. Sometimes this trait is revealed by quality of play, by a moment of brilliance, by a single strike at goal. Sometimes it takes longer: the unfolding of a Test match innings. Sometimes it's a revelation of pure skill, but usually it's accompanied by a revelation of personality. A sense of composure in difficult circumstances, perhaps. Or the ability to seize a moment. Or a willingness to inflict the pain of defeat on an opponent. But it happens: and you know that this person is going to do something great. You just know.

You don't count the times when you're wrong. When you misinterpreted the signal, or when, for all kinds of reasons, the talent failed to mature: failing because of injury, the wrong advice, bad luck. The more sport you see, the more prone you are to these glimpses of future glory, and the more you come to distrust them.

Tim Henman consistently sent out signals that he was the best British player for a very long time. He consistently told us that we were in for a great ride. Did he ever tell us that he was a champion? Perhaps not.

At Wimbledon, Andy Murray was now world number three, heights Henman never quite reached. And he had something that Henman never consistently possessed. Authority.

Poor Ernie!

Murray was drawn against Ernests Gulbis of Latvia in the second round of Wimbledon. It was not the brilliance of Murray's play that was inspiring: it was the authority. The perfect self-certainty. It was not to be confused with the performance of a flat-track bully: this was an athlete taking control of time and place: playing as if he belonged in the thin, chill air of the summits: comfortable in the domain of eagles.

The scoreline was straightforward: 6-2, 7-5, 6-3. The style of play was compelling: mixing depth and power with touch. His defence was masterful and dangerous: frequently shifting bewilderingly into attack. There is no more dismaying thing in sport than to find your best asset transformed into a weapon against you.

It was characteristic of Henman that in such circumstances he would drop the third set from a moment of faulty concentration or, worse, compassion. Henman seldom did it the easy way. Even his straight-sets victories at Wimbledon usually required a wobble, a moment of self-doubt, a rallying of personal resources and a couple of big first serves to dig him out.

This contrast was instructive. Murray took victory as his due, without drama or distraction.

Here's a way of testing a diamond: heat it with a cigarette lighter for 30 seconds and then drop it into a glass of water. If it shatters it's –

Not a diamond.

So what was Murray?

~

In the same way there are sudden or gradual revelations of fallibility in a great champion. Pete Sampras was in a tight match towards the end of his career when he missed a slam-dunk: the one piece of flamboyance he allowed himself on a tennis court. It was still a pretty functional shot: an overhead struck into the ground just the far side of the net, so that it reared unplayably out of the court. When it failed, an expression of unforgettable bewilderment crossed his face: a champion unable to come to terms with his fading powers.

Such occasions are met with a strange mixture of sadness and glee. There are always people, and perhaps there's a small part in most people, that delights in the downfall of the great. Failure is comforting, especially when compared to success. It's so much more our size.

Sporting vocabulary is full of revealing clichés at such times. He showed he was human after all, she showed she was mortal, a god fell to earth. These phrases tell us little about the people involved – and a good deal more about our attitude to them. And then you wonder: does our reckless conferring of immortality on fellow humans affect the way they live, think, understand the world and themselves?

Tiger Woods fell from greatness in the course of a few minutes late one night. He had by then won 14 major tournaments. The fact that he was going to win more and beat Jack Nicklaus's 18 was taken for granted. In 2008 he won the US Open while suffering from a bad leg – a torn anterior cruciate ligament combined with a broken tibia, so not trivial – and this prompted some people to claim that the victory made him the greatest athlete that had ever lived. Certainly he was the richest, with earnings estimated at more than US$1 billion.

He took time off to fix the damaged knee, and failed to win a major in 2009. And then this.

Crouching Tiger, hidden hydrant.

That was probably the best headline. Woods was involved in a late-night crash outside his home, when his car struck a fire hydrant and a tree. This followed allegations in the *National Enquirer* magazine of an extra-marital affair. Soon afterwards, many other women claimed to have had affairs with Woods. Sometime later he released a statement admitting 'transgressions' and took an indefinite break from golf.

Most people assumed that he would resume his career where he had left it. But he didn't.

It was as if his personal myth had been shattered that mad night.

~

Farewell, a long farewell to all my greatness.

It hadn't been much of a match for Andrew Flintoff. He had made scores of 22 and 7; he had taken a single wicket in Australia's first innings and was to take none in the second. But as England moved their way towards victory in the final Test at The Oval and to victory in the series, Flintoff made his inevitable contribution.

In a period of the match in which it seemed that Australia would bat forever and that England might never take a wicket again, Flintoff struck. A direct-hit run-out: Ricky Ponting returning to the pavilion on 66 and, with that, the balance of the match shifted decisively. England were on course for inevitable victory.

Flintoff marked the moment by striking a pose, as if modelling for a heroic statue: motionless, arms raised, face with a slightly self-conscious expression of joyful sternness. Waiting for the others to come and embrace him. As they did.

He had one other gaudy time in that series. England escaped with a draw in the first Test, but in the second, parity was broken by Flintoff's spell of driving urgency, in which he took five second-innings' wickets. There was music in the air again, the stands resounded with a triumphal sound. There was a pose for that occasion too: the fifth wicket celebrated with a genuflexion, the pose held until the congratulators overwhelmed him.

Even by then, cricket had mostly rejected the notion that Flintoff was a great cricketer. That's because, in cricket, longevity is considered essential. A cricketer is judged not on a single work but on his entire oeuvre: and from that point of view, Flintoff was, indeed, unsatisfactory, found wanting.

Other athletes in other sports have found eternal glory in

much briefer spans of time: Roger Bannister in a fraction less than four minutes, Bob Beamon in the space of a few seconds. Flintoff was a great cricketer, a genuine for-all-time great cricketer for the space of about six weeks, in the course of which England won the Ashes in 2005. Disappointments, disasters, moments of farce and naked profiteering – he was always a great man for those little moments of product placement – affected his reputation.

But for six weeks Flintoff was the best cricketer in the world, and because those six weeks took in an Ashes series, Flintoff is surely a great cricketer. Herman Melville is regarded as a great writer, even though a good deal of his work is unexceptional, even unsatisfactory. But we don't judge him on his oeuvre, we judge him on a single masterpiece. It's the same with F. Scott Fitzgerald, whose single masterpiece is scarcely more than a novella. So perhaps that's how it should be with Flintoff. Certainly those who follow England cricket will not forget him: frozen in some self-consciously heroic pose, half-glorious, half-absurd. Like all of sport.

~

A nation can lag way behind the pace in a sport for a while, for some considerable time, and yet still go on to produce champions. It's possible to find greatness in a sport in which your nation has a long history of failure. You need two things to do so. The first is a coaching culture that gets it right: finds that fearful balance between softness and toughness: between shouting and gentle words of encouragement, and does so with a genuine understanding of elite sport and what it entails. The second thing you need is a pioneer.

Gymnastics was already widely beloved in Britain in the 1960s, when the Russians dominated the global culture of the sport and Ludmilla Tourischeva was the most graceful human being the world had ever seen. By the 1972 Olympic Games in

Munich, in which Olga Korbut stole the events with her daring and her love affair with the camera, there was a longing for a British gymnast to challenge the world. Russia and Romania set the pace; the United States followed, along with China and Japan. Britain lagged behind. Way, way behind.

The need for a pioneer is especially desperate in the judged sports. Judges in gymnastics strive for objectivity, but the reputations of individuals and their nations cannot help but affect the way performances are interpreted. And judged. There was a time when being outside the elite nations meant you started half a point down.

Beth Tweddle was the pioneer that British gymnastics needed.

She was driven by the urge to improve. She was a seeker after perfection, knowing that perfection is impossible. Perfection became literally impossible when the marking was changed after the Athens Olympic Games of 2004.

Tweddle was particularly strong on the asymmetric bars, and, swing by swing, release by release and catch by catch, she convinced her sport that being British didn't stop her being one of the best in the world. And eventually best of all: she won gold on the bars at the 2006 World Championships.

Not enough. Especially with the London Olympic Games coming up. Gymnastics is a sport famous for teenage champions, but Tweddle showed that great gymnastic ability and maturity are not mutually exclusive. This love of striving took her to the World Championships of 2009, which were held at the 02 Arena in London, which was to be the site for the Olympic gymnastics in three years. Tweddle was by then 24.

Failure consistently brought the best from Tweddle; that's what made her irresistible as a pioneer. She had a fall from the bars in qualifying at the 02, landing on her head, and that was that.

She was drawn first in the floor final, which is a disadvantage:

judges daren't mark too high in case they have nowhere to go. The new judging made that less of a problem – and so did the home crowd. So did Tweddle herself. She performed a routine that was both bold and clean, and those who followed made a series of those small errors that look so insignificant and cost so much.

Tweddle had taught us something about the way sporting cultures can change. She had shown the way and others were already following: notably Louis Smith, who won an Olympic bronze medal on the pommel horse at the Beijing Olympic Games. But Tweddle was the pioneer and that in itself is a form of greatness.

~

Cheating is the daily bread of sport. The great acts of cheating are met with horror: Ben Johnson's drug-taking, Diego Maradona and the Hand of God, ball-tampering in cricket. Some smaller acts of cheating are accepted as the way the sport is played: shirt-pulling and simulation in football, dawdling over changeovers in tennis, over-vigorous appealing in cricket: and on and on. Varying degrees of moral outrage, ranging from quite a lot to none whatsoever, greet all these forms of cheating. Still-ball games, in which cheating is very hard to get away with, at least in the professional game – snooker and golf – pride themselves on their own virtue. The harder it is to cheat, the more virtuous the players fancy themselves.

Read through today's sports pages and count the references to combat, warfare and death. Or, better, don't. Almost every match report in every sport has some kind of death theme running through it. Perhaps ultimately all sports are about life and death metaphors.

There was nothing of farce in the cheating scandal in Formula One. There was an element of absurdity, as there is in all forms of cheating – why play a game with rules and then cheat? – but this time the absurdity came with horror.

The previous year, the Renault Formula One racing team ordered their second driver, Nelson Piquet Jr, to crash. Oddly enough, this would give active help to the team: it would mean that the safety car would be deployed and no overtaking would be permitted, thereby allowing the team's number one driver, Fernando Alonso, to win a race he would otherwise have not.

It worked, too.

Piquet, the son of the eponymous three times world champion, was out of his depth in Formula One. The team had no compunction in sacrificing his chances – and more than that – in the cause of victory for one greater, nor did they have any compunction in dropping him from the team the following year.

Piquet, who had been horrified by the business, then told all.

And, no, this was not a piece of routine skulduggery. The Renault team knowingly put lives at risk for sporting gain. Motor racing, despite the colossal improvements in safety standards after the death of Ayrton Senna, remains a dangerous sport. In Formula Two that season, Henry Surtees, son of the former Formula One and motorcycle world champion John, was killed. In Formula One that season, Felipe Massa suffered a fractured skull.

Any crash puts at risk the lives of the driver or drivers involved, the lives of other drivers around the crash, also the lives of marshals and the lives of spectators. This was a potentially lethal manoeuvre, done for a few points, a moment of glory and, of course, money.

Sport is not real. The problem is that sport only works if you pretend it's real.

But – boxing apart – sport is a metaphor. Even the dangerous sports like Formula One and eventing are about the pursuit of an ultimately pointless goal.

Perhaps the scandal that surrounded the crashing of Piquet – Crashgate, the newspapers called it – was about metaphor fatigue. People had got so used to the massive importance of the pursuit of victory and the constant metaphorical references to life and death that they forgot motor racing can involve real death.

There are greater long-term examples of cheating in sport, of which the pinnacle is probably the East German state-run drugs system, which for years gambled the future health and well-being and life expectancy of athletes for medals. But as a single act – a single deliberate act of breaking the laws of sport – this probably counts as the worst case of cheating in sporting history.

- Tiger Woods remains on 14 major championships at the time of writing. He has suffered a series of injuries and his future participation in the sport is frequently questioned.
- Andrew Flintoff suffered problems with his knee and retired from all forms of cricket in 2010. He had a single professional boxing bout, beating Richard Dawson on points. He made a return to Twenty20 cricket in 2014, playing briefly for Lancashire and Brisbane Heat.
- Beth Tweddle won a bronze medal on the bars at the London Olympic Games and then retired. The Great Britain men's team also won bronze at the Games, while Louis Smith and Max Whitlock won silver and bronze on the pommel horse. British gymnasts won seven medals at the Rio Olympic Games of 2016, with two golds.

~

BOOK 28

2010

More people see the doctor about stress than any other complaint, apart from back pain.

If stress is so bad, why do we spend our leisure hours seeking it? Why do we actively seek the anxiety of watching Tim Henman and Andy Murray at Wimbledon? Why do we watch the England football team at the World Cup? Why, the previous year, did people watch the final overs of the first Test between England and Australia, a result that came down to the quality of Monty Panesar's leave-shot?

Keith Alexander, manager of Macclesfield Town, died after a 2-0 defeat to Notts County. He was 53. He had had a near-miss in 2003, when he had two cerebral aneurysms removed. He said then: 'There was no evidence in my case that it was brought on by the stress of being a manager in the lower leagues, which is just as well. I reckon the pressure at this end of the spectrum must be greater than the top end.'

Heart problems are a footballing staple. Jock Stein collapsed and died during a match when manager of Scotland. Gerard

Houllier, Graeme Souness, Johan Cruyff and Joe Kinnear all had heart problems. Barry Fry suffered a heart attack while trying to push-start the Barnet team bus.

Sport is about stress. The active seeking of stress. Stress is not an unfortunate by-product of sport: stress is the heart and soul of the matter. The uncertain outcome of meaningful competition cannot fail to create stress.

Often the difference between victory and defeat is about who deals with stress better, or best. Who wants it more; who wants it less. A sprinter must be keyed up – stressed – to make a fast start, but not so keyed up that he false-starts, as Linford Christie did at the Atlanta Olympic Games of 1996.

If we spectators wish to make sport more stressful for ourselves, we take sides. Our team, our nation, our boy, our girl. And we almost always take sides. If there's no obvious affiliation, we make one up to add spice – that is to say, stress – to the occasion. Shout for Venus against Serena because she's the underdog; shout for Barcelona in El Clásico because Messi seems a nicer fellow than Ronaldo; shout for Sri Lanka because they're funky and, besides, that was a lovely holiday all those years ago.

If that's not enough, you can have a bet. You could watch Dancing Brave win the Prix de l'Arc de Triomphe in 1986 and you could watch the same race with your money on Dancing Brave: two radically different experiences. By betting, you deliberately make a stressful experience more stressful.

Arsene Wenger, manager of Arsenal, said: 'At first you think the pressure is unbearable, but then you learn to cope. That is why it is like an addiction.'

Like?

~

Work it. Work it, baby. Work it, work it! *Own* it!

Advice given to Vivian – that's Julia Roberts, of course – in the film *Pretty Woman*.

Own it.

Not just take control. Seize ownership. That puts it at a different level of control. Mine. Not yours.

An Americanism. As if it needed stating.

The Winter Olympic Games were in Vancouver. Which is Canada, not the United States of America, if it needed stating. But quite close. Close enough for all kinds of odd things to matter. Things like precedence and respect.

The idea is that if you get the chance to hold the Olympic Games, you have the honour of playing host to the world. As a bonus, you get home advantage and the chance to win a few medals. Important, then, for all kinds of reasons, to get the balance right. The Atlanta Olympic Games came across, especially to the people who went to Atlanta to watch, as America versus the world. The world being the baddies.

Canada tried to go one better.

Own the Podium!

Exploit every possible advantage. What matters is Canada's medals. Give the visitors a hard time: this is about Canada.

Except it wasn't even that, really. It was about beating the United States: expressing the traditional Canadian chippiness in the form of medals. So they stole an American phrase – own it! – and tried to, well, own it. The Own the Podium business was put together with the Canadian dollar equivalent of £72 million from federal, provincial, territorial and corporate funds. All fine, so far as it goes: but it was not about the pursuit of sporting excellence. It was about doing the rest of the world down. Especially a certain country slightly to the south of Canada.

This involved limiting practice facilities for non-Canadians. Canadians were forbidden to train with non-Canadian training partners. This was a party, and all the guests were gatecrashers, including the world's television audience.

Perhaps inevitably, the Games began with a series of Canadian failures, as if the whole thing was too much. There's an infectious thing about failure at the Olympic Games, just as there is about success. The virus of failure ran through the Canadian team in a way that the watching world found rather gratifying. Every Canadian defeat gave quiet pleasure. Canada had made themselves the villains in their own pantomime. Which wasn't really the point of staging the Games.

Canada came back in the later stages of the Games and topped the table in the end, with Germany second and the United States third.

It's one thing to try to be as good as possible. It's another thing to try to make your opponents as bad as possible.

In two years' time, the Olympic Games would be held in London.

~

The dismal wail of the vuvuzela expressed the national mood. These plastic one-note trumpets were the must-have item at the football World Cup in South Africa. They were curiously satisfying to play on an individual basis: alas, the mad orchestras of tens of thousands of vuvuzelas created a soundtrack of despair. Television sets across the world moaned as if the whole world was in misery: the sun would never rise again, and no birds sing.

The England team danced to the music of the vuvuzela. In their qualifying group, dismal draws with the United States and Algeria were followed by a 1-0 win over Slovenia. That poor showing got them a match against Germany in the round of 16. They fell 2-0 behind, pulled one back with Matthew Upson's header and then Frank Lampard saved the day. Except that his goal was disallowed. The referee ruled that the ball, thumping down off the crossbar, didn't cross the line. This was an error half a billion or so people could have helped him with: televised images showed that it crossed the line by a comfortable distance.

But the simple pleasure of blaming the referee, Fifa, Germany and fate for failure was spoiled by England's dismal response to this setback. Germany won 4-1. It was a terrible confirmation of what had long been feared: England were no longer a major team in international football.

At more or less the same time, Andy Murray went out of Wimbledon in the semi-finals, losing in straight sets to Rafael Nadal, who was devastating. Murray had reached the final of the Australian Open earlier in the year, where he lost in straight sets to Roger Federer. No disgrace to lose to a god, in the manner of Tim Henman facing Pete Sampras, but it was distressing for all those who longed for him to win a Grand Slam tournament. It seemed that Murray was waiting for an opportunity to strike between god and god. But when would such a time come to pass?

Why are we so hopeless? We're a nation of losers. We're all right, but we're just terrible at sport. Such talk stems from a major error: international sport is multilateral, not bilateral. It's not England or Britain against the world: it's lots of nations and lots of individuals all trying to get the same thing. Every victory for one nation makes the rest of the world a loser. There are always more losers than winners: that's kind of the point.

That sense of crushing disappointment is part of sport. To embrace sport you must embrace disappointment and do so fervently. You must dance to the music of the vuvuzela. Only those who know the ecstasies of defeat can truly taste the sweets of victory.

~

Here is a tale about the most confident man in the world, and how he lost his confidence. Here is a tale about the sensitivity of the world's least sensitive man. Here is a tale about the vulnerability of the man who considered himself invulnerable.

Kevin Pietersen batted a single innings in the fourth Test match against Pakistan at Lord's. To his first ball he played a leaden-footed, stiff-legged, cross-batted swipe. And that was it: caught Kamran Akmal, bowled Mohammad Amir.

'I am trying to drag my confidence levels up,' he said. 'They have been hammered over the last 18 months and I am not the person I used to be.'

He had been made England captain, he complained that he couldn't work with the coach Peter Moores, and so they sacked them both. That's the way we do things over here, old boy. Once again, England made their best asset captain and once again the captaincy destroyed everything that made him their best asset. An old story that comes as a shocking surprise every single time.

That glorious innings at The Oval five years earlier seemed like the memory of a different man. Or did it? Those tough guys are always so delicate, so easily upset, so much in need of love. It was one more event in the vuvuzela summer: and England would shortly be leaving for Australia for another Ashes series.

Dismal thought.

~

Where's the hate?

Ever-repeated question of an old-school Fleet Street sports editor.

It was not a story; it was not a contest unless they hated each other. Roger Federer v Rafael Nadal – no one was interested in that. It wasn't sport because they didn't hate each other.

Really?

David Haye was fighting Audley Harrison for the WBA world heavyweight championship. 'It's going to be a public execution,' Haye said. 'It's going to be as one-sided as gang rape.'

Where's the meaning?

Where's the point?

Sometimes it seems that we would all be richer without sport in our lives. F. Scott Fitzgerald believed that his friend, the sportswriter Ring Lardner, devoted too much of his life to sport. He wrote: 'A writer can spin on about his adventures after 30, after 40, after 50, but the criteria by which those adventures are weighed and valued are irrevocably settled at the age of 25.'

He was wrong, if we use the Haye fight as a measure. Not 25. About eight.

At nine you can be too grown-up for sport.

~

It was like watching a butterfly metamorphose into a caterpillar.

A thing of beauty turning into a relentless survival machine.

All right, the zoology creaks a little – a butterfly is a survival machine like everything else that lives – but as an image of Jessica Ennis at the European Athletics Championships in Barcelona, it might have some relevance.

Certainly, it was a revelation of what Ennis had to offer. Apart from talent. Here at the Olympic Stadium at the summit of Montjuic, where Linford Christie and Derartu Tulu had won their gold medals in 1992, Ennis, like so many others, stripped bare her competitor's soul.

Talent and grit. Mix them together in the right proportions and you have your champion. You can't do it without a fair amount of both. Sport is full of brilliantly talented individuals who were never quite as good as everybody hoped; sport is equally full of gritty individuals who rise to a certain level in sport despite their shortage of genius. We see them again and again, opposed archetypes: David Gower and Graham Gooch. We choose our favourites according to our temperaments.

There was no doubting Ennis's talent as a heptathlete. She was small in stature for the event, but she was a runner – and jumper – of brilliance. She was also – comparatively – short on strength for the throwing events, but compensated with very good technique.

A heptathlete is out there on show for two full days of competition and must find a way of coping with the stresses. Ennis's technique was to withdraw into a state of serene contemplation. She looked like the Mona Lisa in a tracksuit, so it was quite easy to miss the grit.

Of the world's elite heptathletes only the American, Hyleas Fountain, was missing. Nataliya Dobrynska, of Ukraine, was looking strong as ever – in fact, she was quite dazzling in the shot, with a throw of 15.88. Meanwhile, Ennis had managed two attempts of around 12 metres with only one throw left. It was at this point that Ennis threw 14.05. It was enough to keep her narrowly in front.

Her warm-up for the javelin was dreadful. It all went wrong. 'I thought I was going to throw it away – literally,' she said afterwards. Her first throw was a lifetime best of 46.71 metres.

But she still had no more than 1.25 seconds in hand over Dobrynska for the final event, the 800 metres. The smart move would have been to track Dobrynska all the way, to run half a pace behind and a little to one side, and follow her no matter what she did – only going for the line at the very end. Ennis rejected such tactics.

She took the race on and led from the gun. Did she know despair as Dobrynska passed her with 200 metres to go?

How simple, how joyous sport can be. As the last bend unwound, Ennis ran away from her rival as if the move was long rehearsed between them.

Do you know what champions do? They find their best when they need it most. Sometimes by soaring high on the wings of their talent, sometimes by finding the answer deep in their competitive guts.

And, either way, it's the same thing: two different forms but the same glorious thing at heart.

Courage.

Is that what sport is for, then?

~

Adelaide. A haunted place. Certainly for all the English people who were there four years earlier. A place of the ultimate dashing of hopes. The vindictive cruelty of it all: as flies to wanton boys.

Now England were back. Again, it was the second Test in a five-match series. This time England had drawn the first, done so from a position in which defeat looked certain. 'Good to see your boys making a game of it!'

In Adelaide Ricky Ponting won the toss for Australia and chose to bat. The match began: 16 minutes and 13 balls later, Australia had scored two runs. And lost three wickets.

Joy is too feeble a word for the England supporters who had been in Adelaide in 2006. This was jubilation, ravishment and rapture: this was the high and refined ecstasy of partisanship that sport can bring – but rarely, rarely. It was combined with a hideous delight in Australia's discomfiture. Those 16 minutes were worth all the years of defeat: and yet it was to get better.

Simon Katich was run out without facing a ball, a diamond duck. Two wonderful swinging deliveries from James Anderson, two edges, two screamers, both caught by Graeme Swann. Australia were three for two, or if you prefer, two for three. There was a feeling of being transported to a magic land where every glorious thing is not only possible but easy.

Kevin Pietersen was a batsman with as much grit as there is vermouth in a traditional Martini: reliant almost entirely on the pure vodka of talent. His attacking style was a policy dictated by his own nature, and therefore, presumably, unavoidable. It had brought him disaster and triumph in equally lavish measures. In Adelaide, he played an innings of murderous certainty.

That big, bullying stride towards the bowler, that extravagant arc of the bat: how pathetic such things look in times of failure. How majestic, how perfectly unstoppable in times of glory.

Pietersen was at last out, having scored 227. England finished on 620 for five declared.

But it didn't seem as if Australia would lose. They looked capable of batting forever as the fourth and penultimate day moved towards its close. Then Andrew Strauss, the England captain, had one of his wild intuitive punts and asked Pietersen to bowl the final over. Michael Clarke was out for 80, edging one to Alastair Cook at slip, and Australia were four down overnight.

Rain in the air that next morning. Couldn't be long delayed, could it? There wouldn't be, couldn't be time for victory. Australia were going to get away with it. It's all been very lovely, but – well, the disappointment will add to the match's poetry.

And poetry is all very well, but the combined brilliance of Anderson and Swann was rather better. They bowled England to victory as Australia collapsed in the early afternoon. Within an hour of the finish the city was brought to a halt by an ark-building downpour. Under a coal-black sky regularly rent with jags of gilded lightning, the hammering of the rain interrupted by gasp-making detonations of thunder, the England supporters celebrated.

It was a match sanctified by excellence, glorified by drama and made unforgettable by partisanship.

- The football World Cup was won by Spain, who beat Holland 1-0 in the final; Fabio Capello remained in place as England manager.
- David Haye beat Audley Harrison comprehensively; the fight was stopped in the third round.
- England won the Ashes series 3-1.

BOOK 29

2011

Sometimes television coverage of sport has a rawness and immediacy that live action can't compete with. So it is with the Grand National, in which the viewer sits motionless while horse after horse falls in front of him and jockey after jockey crashes to the ground.

At the fourth fence, Ornais fell. At the sixth, Becher's Brook, Dooneys Gate fell. On the other horses galloped, some falling, some not, some completing the first circuit, over the Water Jump and the Chair. On, then, to the second circuit, but neither the fourth – or rather 20th – nor Becher's, this time round the 22nd, were jumped. Instead, the runners ran around them. Cameras mounted high on cherry-pickers showed the runners snaking around the fence, directed by officials. And pitilessly, the cameras showed why: beside each fence a green tarpaulin, each one covering a dead horse.

It was a sight that left no room for euphemism.

A beautiful day, spring sun warm, even hot. Weather that

examines a horse's stamina at the closing stages of a long race, more than four miles, all taken at a rapid pace, interrupted by 30 – no, 28 – huge jumping efforts.

Ballabriggs was exhausted coming over the last. He'd given the lot. At the end of his physical and mental strength. But somehow he kept going to win. That somehow was held in the hand of his jockey, Jason Maguire.

It's called a whip.

Ballabriggs was beaten all the way to the line and won: whereupon the jockey and all the horse's connections gave themselves up to celebration.

Maguire was banned for five days for excessive use of the whip. But there was no thought, and no opportunity within the rules, of disqualifying the horse for the crime of the jockey.

Hence the celebrations.

Perhaps it's just one of those personal frontiers. You make your own choice of sport. But perhaps the more sport you watch, the less appetite you have for certain kinds of sporting cruelty. If sport isn't fun it isn't anything very much at all – and ideas about fun can change, especially when the pitiless cameras make the cost of fun so very plain.

That same day, but in a different race, the jockey Peter Toole suffered a terrible fall and, by the time the Grand National began, he was in hospital and in an induced coma. Did it make a difference that he had chosen to take part and that he had some idea of the risks involved?

For some, the Grand National remains one of the greatest sporting events of the year. For others ... there remains the 'off' switch.

~

The champion lady rider in 1990 was Clare Balding, who went on to become a television presenter of genius. A week or so after the victory of Ballabriggs and the death of Ornais and

Dooneys Gate, she was due to front up the BBC coverage of Badminton Horse Trials. 'A horse may get killed at Badminton Horse Trials this weekend,' she said. 'I cannot guarantee that it won't. But I can guarantee that I won't see an exhausted horse being battered.'

Even if an event rider had decided to go for the battering option, it would do no good: try such a thing and you'll be disqualified on the course, before you've finished. That happened at the Barcelona Olympic Games of 1992, when a Russian rider Oleg Karpov (representing the Unified Team) was stopped before finishing the cross-country course. His horse Dokaz collapsed but later recovered.

Another hot, bright day. The event was won by Mark Todd, riding NZB Land Vision. Todd had retired and unretired and come back as good as ever. And, as ever, nothing spectacular: just calm and inimitable excellence. He did nothing, or so it seemed: beneath him the horse danced and leapt. His rider at times apparently half-asleep in the saddle.

～

Excellence is not to everybody's taste. When it comes in a very pure form, it can be deeply alienating – so unlike the way we do things ourselves. It can be hard to find affection for the purveyor of such excellence; even admiration can be reluctant, as it was for Pete Sampras.

A little partisanship can ease things, but by no means completely. Alastair Cook was opening the batting for England and scoring ridiculous quantities of runs against all opposition: and yet everything except the numbers was hard to relate to.

He scored 106 against Sri Lanka at Lord's, which was his third century in four innings; the blip had come in the previous innings in the same match, when he was out for 96. He had scored six centuries in nine matches, highest score 235, second highest 189. Three more innings above 50, average in that period a shade over 102.

And yet it was hard to recall a single shot he had played. There had been no character-revealing vignette. He had, it seemed, gone out and played the cricket ball almost with indifference, as if the batsman himself had been refined out of existence.

This was excellence of a kind that can only be understood by grasping what it was not: not flamboyant, not crabby, not aggressive, not defensive, not a hitter, not a blocker, not stylish, not ugly, not classic, not unorthodox. There was no relishing of the duel, no seeking of enmity, no defiance, no apparent fear and, for that matter, no apparent courage.

Had he been anything other than English, followers of English cricket would have said he was boring, as people said of Sampras. As it was, they had to deal with the uncomfortable phenomenon of impersonal excellence: no delight in the opposition's pain and no concern for it either, a callous indifference to everything save the pursuit of runs and excellence.

And if there was something disturbing about the nature of the century and of the centurion, this was precisely the sort of thing that sport is there to create, to encourage, to showcase, to admire, to aspire to.

~

Yes, but do I belong?

Am I really of this company?

It's an extension of the old saw that cheap horses know it. The top performers believe that they are top performers. It's not something they want, it's something they are. The great occasions, the great opportunities are there for them to take, and the great opponents are themselves both siblings and opportunities.

It's the conundrum of Graeme Hick, of every flat-track bully.

It's the conundrum of Graham Gooch, who began his Test match career by making a pair – two ducks, two noughts – at

Lord's, and who went on to become one of the great cricketers of history.

And it's the conundrum of Novak Djokovic, whose road to the summit of tennis was blocked by two of the greatest players of all time, Roger Federer and Rafael Nadal. How could he aspire to that company? Must he too seek to strike between god and god? He won a Grand Slam event, the Australian Open in 2008, but the big two still held tennis as a joint fiefdom.

Was there a moment, perhaps a long moment of realisation, as Djokovic led Serbia to a Davis Cup victory in 2010? Did it come from the major changes in his lifestyle and diet that same year? Was it the realisation that to be a modern champion, you must devote every waking and every sleeping second of your life to the pursuit of excellence? Everything is part of the process. 'I turned the head off,' Martina Navratilova once said, looking back at her own career. 'I never turned the body off.'

The edge in fitness was there to see: getting to balls with time and balance to play the optimal shot. It's always too easy to put everything down to the matter of belief, but when Djokovic went to Wimbledon, having won his second slam in Australia earlier in the year, he was beginning to add a certain certainty to his game. It seemed that he had also added something to his personal myth.

Andy Murray went out in the semi-finals, having taken the first set against Nadal in a storm of brilliance. Was that, too, a question of belief? Djokovic played Nadal in the final, having lost one match in the course of the calendar year, and won 6-4, 6-1, 1-6, 6-3. He had broken the cartel of champions. Comfortable in the domain of gods: no, a god himself now.

As for Murray, he now had not two gods in his way but three if he wanted to win a Grand Slam tournament.

Paul Dobbs died for sport. He was killed in the TT races on the Isle of Man in 2010. The following year, his widow Bridget went back to the island. For the races, naturally. That, and a blessing at Lonan Parish Church near Douglas. Back then the score was 234 deaths on the Mountain Course on the island, in TT races and the Manx Grand Prix. 'I'm not bitter,' she told the journalist Rick Broadbent. 'It's common knowledge that people who go through grieving are meant to get angry, but I can't see anything to get angry about – there was nothing wrong with the bike, it wasn't another rider who caused it. He just got it wrong. In a way that has been a help.'

It was a loss not a waste. That's what she said.

The alternative was a longer life half-lived.

~

The great artists who make the mightiest Islamic carpets create a near-perfect symmetry. But always with an imperfection, deliberately included. It's there to show that they have no ambition to rival God. But is there not an implication that they could rival God all right, if they chose to? That they just chose not to, from sheer modesty?

The great players in all team sports tell us they do it for the team. Why, then, do personal statistics and personal milestones matter so much – not just to the individual, but to the watching world? Everyone who follows cricket knows that the highest individual Test match score is Brian Lara's 400 not out in 2004. Very few know without looking it up that the highest team score is 952 for six declared, scored by Sri Lanka in 1997.

At The Oval there was a sense of triumphalism in the air as Sachin Tendulkar moved towards his hundred. His hundredth hundred: that is to say, his hundredth international century, gathered from Test and one-day cricket. The fact that India looked doomed to lose the series 4-0 was perfectly irrelevant, utterly forgotten.

Tendulkar was widely recognised by the most begrudging as the second greatest batsman to have played Test cricket; the rest said he was as good as Don Bradman. As is cricket's way, this was a greatness decided over time. Bradman's most important statistic is his Test match batting average, which is – so many cricket people can recite without a moment's pause – 99.94. It would have been more than 100 but for his final innings, which was a second-ball duck – bowled Eric Hollies – at The Oval. Bradman's minute imperfection is a greater thing than a perfect 100 could ever be: his flawed number contains poetry and humanity and fallibility: and all these things set off his greatness.

Tendulkar's Test match average was in the mid-50s, remarkable enough. And not comparable: Bradman faced more third-raters than Tendulkar, and very little sustained short-pitched bowling. The stat that mattered about Tendulkar was the number of centuries.

Both players had important symbolic roles to play as their countries emerged from British domination. Both were symbols of a new nationalism, a new kind of self-certainty, one for Australia, one for India. It was important, then, that both had an unanswerable number: an objective measure of greatness.

This was not a great Tendulkar innings. At his best, Tendulkar had that Zennish Sampras touch: nothing going through my mind, just me and the ball. The context of the match seemed irrelevant to him: his strength, and, therefore, his weakness. Some followers of Indian cricket complained that he never did it when it mattered: that he never rose to a great occasion.

But at the end, the approach of the most massive and perhaps never-to-be-repeated milestone seemed to get to him. That, and his increasing age. He had been playing international cricket since he was 16; he was now 38. By the time he was in the 90s he had been out five times, or should have been: two dropped catches, both off Tim Bresnan, two leg-before decisions that went the wrong way (and England had run out of reviews) and, preposterously, he was also out stumped but the wicketkeeper, Matt Prior, for the first and last time in his life, failed to appeal.

Tendulkar was out on 91; lbw Bresnan.

Marooned still on 99 international hundreds.

The beauty of imperfection suited him. Suited cricket. Suited sport. Not seeking to rival God.

~

Magic.

A leader's defining quality is often described that way. Often with perfect seriousness. Something that can't be explained or defined, and certainly not acquired or learned. Something innate: some are born to lead as others to follow.

The English are said to place overmuch faith in this notion. And certainly, it was the notion at the heart of England's disastrous showing at the rugby union World Cup.

Martin Johnson was a great England captain and led his team to the World Cup victory of 2003. He always claimed that he never set out to lead: perhaps his gift was for inspiring the finest forms of followership in the rest of the team.

It was a belief in these magic qualities that persuaded the (English) Rugby Football Union to make Johnson head coach. He had never coached before, but so what? The magic that he had within would surely be enough.

He was appointed in 2008, and his England team won the Six Nations Championship in 2011, though not with a Grand Slam. Johnson's strengths were in his loyalty and his trust: loyal to his coaches, loyal to his players.

On, then, to the World Cup, which was held in New Zealand.

After beating Argentina 13-9, the England team visited a bar that offered 'Dwarf Wrestling' as an attraction. It has to be said that this was poor PR. In the days following, footage (from security cameras) was released; it showed the England vice-captain, Mike Tindall, clearly drunk and apparently making a rhinoceros-in-heat pass at a 'mystery blonde'. Sport becoming farce again. Tindall was engaged to the Queen's granddaughter, Zara Phillips. The Queen and dwarf wrestling in the same headline: unimprovable.

From there, bit by bit, the team and the tour destroyed itself, and, with it, their trusting, loyal leader. Courtney Lawes was banned for kneeing an opponent. The team were caught illegally substituting the ball during the victory over Romania, for one more sympathetic to Jonny Wilkinson. There was some distasteful horseplay with a female hotel worker that went public. Delon Armitage was banned for a high tackle. They beat Scotland 16-12. Manu Tuilagi was fined for wearing a sponsored mouthguard. England were beaten 19-12 by France in the quarter-finals. Tuilagi was fined for jumping off a ferry.

And then things took a turn for the worse.

A report on the tour was leaked, revealing hopeless divisions, bogus assumptions of entitlement, a stinking atmosphere, a manager castigated for his inexperience, a bad tour, a broken team and a self-serving administration.

No athlete goes into sport seeking only money, content with mediocrity and failure. You only settle for these lesser things when something has gone wrong. And, ultimately, that's a problem of leadership. Not coaches or captains but people higher up: the people who run the sport and, while doing so, forget what sport is for.

Love gone sour. Sport is full of it.

～

Throw your heart over the fence and try to catch it the other side.

The art of jumping a horse over an imposing obstacle has often been described in such terms. A lot of things in life are like that: an uncertainty that must be treated as a certainty if any good is to come from it. The only possibility of success is complete commitment to uncertainty.

Greenwich Park radiated this sense of commitment. At almost every Olympic Games, the equestrian events take place well away from all the other sports: cut off, with only a tenuous connection with the rest of the proceedings. It requires something of an effort to get there, and is normally a specialist event for the horsey people. The equestrian events at the Beijing Olympics were held more than 1,000 miles away in Hong Kong.

The London Olympic Games had decided to hold the horsey events right in the middle of London: in Greenwich Park, just down the road from the 02, where the gymnastics would be held, and 20 minutes by road from the Olympic Stadium.

They held a test event to pre-empt problems. A two-star event involving dressage, cross-country and showjumping, in the classic format, and it was as if this pleasant London park had been designed across the centuries for equestrian sport, the backdrop of the naval museum perfect for the formalities of dressage, and the hills of the parkland offering a demanding test of stamina for the cross-country.

Carl Hester was not competing, being a dressage specialist. He was there to spread the word of his sport, languid, elegant, charming and funny, speaking in his chorus-boy drawl. He was the pioneer for his sport. The Germans and the Dutch excelled at dressage – as in the great Bonfire v Gigolo duel at the Sydney Games of 2000 – and joined together to laugh at the British, who might ride like madmen over fences but lacked the grace, accuracy and power of the purest discipline of them all.

Hester had shown them otherwise, and in a sport that struggles to achieve objectivity he forced judges to set aside their prejudices. He talked of the strides taken by the British team, of the increasing excellence of his former stable-hand, Charlotte

Dujardin, and their chances in the European Championship coming up. The British team were to go into the London Games with hopes for a medal. That would once have been absurd. Now, for those who love the discipline, it was quietly enthralling.

It's the cross-country course that brings non-horsey people into the equestrian sports. And there, at the top of the steep rise, was a fence that seemed to require the horse to leap clean off the summit of the hill and land in Canary Wharf: as if the sweet Thames was a water jump: a perfect example of the principle of getting the horses round safely while terrifying the life out of the riders.

And here too was the perfect image of sporting adventure. The Olympic Games must be approached in the same manner: jump – and hope that the catch is safely made on the other side.

There was anxiety in the air, of course there was, but beyond that a surpassing hope, or perhaps even a realisation.

This was going to be all right.

This was going to be bloody good . . .

- There have been a series of reviews and changes to the Grand National course. The start has been moved 90 yards, there has been further levelling of the landing area at Becher's Brook, changes to the landing areas at some other fences and a new catching pen was created. The maximum number of runners remains at 40, despite calls to reduce this.
- Peter Toole recovered and two years later was able to ride again.
- Novak Djokovic became the world number one player. He had won 12 Grand Slam titles at the time of writing.
- Sachin Tendulkar scored his hundredth and last international century the following year as India lost a one-day international against Bangladesh in Dhaka.

- Martin Johnson resigned as England head coach. No one at the Rugby Football Union resigned his position.
- The British dressage team won the European Dressage Championship in Rotterdam a few weeks later.

~

BOOK 30

2012

Even the train was a thing of joy.

Out of the stadium and past the great stretches of flowering meadow, still visible in the brief summer darkness, footways lit by the courteous light that guided the crowds. All heading for the train.

The English dominated, though narrowly. This was a crowd of all the nations, people making for the station with joy in their hearts: the sort of joy that comes from sport: from partisanship, drama and excellence and sometimes from a collision of two at once or even all three.

The walk, the brief queue, the short wait on the platform, the eight-minute ride to St Pancras station, all these were accompanied by conversations between stranger and stranger. It was a crowd full of after-yous and thank-yous and what about him and did you see her?

It was as if the normal stresses and irritations that govern human life had been set aside: as if everyone was living under a dispensation from everyday life. There were plenty of pushchairs and wheelchairs and other things to inconvenience the harried, but people parted and made room and exchanged good words. There were many families, often with quite young children, whose occasional weariness-driven moments of intemperance were greeted with calm tolerance.

A crowd united by a feeling of gratitude: that we could all see such things and experience such things and do so together.

Life should always be like this. For one summer it was.

~

For two days in London, Jessica Ennis was us. Every one of us. She was England; she was Britain; she was everywhere; she was Jerusalem, the green and pleasant land we long to live in. She was beautiful and talented and strong and vulnerable. She seemed to belong to no social class and no race, or to all social classes and all races. And with all those other things she seemed never for one second to have considered the notion that just because she was brilliant and talented and beautiful and wonderful and beloved, she should be treated any differently from anybody else in this world.

Ever since she won the heptathlon at the World Championships in 2009 she had been The Olympic Games so far as Britain was concerned: a symbol of the triumph in hosting them, of the humility required for making a good job of them, and of the hopes for great sport.

She entered the Olympic Stadium almost bowed down beneath the weight of all that love, all that symbolism. She had to do what Cathy Freeman did in Australia 12 years earlier: but she had to do it seven times.

Seek serenity, then.

Always her chosen method. The way of the Mona Lisa: calm, seraphic, lovely, older than the race in which she runs. Though before the first event, the 100 metres hurdles, she looked a little like Mona Lisa about to sit her A-levels. The event is both explosive and nigglingly technical: get the stride pattern wrong and you can hit a hurdle and lose yards and points; hit it hard and you can be on your face and out of the competition.

What do the great ones do?

They turn fear into fight, they turn stress into achievement, they turn disadvantage into advantage. When you ask them the overwhelming question, they find the answer.

Bang. 12.54 seconds. A time that would have won the specialist hurdles event in Beijing four years earlier.

High jump: struggling against rivals six inches taller. She looked like the underdog even in triumph and that made her still more greatly loved. She struggled, and for the first time asked the crowd for support, rhythmic clapping – and cleared 1.86 metres, worth a sudden smile. A smile of relief.

As usual a struggle in the shot, but the mongrel that lies behind the Mona Lisa found a decent throw, 14.28, that dropped her into second place.

Which left the 200 metres to finish the first day of competition. Not a bad moment to run a lifetime best: 22.83 seconds put her back in the lead.

Tomorrow was easy. All she needed to do was to go beyond her very best all over again, while the expectant love grew heavier with every passing hour, every passing event, every single stride. All that expectation, all that love: and, at the end of it all, alone. Absolutely and completely and eternally alone.

∼

Alone.

If not now, when?

Kohei Uchimura was perhaps the greatest male gymnast in history: the only one to have been the all-around world champion three times running. And now, in London at the Olympic

Games, he knew it would all count for nothing unless he won the gold medal.

Gymnastics is one of the heartland Olympic sports. Olympic gold is everything: every other victory in every other competition is but a consolation prize.

It's not about getting it right. It is about getting it right right *now* – today, this hour, this second of all the other seconds in your life. For this is the one in which you will be judged.

To embrace that concept and use it to find your very best.

Uchimura had won silver in Beijing four years earlier. In qualifying in London he fell off the high bar; something he never normally did. He had a disaster in the team event, and that was the one he had set his heart on. Japan were left with the silver medal.

It takes nerve to let go of the high bar and catch it. It takes something beyond nerve to catch the single second of your life that really matters and to make it yours forever.

That remote, uninvolved, absent look. Uchimura had the body of a waif and the shoulders and upper arms of a giant, all beneath a manga-comic thistledown haircut. The eyes seemed to go dead. Nothing existed in the world but the six pieces of apparatus. Uchimura entered a long tunnel of concentration: utterly involved, totally detached, in a perfect balance, a self-induced trance of competitive perfection.

The third event was the vault. That moment of transition from his high and rapid double-twisting flight to the perfect stillness of his landing was enough. It was everything.

He continued, making the strength moves look like ballet and the leaping moves look like flight: a perfect expression of the Olympic heartland.

～

Once again sport found a symbol and drove it deep into global consciousness. Sarah Attar bore the symbolic load for the world at the London Olympic Games – and no victory was required.

She completed a heat of the women's 800 metres and finished in 2 minutes 44.9 seconds, half a minute behind the rest, and last by a distance. She was given a standing ovation, not for her performance but for the symbolic role she embraced.

She was running for Saudi Arabia. This was the first year that Saudi had an Olympic team with women in it. She covered every square inch of skin but her face: long jogging trousers, a green top and a white hood. She was a walking, no, a running symbol of all the cultural collisions involved.

The details did not matter. She was studying at Pepperdine University in the United States, had seldom been to Saudi, had dual nationality, American and Saudi. She was not the first Saudi woman to perform at the Olympic Games: that was the judo fighter, Wojdan Ali Seraj Abdulrahim Shahrkhani, who had competed a few days earlier. But she wore judo kit like everyone else, and pictures of her were historically rather symbolically interesting.

All symbols can be interpreted in many ways. Was Attar representing a new freedom? A new hope for the world? Or was she the point at which the great wave of liberalism broke and rolled back?

Your call. The point is that Attar, in her hood, was unforgettable. As symbols always are.

~

The Olympic city does not contain the sporting arenas. It is the sporting arena. All the city's a stadium.

The Games subverted London, took familiar places and turned them into pleasure domes. The beach volleyball on Horse Guards Parade, the archery at Lord's, tennis (obviously) at Wimbledon: and then the free events, the marathons, men's and women's events, beginning and ending on The Mall, the walking events which also looped around London, the triathlon in Hyde Park, the road cycling, which began and ended at Hampton Court.

It was as if nothing mattered but sport. It was as if London's long history of warfare, plague and fire had been designed to lead to this one goal: a 17-day festival that celebrated the glorious trivialities of sport. And a few other things as well.

The open-water swimming took place in the Serpentine in Hyde Park, the women's event on a day that seemed to have been painted by Monet. No occasion more perfectly captured the disconnect between those who watch and those who do: a lovely day of summer sunshine in this lovely park with half a millennium of history behind it, sun bouncing off the water, grebes and terns on, above and below the lake's surface, a day of frivolity and sunshine and shirtsleeves and cotton dresses – and two hours of sheer bloody hell for the competitors.

The course was six laps of the Serpentine, ten kilometres in all. In the open water there are no lanes, so blocking is a legitimate tactic. Pushing and pulling and boring are not, but are frequently employed. In every way, this is an event that hurts.

Eva Risztov of Hungary took an early lead and held it. This is a strangely static race. It contains six episodes and every episode seemed to be the same, the swimmers holding their positions for lap after lap, visible as a vague watery disturbance on the far side of the lake, slowly coming closer, revealing arms and legs and heads, and a curious mat of disturbed water. Keri-anne Payne, still there, swimming for Britain, still in fourth, always just about to make her big move.

There was time to get an ice cream, despite the queues, while the swimmers rounded the most distant buoys, time to consume it before they were back after yet another lap, faces unreadable behind goggles.

And then the finish, Risztov, the winner by a distance, the not inaptly named Payne still fourth at the end. The faces of winner and loser likewise contorted, showing equal agonies, though for one, the agony would last longer.

A lovely day.

~

I am the champion.

I have a right to be here, I have a right to be in front, I have a right to win.

That was the transformation that took place with Kelly Holmes at the Athens Olympic Games of 2004. It's often said in sport that the last step is the hardest of all: to believe that you genuinely deserve the prize you have spent your life working for. Second place – being relatively ordinary – being first-class of the second class – is so much more comfortable.

In distance running the East African runners had for years dictated terms and made it clear that no one else had a right to the big prizes. Mo Farah, a British runner of East African extraction, had been pushed into what seemed his rightful place on many occasions past: that is to say, first-class of the second class. He was expected to do well at the London Games: but no one knew if he would be able to take that final step.

The answer came early in the 10,000 metres. The Kenyans traditionally run team-handed, and one of their number dropped back into the pack to mind Farah. He plonked himself right in front: a message: this is our race, forget it, you're out of your class.

Farah dropped back half a pace and then ran round his minder, breaking his rhythm, something distance runners normally avoid, before picking it up again. As an expression of confidence it even had a little touch of contempt. As Clint Eastwood said when facing down the bad guys: 'I'm faster than you'll ever live to be.'

The rest was merely running.

～

Self-sacrifice. Not a quality you associate with sport.

Carl Hester could ride the horse with brilliance. The problem was that his stable-hand, his pupil, could ride him even better. One of those things that horsey people can't really explain.

They just click, they will say. Something beyond analysis: and yet clear to all who look with knowing eyes.

So Hester gave up Valegro for Charlotte Dujardin. Hester was the pioneer who gave British dressage credibility, but it was Dujardin who took things up to the next level. Did the horse, did the rider feel they had a right to be the champions? Or was it a simple outpouring of talent?

The British team, which included Hester riding a different horse, won the team gold medal, but the best was yet to come. That was in the individual event, the kur, in which horse and rider perform a routine to music. Dujardin and Valegro didn't win in the usual sense of the term: they surpassed anything ever seen before in the glorious and mystifying world of dressage.

Not only did they win by a world record score, they made the sport startlingly accessible, with an artfully compiled routine set to patriotic music: canter pirouette to the Westminster chimes, extended canter to 'Land of Hope and Glory', with 'I Vow to Thee, My Country' and the James Bond themes thrown in. The most esoteric sport in the Olympic Games was a populist success.

More than that. It was as if this sudden strange triumph told us all we needed to know about the heart and soul of sport. The three great desirables of sport were there in unison: and with them the added dimension of beauty. Twice in a week, dressage thrilled a nation, twice in a week dressage was front-page news, twice in a week the world stopped for beauty.

~

The face of the Games.

The load that Cathy Freeman successfully carried in Sydney. The load that Konstantinos Kenteris carried in Athens four years later; he was involved in a motorbike accident on the eve of the Games while apparently fleeing a drugs test. The load carried by Liu Xiang in Beijing; he broke down with injury at the start of his first heat.

Kenteris never got to present himself to his own public; Liu did for about five minutes, Freeman for a little longer. Ennis had to do so for two days, two long sessions of sport in which her long event unwound itself towards its conclusion. All that time she stayed in her trance of concentration, the world shut out.

On that second day she threw a personal best in the javelin, her third PB of the competition. In the long jump she began with a poor but at least safe and legal jump, and then nailed the second. At this point she briefly joined the rest of the world and performed a little dance of maybe five paces in total, with a double-arm wave. Then she was back into her own private place again.

She led the final event, the 800 metres, from the start, and was passed. She then repassed and won.

At last, at last the tears.

This was sport. This was sport as we long to experience it. Grace, beauty, perfection, fight, struggle and victory.

And all for us.

~

Sport is different from chess or bridge or poker or Monopoly or Spoof. In all these games you try to beat somebody else – be better than somebody else – be further up the dominance hierarchy than somebody else – but in sport you attempt to beat them with your body. And your mind, yes of course with your mind as well, but you try to win in sport by means of physical skill before anything else.

Put your body on the line. That's what people in sport like to say: you risk, you commit and you accept whatever pain and damage to your body that comes by doing so.

When your body forbids you to perform many of the skills that great athletes command, the willingness – the desire – to put your body on the line – to test yourself physically – does not necessarily die. Intense physical limitations do not turn you into a Zen monk. You still want to play. You still want to win, you still want to lose, you still want to risk, you still want to suffer and you still want the opportunity to roar in triumph.

Perhaps more than before.

Boccia.

As in gotcha. An event at the Paralympic Games, taking place in the wide, lofty spaces of the ExCeL. The first shock is the sight of so many wheelchairs, so many bodies with such limited movement. Boccia was one of three sports at the Games that were invented for disabled athletes. The game is played by people with 'functional impairment' in all four limbs. Many, perhaps most, contestants suffer from cerebral palsy. The sensation of horror and pity at seeing such a thing replicated so many times in a confined space is at first overwhelming.

Sport is a treacherous thing. It gets beneath your guard. Soon you stop thinking about the problems that the athletes face in their daily lives: all you care about is whether the next ball will land closer to the target than the one before. Who wins, who loses.

As if it actually mattered.

Britain were playing Argentina. It was a tense encounter. The game is played by propelling small cushions – large juggling balls – at a target, so it's quite a lot like bowls. Some competitors had so little movement they propelled these balls along a ramp, by giving them a nudge with a rod attached to their heads. Pathetic, you might say. Pitiful.

The clinching shot. It gave Britain victory. And at once an involuntary cry came from the packed stands: 'Yes!'

Yes, yes, he won, yes – we won. Yes! The great cry of Molly Bloom, the great cry of all people in sport, a universal affirmative, for this was not about horror and pity, this was just sport, oh no when you lose and when you win – yes!

'It was a tight one all right,' said Nigel Murray afterwards; he was the British and the world number one player. No one thought of asking him how he got like that, or what difficulties he faced in his life. That didn't matter, not then. What mattered was not what divided us but what united us.

Sport.

Yes.

~

Bestriding, uniting the Olympic Games with the Paralympic Games – uniting the able-bodied with the disabled – who else but Oscar Pistorius? He was the man who took pity out of the equation.

South African. A runner who seemed to unite also the ancient and the modern mythologies: a hero who should be carved in marble and a superhero who might have been drawn by Marvel.

Here was a man gloriously put together for his sport, an Achilles brought back into existence in London, the fastest of them all. In action his movements demanded the extravagance of the feature film. He was a figure from the epics of the ancient world and from the epic cinema.

A double amputee propelled on blades that might have been ripped from the wheels of a chariot. An amputee, yet fast enough to make the Olympic Games and compete against the fastest able-bodied runners in the world. At the London Games he was second in his heat in the 400 metres, eighth and last in his semi. He also ran in South Africa's 4 x 400 metres relay team; they finished eighth of nine.

It wasn't results, though. It was the amazing nature, the amazing physique, the amazing speed of the man himself. He had made misfortune a positive asset: so much so that able-bodied runners complained that he had an unfair advantage.

A legless man with an unfair advantage over the greatest runners on the planet. Glorious.

He carried the flag for South Africa at the closing ceremony at the Olympic Games; he carried the flag for South Africa in the opening ceremony of the Paralympic Games, where he won gold medals in the 4 x 100 metres relay, and in the T44 400 metres, plus a silver in the 200 metres.

This wasn't about disability to be tolerated and accepted. This was disability to admire. Almost, it seemed in that enchanted time, to envy. He moved on those blades with a hero's swagger.

～

One of the lucky ones.

Seven years earlier, Martine Wright was going to work. It was the day after London was awarded the Olympic and Paralympic Games. She was one of the last people to be taken from the wreckage at Aldgate. She was in a coma for ten days, in hospital for ten months. She had both legs amputated from above the knee.

One of the lucky ones, she said; 52 people died in that series of attacks. Now she was competing for Britain at the Paralympic Games in the sport of sitting volleyball.

The competitors hop, slither, crawl and writhe to their starting positions. As soon as the ball is in play each side of the net is a mass of rolling bodies. Personal dignity is abandoned; all that matters is the ball. 'Once you've got your bum on the floor all disabilities are forgotten,' Wright said. It was also a liberation: 'Full-on physicality without a wheelchair.'

She was married, had a son, worked as a property manager, and had campaigned for fellow victims of the attacks. And as Britain played Ukraine, she played a game that is as glorious and as daft as any other and she did so as if her life depended on it, knowing full well that it didn't.

Sport, eh?

～

The Javelin train service from the Olympic Park to St Pancras was now in its final days, but the good cheer remained. During the Paras there were many more wheelchairs, and many others who required a little consideration, but the good vibes continued. Many more of the spectators were sports enthusiasts who had tried and failed to get balloted tickets for the Olympic Games, and took tickets to the Paras as a second-best ... discovering in the process that it was nothing of the kind. New vistas of understanding opened up for everyone.

The Games had begun seven years earlier with division and death and mutilation and hate. But it's no use. Force, hatred, history, all that. That's not life for men and women, insult and hatred. And everybody knows that it's the very opposite of that that is really life.

- Kohei Uchimura was part of the gold medal–winning Japanese team at the 2016 Olympic Games in Rio. He also won the individual all-around gold again; the first man to win successive gold medals in the all-around competition in 44 years.
- Sarah Attar competed for Saudi Arabia at the 2016 Olympic Games, this time running in the marathon. She was not named on the official Saudi website. She ran with arms and legs covered, but a baseball cap rather than a hood or hijab. She finished 132nd out of 133 runners, 52 minutes behind the winner, Jemima Sumgong of Kenya.
- Eva Risztov retired for the second time after winning the open-water swim in London; she was 19 when she retired the first time.
- Mo Farah won the gold medal in the 5,000 and the 10,000 metres at the London Olympic Games, and went on to do the same thing at the Rio Games four years later. His coach Alberto Salazar acquired an equivocal

reputation and Farah was urged to dissociate himself, but declined to do so.

- Carl Hester was part of the British team that won a silver medal at the Rio Games. So was Charlotte Dujardin, who also won the individual gold. Valegro was retired later that year.

- In 2014 Jessica Ennis gave birth to her first child, Reggie. She won the silver in the heptathlon in Rio two years later and then retired.

- Nigel Murray was part of the team that won a bronze medal at the London Paras in the BC1-2 category.

- The British women's sitting volleyball team failed to make it beyond the preliminary stages at the London Paras, but they did a good deal to establish the sport in this country.

~

BOOK 31

2013

What did it mean, the gun in the night? The shots? The shouting and screaming that came earlier? What was the meaning of the death of Reeva Steenkamp?

Did it mean that the heroic life of Oscar Pistorius was in truth a living hell? Some had claimed recklessly that Pistorius was the man who made disability 'cool'. The events of Valentine's Day seemed to contradict that.

Information was slow to come out. At first all that was known was that Pistorius had fired a gun and that his girlfriend was dead.

There's always a difference between a hero, as we perceive him, and the human being who does the actual living. What's he like? That's the question people always ask of those who have met sports stars. What's he *really* like? He's actually quite shy. Oh, he's just as you'd expect him to be. He's quite a funny guy. He's astonishingly polite, genuinely considerate. He's actually pretty smart. He's a much better talker than you'd think. He always acts as if he's genuinely pleased to see you. Oh, he's a pain, only likes sycophants. Oh him, he'll talk to you, but he's always looking over your shoulder for someone more interesting. He's great, always remembers your name and says hello. No side to him at all ...

And on and on.

What about Oscar? What's he really like?

That strutting, confident figure on his blades with the torso of a god: was he in fact eaten up with a sense of personal and physical inadequacy? And sexual inadequacy? Was his life defined by resentment and crippling envy of the able-bodied?

Pistorius was a great athlete, so we assumed his life must be great. Pistorius helped us all to find a better understanding about disability.

Perhaps we didn't understand enough.

～

Sport has always had an attraction for hypocrites. As a haven for hypocrisy, sport makes a panting but enthusiastic third behind politics and religion. That's because sport has primordial associations with virtue. Sport was encouraged by 19th-century educationists because it was supposed to teach virtue – sinking self into common cause, unquestioning obedience to authority and exhausting physical labour that left boys too tired to masturbate.

The equation of sport and virtue has survived two centuries of discouraging reality. We want sporting heroes to play their sport and, if possible, conduct the rest of their lives in a manner that we find acceptable. It's also where the money is: if you want to grab the best endorsements and sponsorships, you'd better be what's called 'a role model'.

Which is an invitation to hypocrisy.

There have been three classic hypocrites in modern sport.

Not people who have been a little smarmy, a little insincere, a little inconsistent: people who constructively lived their sporting lives while espousing virtues they had no intention of living by.

Hansie Cronje, the South African cricket captain, had a tattoo that read 'WWJD', meaning What Would Jesus Do. Possibly Jesus would not have fixed matches and corrupted young cricketers in exchange for a few rands and a leather jacket.

Tiger Woods set himself up as a pillar of middle-class virtue, with a perfect home life and a perfect blonde wife, the sort of thing the whole world aspired to – and all the time he devoted himself to cocktail waitresses when the world wasn't watching.

Amateurs. Small-timers. People of limited ambitions and limited scope.

Lance Armstrong made the first guarded public admission that he had taken performance-enhancing drugs. He made it to Oprah Winfrey, to add a bizarre note to the business.

Armstrong hadn't just won the Tour de France seven times. He had also 'beaten' testicular cancer. The message from his extraordinary, inspiring book, *It's Not About the Bike*, was that if you're mentally strong enough, you can achieve anything. You could buy a yellow wristband with the legend LIVE STRONG. It showed that you too aspired to such mental strength. Armstrong was empowering a generation, telling us new things about the possibilities of life. All down to you. You and the strength of your mind.

The United States Anti-Doping Agency said that 'it was the most sophisticated, professionalised and successful doping programme sport has ever seen'.

Winning wasn't enough. Cheating wasn't enough. Armstrong had to be an icon of impossible virtue as well.

Being a hero wasn't enough. Armstrong had to be a secular saint as well.

～

Here's the thing about last-wicket stands: they're great until they get serious. They're like a dorm romp, a classroom frenzy: tremendous fun – until the headmaster walks in. He doesn't need to shout. He doesn't need to issue punishments, impositions and canings. He just has to stand at the door and there's an instant return to silence.

Watching cricket has always been a hard thing for people who support England. Especially as success turned out to be as hard to bear as the years of failure. England mastered failure: but they never mastered the art of success without anxiety.

There's a human constant in that, though it often seems like an English constant. Call it open-topped bus syndrome: one whiff of triumph and they're on the floor, like the tyro drinker and the barmaid's apron.

Another Ashes series: at this time in history they were coming thick and fast, losing something of their meaning and perhaps a little of their intensity as well. Was that why the first Test, at Trent Bridge, was so peculiar? England, a team in their pomp, were bowled out for 215. But then, largely thanks to the bowling of James Anderson, they reduced Australia to 117 for nine. Which brought in the last-wicket stand.

It was one of those days dominated by the Lord of Misrule. But of course, when it got serious, when it seemed that the debutant, Ashton Agar, might become the first Test match number 11 in history to make a century, he was out for 98. England replied and Ian Bell, previously considered a player better at decorating than dominating an occasion, held everything together with 109.

England's bowlers, led by Anderson, had Australia beaten at 231 for nine chasing 310 – and then came another last-wicket stand. This, too, was all right until it got serious. It happened because Anderson left the pitch for treatment – and then at once there was a light-headed feeling in the air. Somehow everything was possible. Brad Haddin and James Pattinson moved towards an impossible victory, and so it continued – until the headmaster walked into the classroom.

Anderson, who had taken the previous three wickets, came back and restored order. He took the wicket of Haddin, caught behind off a faint nick. He bowled 55.5 overs in that match, took ten wickets for 158 runs and overtook Fred Trueman's record of Test wickets for England.

This was a performance of true authority. It wasn't a victory against the odds, despite England's attempts to make it look so. It was the deserved victory of a superior side: and if only Anderson and Bell seemed to possess that sense of authority, it was enough. When Anderson had the ball, things were serious. Immense skill married to immense stamina and immense will made a devastating combination.

This, then, was the heady experience of watching England take hold of a Test match against Australia as of right. Many of the players seemed uncertain about the nature of this right, but not Anderson. England won by 14 runs. They did so because Anderson knowingly used his authority.

~

There are rare, rare occasions when the impossible becomes the inevitable.

Normal life is set to one side. The notions that enable us to cope with day-to-day existence – making the best of things, knowing that life is what it is and not what you want it to be – could be forgotten.

It was as if the same audience had sat in the same seats in the same place for endless years, years in which local success was at first unthinkable, then a teasing long-range possibility, and, finally, a tantalising thing doomed to be forever snatched from their grasp.

And then, with an hour played, the same thought spread

across everyone who was sitting in Centre Court: my God, he's going to do it in straight sets. We don't even need to worry. Our prayers have already been answered. It's already happened: we are watching something already decided, something that cannot be changed.

Andy Murray was about to win Wimbledon. He played with complete authority: taking control of space and time. What a nation had fretted about and feared about and ooh-erred about for 77 years – for that was the length of time since a British player last won the men's singles at Wimbledon – was now unfolding with something not far from serenity.

Novak Djokovic, the world number one, was playing well: it was just that Murray was playing better. He was playing better because, it seemed, he had a right to win. Uncertainties had been set aside. What we had fretted about for those seven or eight decades was now happening without fuss. As if all you need to do to walk along a kerbstone a thousand feet above the ground is to put one foot after another. It really is that simple.

How well that audience had got to know Murray: those marvellous passages when he played so well, those terrible black moods of self-loathing when his standard slipped a little. That day he played with an air of slightly spooky calm.

Oh, there was a little faffing about in the last set: a little tease, as if to recall the great days of Tim Henman. He was two sets and a break up when he performed that Henmanesque wobble: got broken and broken again. But then he broke back and then broke again to restore the initial break and, after that, all he had to do was serve out for the championship.

Just a soupçon of drama, then. He held three championship points: and perhaps then the terrible thought entered his mind: wouldn't it be just awful to lose from here? Back to deuce. And now break points: he saved three of them. But then he served again and Djokovic dumped the ball into the net and, yes, there it was: as if everyone in the stadium had been sitting in the same seat for the past 77 years waiting for this to happen.

Expecting just about anything other than that, at the very last, it should be almost easy.

This crowd had watched him from an awkward teenager, who first attracted attention by vomiting on court: a signal that things might get ugly, but effort and desire would dominate everything that he did. He went from promising boy to one of the top four players in the world. Alas, the other three were all among the greatest players of all time: in this band of four Murray was always doomed to be Ringo.

But every album has its Ringo track and here was Murray's triumph: his second Grand Slam singles title after his victory in New York the previous year. He also won a gold medal in the singles at the London Olympic Games, where he was more lavishly supported than ever before.

Sport can do many things. Just occasionally, it provides an afternoon of perfection.

- In 2017 James Anderson took his 500th Test match wicket, the sixth bowler to do so.
- In 2015, Andy Murray led the British team to victory in the Davis Cup, their first win for 79 years. The following year he won Wimbledon again.

BOOK 32

2014

Team spirit. Not, as the footballer Steve Archibald famously said, an illusion glimpsed in victory. Not for most people anyway.

Team spirit is perhaps a reality that is lost in defeat. Or if not in defeat, then in humiliation. In the kind of humiliation that makes people doubt their own identity, their own meaning, their own purpose.

A cricket tour is relentless. Test matches last for five full days, and when an England cricketer travels in Australia, there are five of such matches. Effective fast bowling unmans an individual. Consecutive humiliations destroy the soul. It was terrible when England were beaten in West Indies in the 1980s, but at least they knew they were going to lose. This time, after three successive victories against Australia, they were pretty certain they were going to win: or at least be worthy opponents until the last ball was bowled. They were out of it from the first moment that Mitchell Johnson began to bowl at them.

Mitch! A joke bowler, a player every England batsman had

got top-sides of. But then he grew a moustache and decided he was Dennis Lillee, but left-handed. Late in his career he found the best of his form: and it was this transformation that England couldn't stand.

In such circumstances you search for unity. Anything that gets between you and the night: you and despair. And so the England team united behind the former captain and their best batsman, Kevin Pietersen. They all hated him. It was all his fault.

It was the only way in which the trauma of humiliation could be managed. Pietersen was top scorer in a broken team. It was a team that kept losing people, players who had lost their nerve: Jonathan Trott, Graeme Swann, both serial winners, running back homewards, broken.

When the team got back to England it was decided that the only way forward was to sack Pietersen. In any debate between individual brilliance and team-first loyalty the default setting is towards the loyalists: the faceless second-raters, those who are first-class of the second class. Sports psychologists call such people 'membership individuals'. To argue otherwise is to side with the madness of personal excellence: to claim genius for yourself.

The sports psychologists' model for team-building is that all players who bring something to the team are by definition acceptable: and must be accommodated. If you fail to accommodate a genius, the team culture is at fault. And yet it was said that West Indies of the 1990s were stronger without Brian Lara: a better team when deprived of one of the greatest batsmen in the game's history. If you can't make the adjustments required to accommodate a genius, you are the lesser team – and team-mate. And the same goes for a genius who can't fit into a team. What is remarkable is that Pietersen lasted as long as he did: ten years of awkward, intermittent and occasionally outstanding brilliance.

At once this became not a sporting but a moral debate, as if we were back on the Victorian playing field: what matters is not the result but the moral lessons learned. Some took Pietersen's side, others the side of the rest of the team, especially the captain, Alastair Cook. It was a moral debate about why people like me are better than people like you.

And at bottom it was all a way of avoiding the truth about defeat, rather than confronting it. About the way that defeat – yes, even in the great eternal triviality of sport – can break minds and hearts and spirits. The traditional response is to find someone to blame and then move on. Sport can be a lowering business, in defeat as in victory.

~

Genius is an easier thing to bear in the individual sports. The genius becomes you, the spectator – or at least what you long to be, with no ambiguities.

It is the fate of the great to fail us, if only at the very last. They are never quite as great as we long for them to be, so their fallibilities cause us disproportionate pain. Perfection seldom lasts long in sport, for every second there are people seeking to destroy it.

No one played the role of champion better than Roger Federer. At his height, he used his number one status as a weapon, inflicting his cruel serenity on a string of lesser opponents. But his relative decline seemed to have no effect on him, any more than demotion from the number one position.

Years ago Bjorn Borg retired from tennis at the age of 26; when he lost his number one status, he lost also the will to play. He lacked the grit required to go slumming for victories. By retiring he robbed his greatest opponent, John McEnroe, of something too. Not to mention the watching world.

But Federer never lost heart. Perhaps he loved tennis too much: not just the struggle but the sublime art of hitting a tennis ball with sweetness and power. Perhaps one or two perfect points in a match were enough to sustain him.

At Wimbledon he reached the final again and was cheered every step of the way. Cheering for Federer was a pursuit of the fantasy of perfection. His powers were waning, but at Centre Court on Finals Day there was joy in the air once again as he came back to level the match at two sets all.

His opponent was Novak Djokovic, much admired, but never much loved outside his own country. He inspired the most colossal respect: but for the Wimbledon crowd Federer was an embodiment – however absurd that is – of every good thing in the world.

How cruel sport can be. Centre Court stood and applauded as Djokovic closed out the final set. The place has often been described as a cathedral: here was a Mass that celebrated the ending of hope.

At least for today.

In sport there is always tomorrow.

Even for ageing champions.

And always for you – *hypocrite spectateur, mon semblable, mon frère.*

~

Love makes one little room an everywhere. Sport makes one town an everywhere: the whole world is here in these few streets, at least for a time: a decent, cheerful, reasonably loving place with no great need to worry about tomorrow. Here is only victory and defeat, partisanship, drama and the eternal search for excellence: excellence in a piffling medium perhaps – but true excellence can never be truly piffling, for it elevates us all.

Glasgow was not only Glasgow. It was Seoul and Sydney and London; it was Rome and Los Angeles and Mumbai; it was Minneapolis and Adelaide and Lisbon; it was everywhere that good sport has ever been played.

The perfect ubiquity of Glasgow was best observed from the top of the stand at Kelvingrove Lawn Bowls Centre, for this was the Commonwealth Games, contested by 71 nations brought together by the ambition and rapacity of one (or perhaps more, you do the sums and the politics) of their number.

Australia were playing Norfolk Islands in the women's fours. Papua New Guinea were playing the Falkland Islands in the men's triples. Sharp cries of encouragement to the rolling woods could be heard even from this eminence. The applause was fulsome but by no means excessive.

The security people were cheerful. A policewoman smiled and became beautiful. Glaswegians directed visitors and visitors did their best to understand. Competition continued all over the town: netball, judo, rhythmic gymnastics, women's weightlifting. Everywhere you went people were winning and losing – mostly losing, of course, because that's the nature of sport, but even for the most dreadful of losses there are the consolations of heartbreak and the certainty of the sun's efficient performance on the good morrow.

Lower in the sky now, the sun. The crowd at the bowls a little thinner. No matter: there would be more sport tomorrow.

I folded the laptop shut and slid it into my bag, the one they gave me at the Beijing Olympic Games.

Tomorrow I would look for eagles on the island of Mull.

Perhaps all of the last 32 years I've been looking for eagles. Sometimes finding Icarus. Sometimes ... sometimes not. Sometimes very much not.

Behind me the sport continued.

As if it would do so forever.

Epilogue

And then he danced, and it was the fastest dance that has ever been danced.

Not noon. This time it was late; the sky above the Bird's Nest stadium in Beijing that night in 2008 was an impenetrable, starless black above the blazing lights.

He had stumbled coming out of the blocks in the semi-finals but still won in 9.85 easing up. And now the final of the Olympic 100 metres for men.

The same hush. The tension of all the ages in one long moment.

Bang.

The sudden roar seemed to express disbelief that such a thing could be happening before our watching eyes.

A line of runners, all abreast at 30 metres or so. The man we were all watching most closely had started poorly. Again. And then in the space of a single stride it all changed.

Usain Bolt.

Usain Bolt took over the race, took over all of sport. In the space of that single stride it ceased to be a race and became a detonation of glory.

The seven other fastest men in the world looked slow. Usain Bolt entered a different order of being.

No one was close. And so he danced.

He dropped his arms, held them still by his sides in aeroplane mode, then slapped his chest and lifted his knees.

A dance of joy.

A stadium filled with joy, and a world, that such a thing could be.

Athletics purists had to criticise, saying he could have gone much faster had he run properly to the line. How much faster? Perhaps 0.11 of a second faster, as he did at the World Championships in Berlin the following year. Some said he was showing off, showboating, showing disrespect to his sport and his opponents. 'I was just happy.'

Then the time.

The poetry of numbers, the numerological magic of a new digit: a six, not a seven. He had finished in 9.69, beating his own previous record by three-hundredths.

There's a fizzing, incredulous joy that fills an athletics stadium when a new world record has been established, and that joy is greatest in the greatest race of them all.

Here speed was beauty and truth and meaning and hope.

And joy.

At least for now.

And the world shared it.

Sport can do this.

Yes.

～

Somewhere else in the world a surfer with no need for opponents or audience commenced the perfect coupling with the perfect wave.